POSTCARD HISTORY SERIES

# *Roycroft Campus*

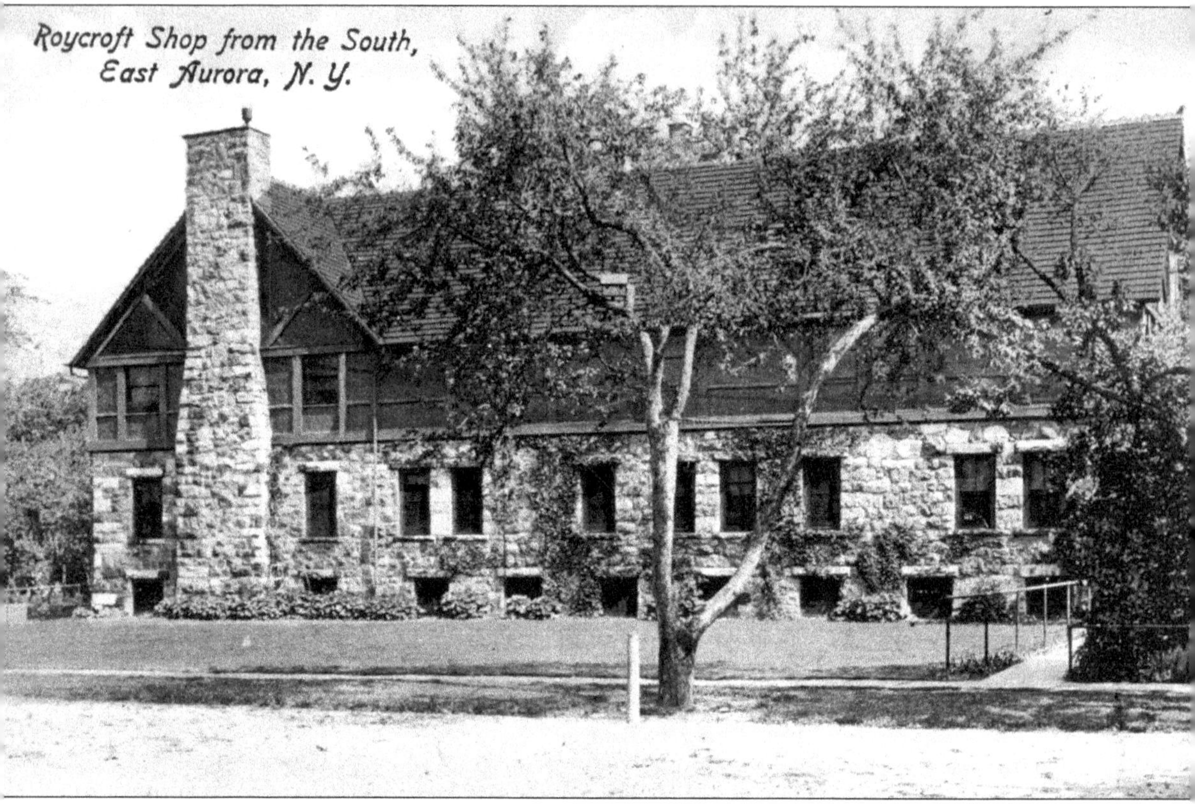


**ON THE COVER:** This view is of the south side of the Roycroft Print Shop in East Aurora, New York. It was built between 1900 and 1901 in an English Tudor Revival style, across the street from the previous Phalanstery and first Print Shop. The exterior remains today virtually unchanged and is owned by the Cornell Co-Operative Extension, though possibly is to be sold to one of the nonprofit organizations associated with the present restoration and revitalization of the campus. (Author's collection.)

POSTCARD HISTORY SERIES

# Roycroft Campus

Robert Charles Rust

ARCADIA PUBLISHING

ISBN 978-0-7385-9906-9

Published by Arcadia Publishing
Charleston, South Carolina

Library of Congress Control Number: 2012951437

For all general information contact Arcadia Publishing at:
Telephone 843-853-2070
Fax 843-853-0044
E-mail sales@arcadiapublishing.com
For customer service and orders:
Toll-Free 1-888-313-2665

Visit us on the Internet at www.arcadiapublishing.com

*To the many original Roycrofters I had the honor of knowing as friends: Miriam Hubbard Roelofs, Rixford Upham Jennings, Nancy Hubbard Brady, Emil Georg Sahlin, Muriel Jennings Case, Leon Varley, and the many others connected with the Roycroft Inn and Shops during its long history.*

# Contents

# ACKNOWLEDGMENTS

Though my collection is a work of over 30 years, I am sure there are many collectors who have been more focused than I in their collecting skills. So they might have a postcard or two that represent some aspect of Roycroftiana not found within these pages. One such collector is Jack Walsdorf, Morrisian scholar and bibliophile par excellence and longtime friend. He has loaned a dozen from his extensive library to add some additional color into this work. I thank him for the loan of those cards. I also must thank my fianceé and fellow postcard collector Pam McClary, who puts up with my Collyer Brothers' inspired ephemeral habit, not just in collecting Roycroft but all of the paper, be it books or letters or old catalogs and magazines that find their way into our home and add to the collections. Unless otherwise noted, all postcards are from the author's personal collection.

# INTRODUCTION

The history of the Roycroft is the history of the Arts and Crafts Movement in America. The once and now again world-famous group of 14 buildings in the little village outside of Buffalo, New York, has reinvented itself almost as many times as a cat with nine lives. The Roycroft began as a voice for the philosopher, heretic, ad man par excellence, and son of a country doctor, Elbert Green Hubbard (1856–1915), as a printing operation in a small building next to his home and grew into a campus of English-style stone and wood structures. Postcards were issued documenting the growth of this Print Shop into a craft commune of over 500 workers only one year after the Phalanstery, the first building, was constructed.

Hubbard, following in the footsteps of Englishman William Morris (1832–1896), furnished his interiors with furniture now known as Mission or Arts and Crafts. The images in this book feature items of art and decorative arts now only seen in museums throughout the world and highly regarded as some of the first interiors in this style. The people, both visitors and craftspeople alike, were able to enjoy an environment unlike any other with a parklike setting, farms, and even hostelries built for many of the workers and guests. Many of these guests were the literati and famous of the day, including Carl Sandburg, Frank Lloyd Wright, Ellen Terry, Clarence Darrow, and Henry Ford, among others. Famous craftsmen and women like Dard Hunter and W.W. Denslow were drawn to Hubbard and his philosophy of life and work, and their artwork and designs were showcased in Roycroft Press books and magazines in addition to the postcards and motto cards sent throughout the world.

This book will cover the Roycroft's eras of Elbert Hubbard and his son Elbert Hubbard II (Bert) from 1898 to 1938, when the shops and inn were forced into bankruptcy. It will also show images from the intervening years of 1938 to 1988, which highlight many changes and were documented in their postcards. Two of the campus buildings became churches, and one even became the town hall of the town of Aurora. The most major change began to happen once it was listed in the National Register of Historic Places in 1978. It was then further recognized as a National Historic Landmark in 1986. In 1995, the Roycroft Inn reopened after an $8-million restoration and renovation. The years leading up to this "Campus Restoration Project" are the focus of this book, and the Roycroft Renaissance is documented in this collection of picture postcards owned mostly by the author and one other major collector of Roycroftiana.

# *One*

# East Aurora before the Roycrofters

## Presidents and Horses

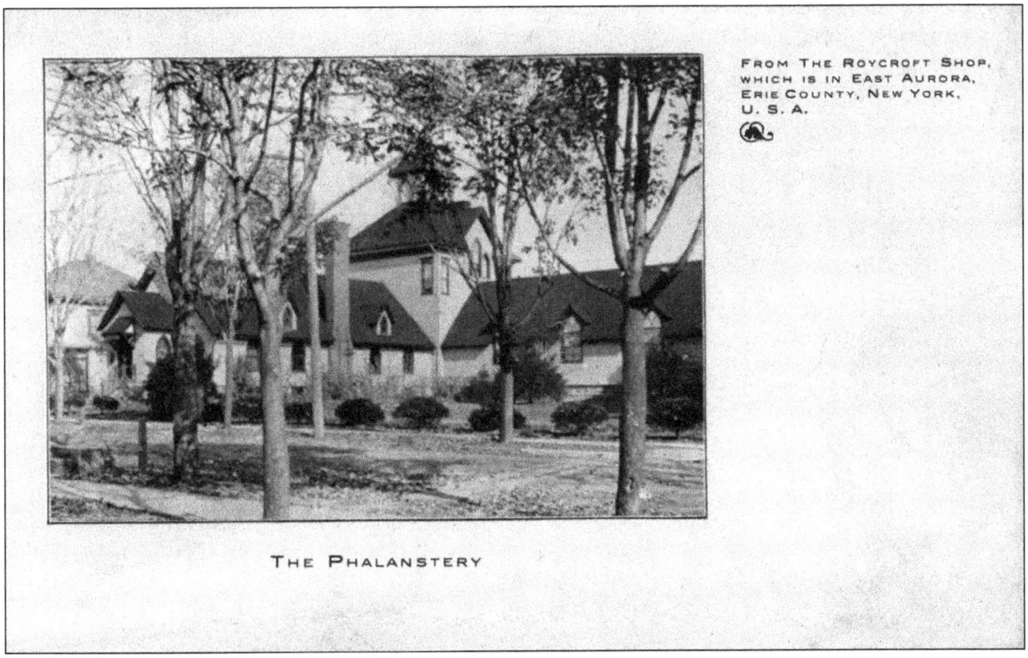


The Phalanstery, literally the communes meeting place, was the first of the Roycroft Campus buildings. This church-like structure was built in 1897 and 1898, and it has been said that it was modeled after St. Oswald's, known as Wordsworth's Church, in Grassmere, England. The Roycroft's presses had been moved from Main Street to the cellars of this Print Shop, and the binders, editors, and illuminators were accommodated on the upper floors. The entrance, through a large oak door, led one into a room that has undergone many changes in the last 100-plus years, as will be shown throughout this history through postcards. Once this building was constructed, Aurora would never be the sleepy little horsey town it had been.

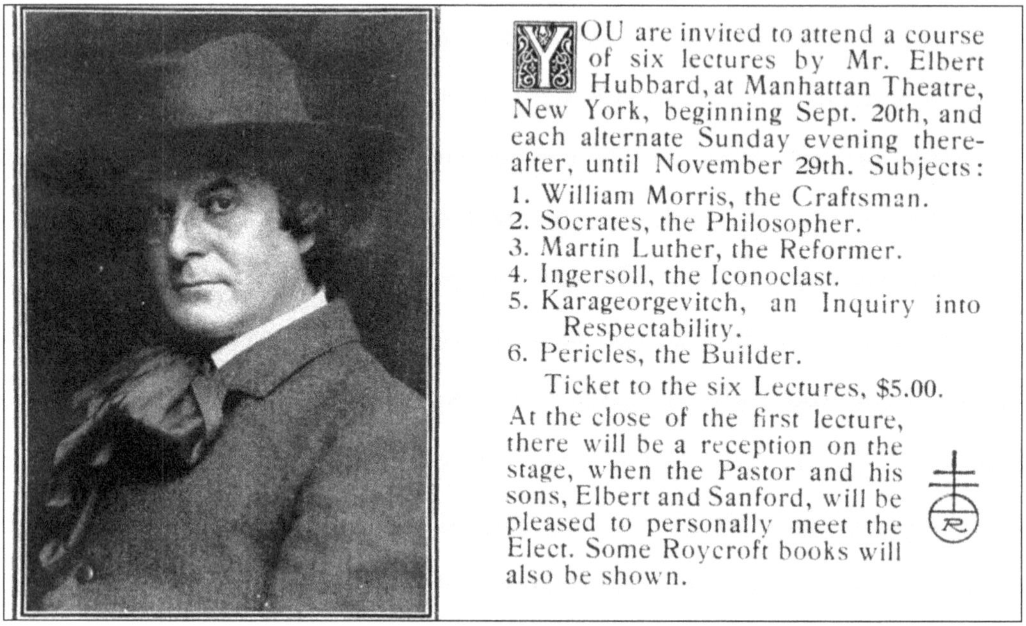


Elbert Green Hubbard (1856–1915), a soap salesman, businessman, advertising genius, and founder and proponent of the Arts and Crafts Movement in America, was to change the world in many ways. He invented the premium sales method while he was the vice president of the Larkin Soap Company in nearby Buffalo. In the late 1880s, he then moved his family to the village to be able to enjoy his horses and the fresh air of the countryside in the Cazenovia Valley. Selling out his substantial share of the soap business to his brother-in-law for $75,000 in 1893, he embarked on a new career as a writer.

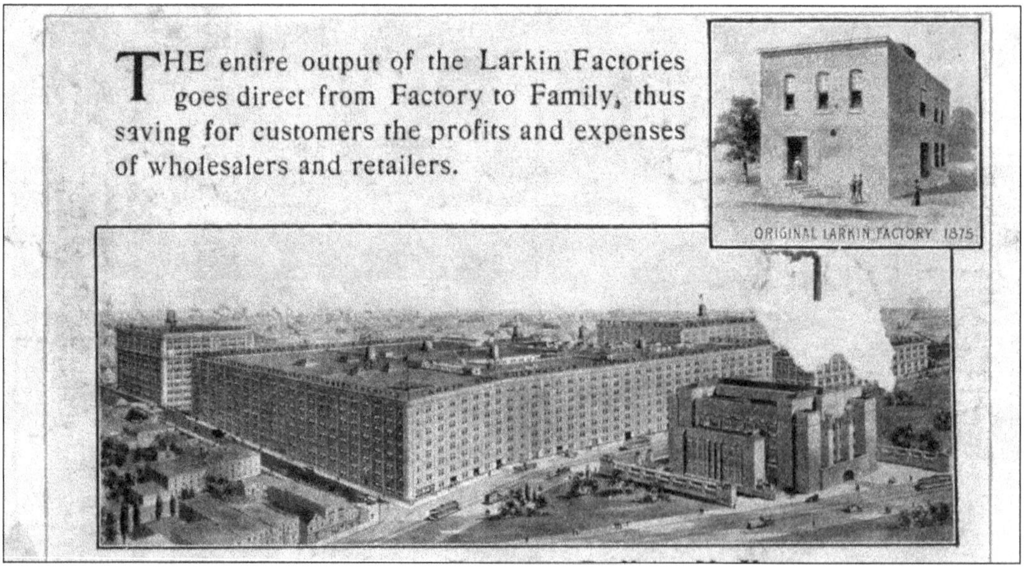


This card, actually a foldout of the extensive acreage of the Larkin Soap Company in Buffalo, New York, shows the original building still standing at the time of this printing. Elbert, John Larkin, and a few helpers grew this into a multimillion-dollar business. At the time of Hubbard's departure, the Larkin Soap Company was a company the size of rivals Sears and Roebuck and Montgomery Ward. Mail-order enterprises were what America needed to fuel its growth in the Industrial Age.

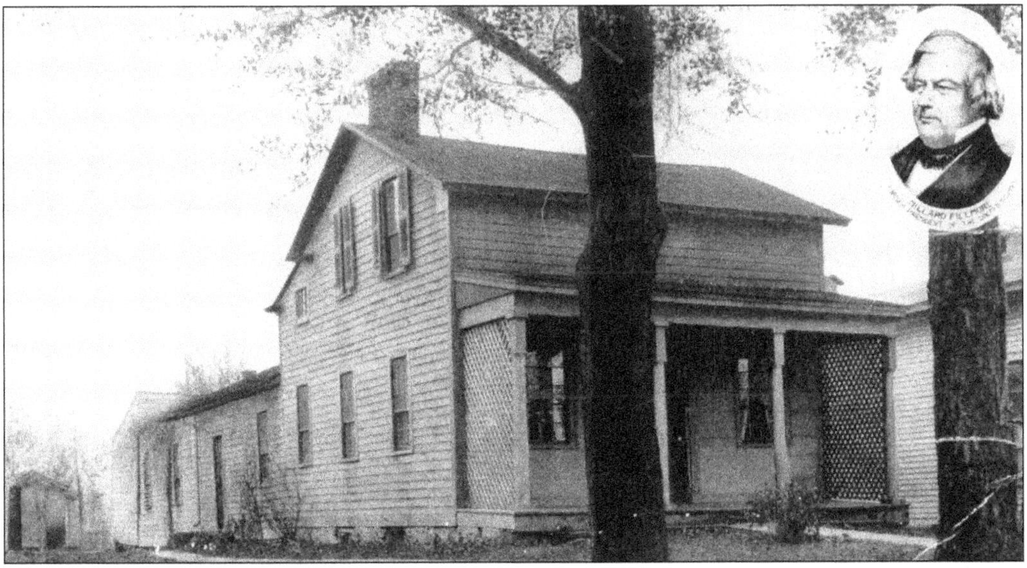

Almost two generations before the Hubbards' move to South Grove Street in East Aurora, Millard Fillmore, the 13th president of the United States, built his wife, Abigail, a home on Main Street in 1826. They lived in this home until 1830, when they moved to Buffalo. He was the village's only lawyer and began his political career from his law office, also located on Main Street. In 1930, the derelict building was moved off Main Street to its present location by Margaret Evans Price, an artist and illustrator of children's books who used it as her artist's studio. Bought in 1970 by the Aurora Historical Society, who meticulously restored the house now located at 24 Shearer Avenue, it serves as a museum for the president and his life around 1830 and was named a National Historic Landmark.

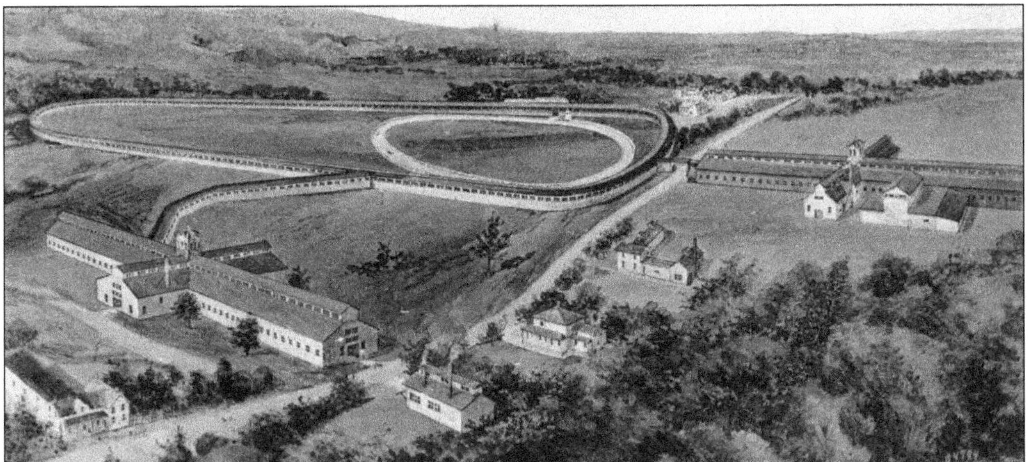

East Aurora and the surrounding town were the home to two of the largest trotting horse farm operations in the world at the time just after the Civil War. The Hamlin and Jewett Farms (pictured here) were also the largest employers until the arrival of the Roycroft Press and Shops. The Jewett Farm and its mile-and-a-quarter covered wooden racetrack was the only one known in the world and drew visitors from many countries. Due to Western New York's famous weather, the track started deteriorating quickly and a few horses ended up with broken legs while training, so the track was dismantled and many of the late-Victorian-era homes, possibly even Hubbard's own, were built with the stacks of aged lumber.

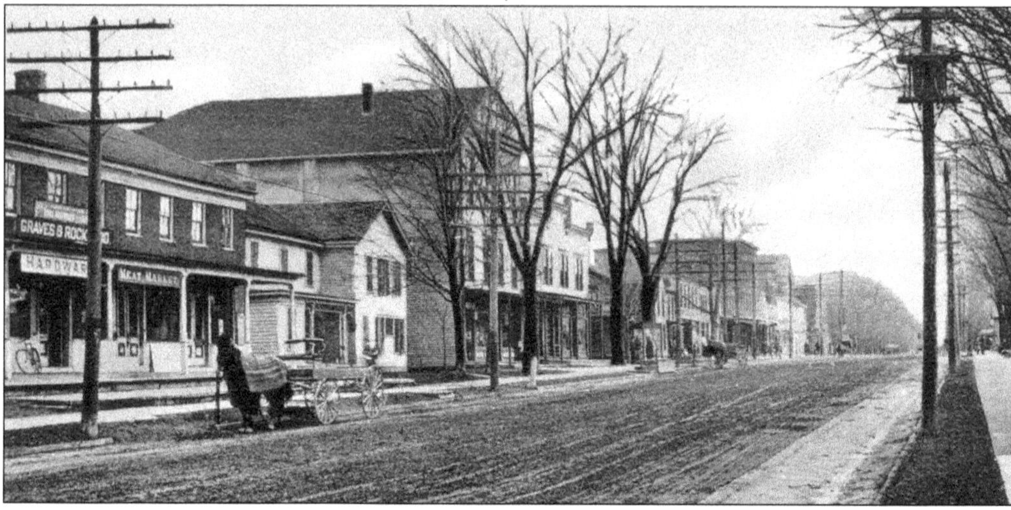


This view of Main Street is how Elbert Hubbard and the Roycrofters would have known it in 1900. Many of these buildings along this block are still standing; only a wonderful Art Deco–era movie theater with Margaret Evans Price murals and a stunning original neon marquee has been built where the Fillmore's home was located in 1930. Unfortunately, like many small towns in America, the hardware store and meat market are now in a plaza at the edge of town. Opened during the Depression, the famous Vidler's 5 and 10 store is still located across from the Aurora Theater. Every storefront and office is filled today with restaurants, small locally owned shops, and the hometown newspaper, *The Advertiser*, which has been in its original location at 710 Main Street since 1872.

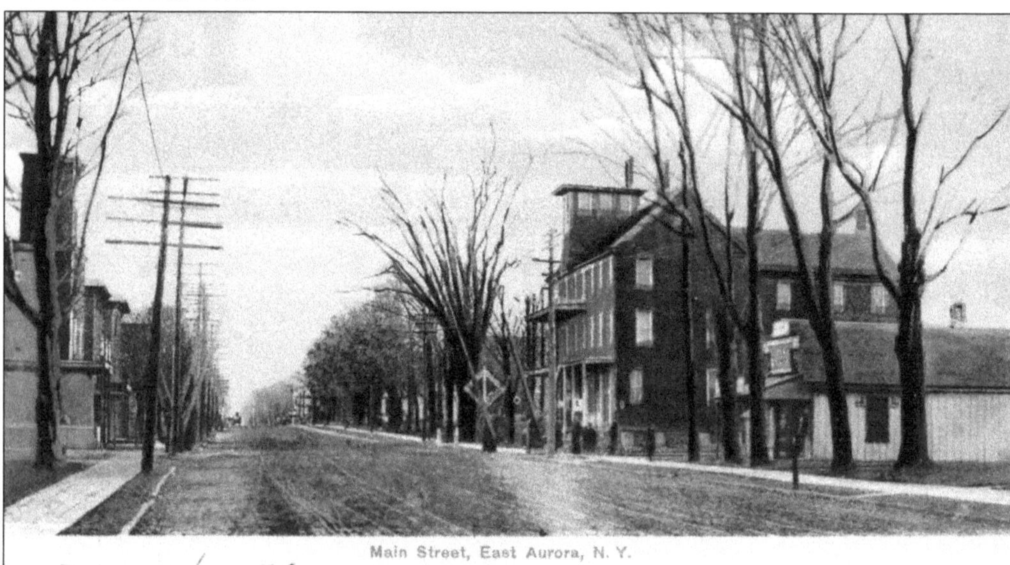


The village at the turn of the 20th century had a population much the same as today with a little over 6,000 people. It has also become famous as the home of Fisher Price Toys, founded in 1930 by two ex-employees of the Roycrofters and was funded by a loan from Elbert "Bert" Hubbard II. Bert also was elected mayor of the village in the 1930s during the Roycroft's last years in operation. Just a few years after this photograph was made, the railroad crossing shown here was raised above the street and a viaduct with stone pavers was installed.

Anson Blackman, known around the Roycroft and from Hubbard's many writings as "Ali Baba," was a local horseman who Elbert hired before the press was founded to take care of his horses. He became a friend, babysitter, traveling companion, valet, and alter ego for Hubbard's pragmatic epigrams. One motto credited to the Baba was "Art is only a matter of haircut." Blackman lived with his wife in a house given to him by Hubbard on the corner of South Grove Street and Oakwood Avenue, three houses down from his own. The alleged theft of a bowl's worth of tobacco by Anson Blackman is the supposed beginnings of the nickname by the Roycrofters. Hubbard even went so far as to issue an autobiography of Ali Baba in 1899; a signed limited edition with his "X" signature included. This postcard was in the first group issued in late 1899.

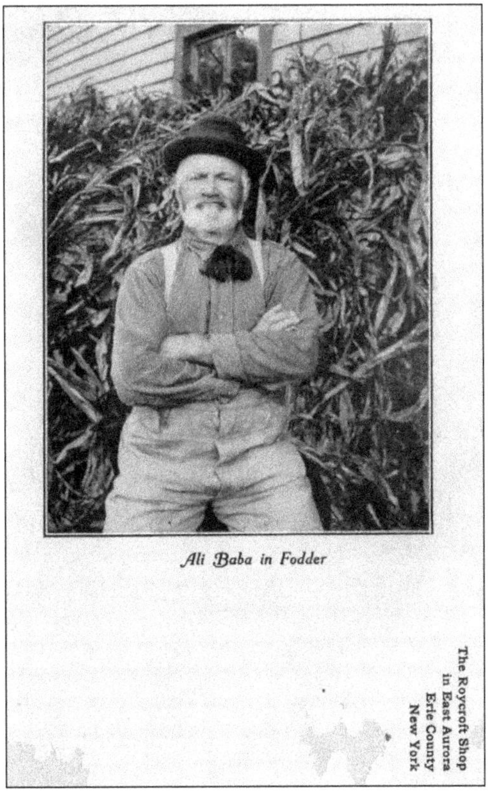


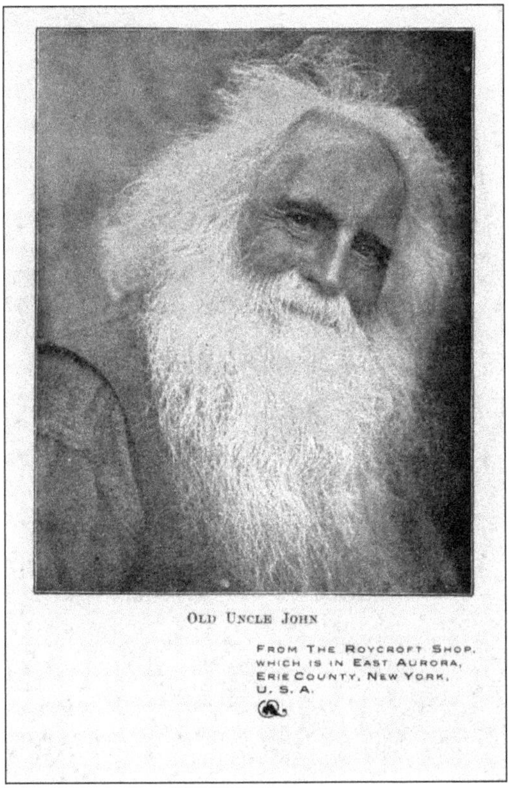


Old Uncle John was one of the characters in and around the village. This is one of the first Roycroft postcards of the Private Mailing Card type first issued in 1898. They were restricted to comments on the pictorial side and only the address could appear on the reverse, so many are found in very good condition today and have been collected since they were issued. John, whose surname is unknown to the author, was seen in many images printed in the early magazines. This picture as taken by Paul Fournier in the studio he shared with his father, Alexis, on Walnut Street.

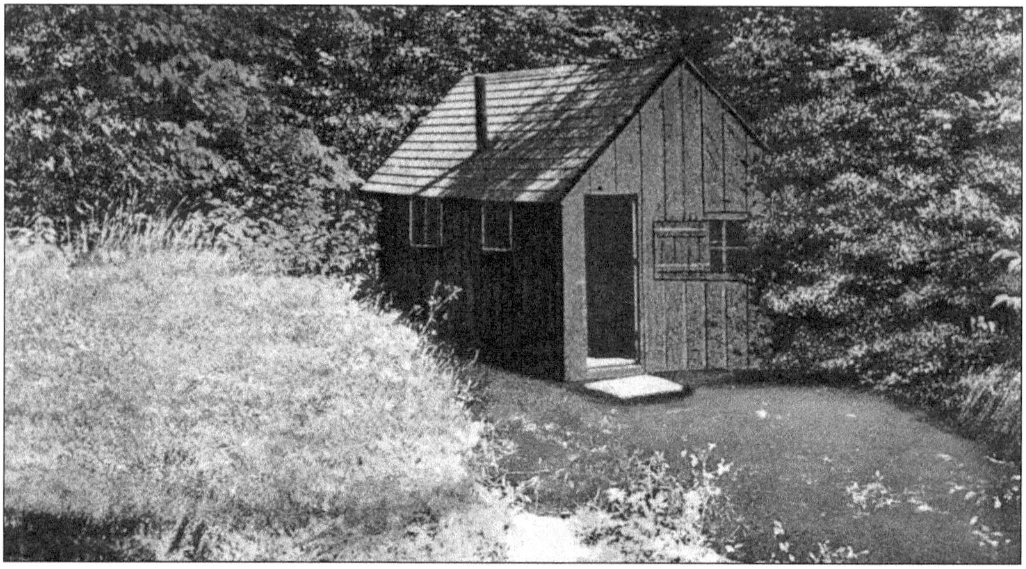

This small cabin nestled in the woods was Hubbard's retreat away from his home filled with children to write his articles and essays. Called "the Little Journey's Cabin," it was a nice bit of exercise on horseback and less than 30 minutes from South Grove Street. Heated in winter with a wood stove, it was also a popular destination with visitors at the Roycroft Inn in the early 20th century. The East Aurora Paint and Varnish Club artists used it as a studio and meeting place after 1928. Its foundations can still be found by those who know the location.

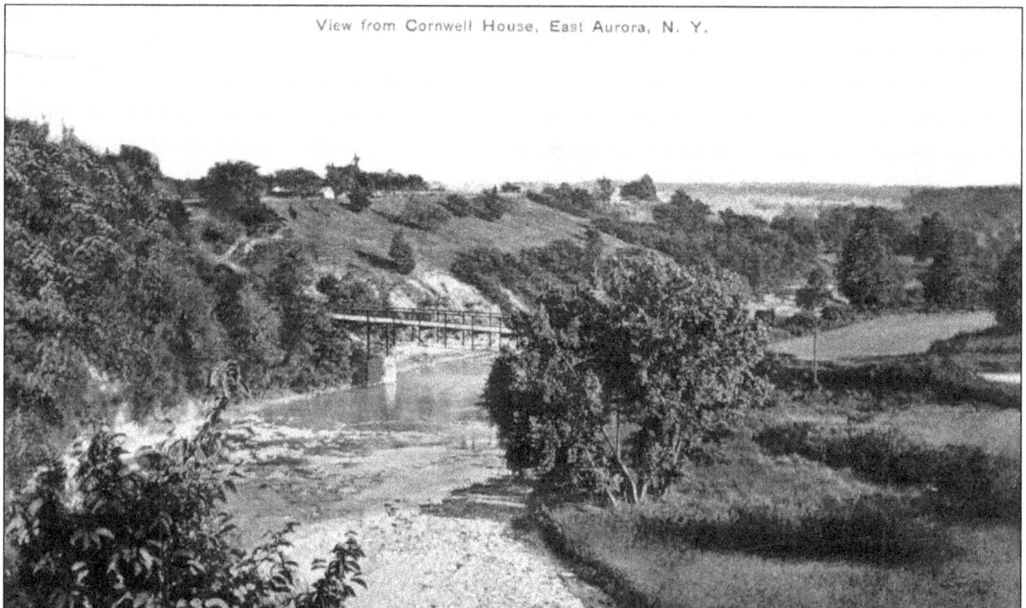


A view from the edge of the village looks toward the south into the creek bed of Cazenovia Creek, which flows along the borders of the village on the southern and western sides. Farmland reached to the edge of the village proper. The iron bridge was replaced with a concrete structure with the advent of the automobile and its use along what is now New York State Route 16. This road travels to the village of Orchard Park, now famous for being the home of the NFL's Buffalo Bills and their Ralph Wilson Stadium.

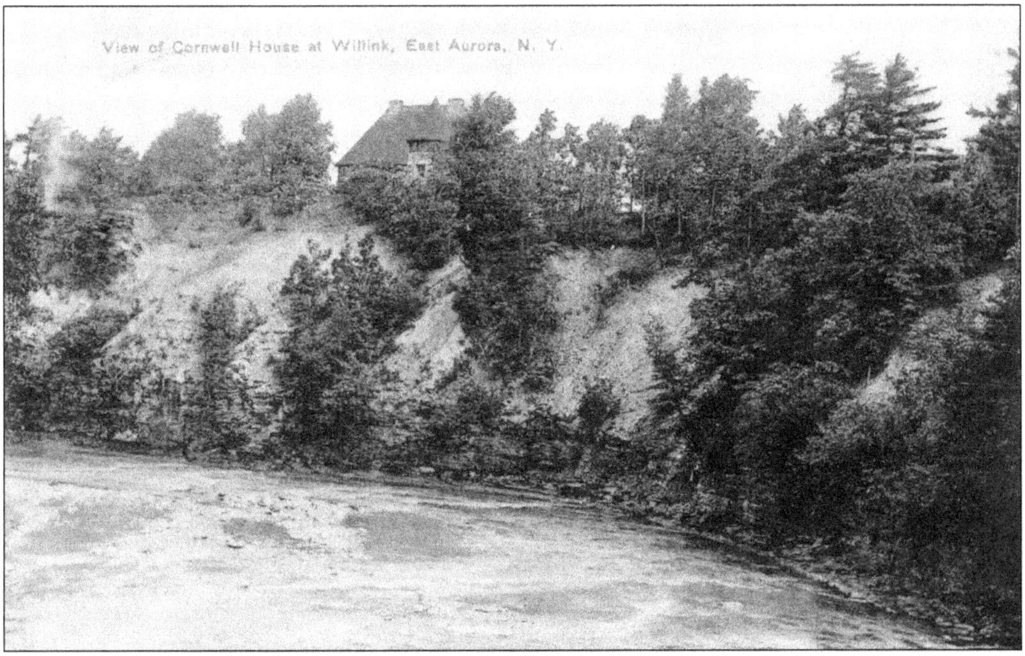


This image, taken from the bridge over Cazenovia Creek looking northeast just west of the village, features the Cornwall House. Built in the Richardson Romanesque style, this home was constructed in the late 1880s by Lyman Cornwall, Aurora town supervisor from 1881 to 1882. It was advertised in Roycroft's magazines as a health house and a rest home for weary businessmen in the 1910s. Some say that it was what is known today as a place to dry out from the effects of the evil drink. Elbert Hubbard, himself a teetotaler, had little patience for his workers with this addiction. The home is privately owned today and has a wonderful view of the sunsets over the creek's twists and turns below.

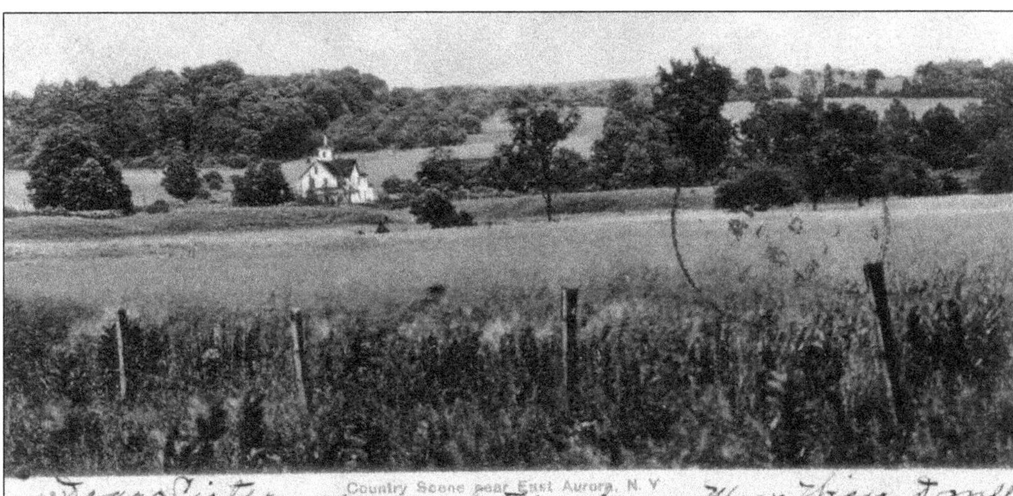


A scene of the very fertile land surrounding the village around 1910 is seen here. Many of the farmers, both then and now, send their produce into Buffalo. Many, like Arden Farm, which was a farm that supplied the Roycroft and is still owned by Arden's grandchildren, provide organic vegetables through the Aurora Farmers Market held from late spring until late fall each year.

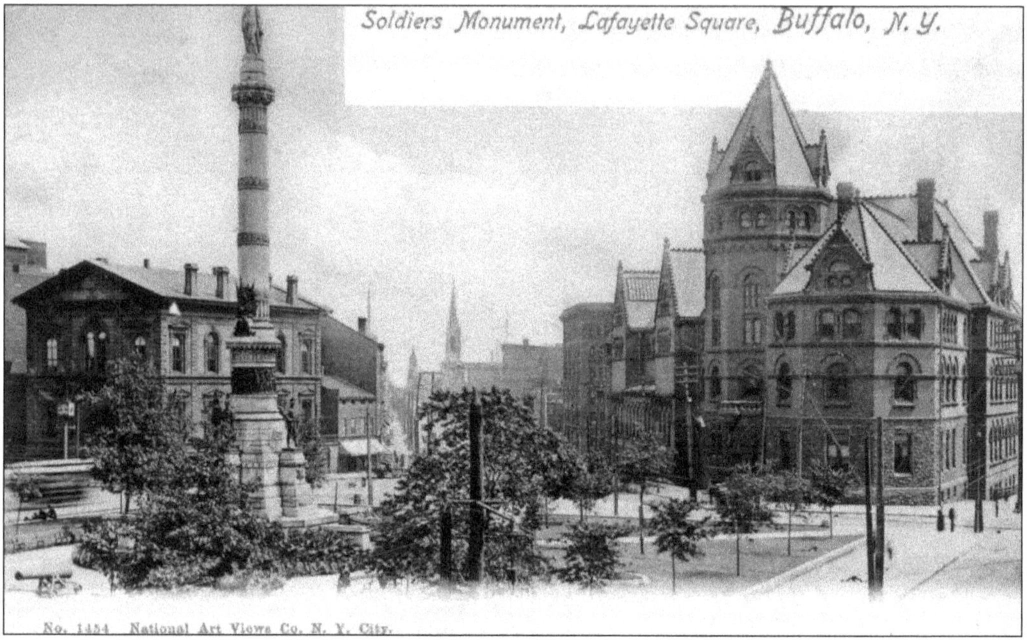


Lafayette Square, in the center of downtown Buffalo, is 17 miles from Hubbard's home in East Aurora and would have looked as pictured here when he still worked at the Larkin Soap Company. The Soldier's Monument still stands but all of the other buildings have been replaced. The recently restored Lafayette Hotel is now located to the left side of the monument. The building on the right was the public library where Hubbard spent many hours of his time off from work, prior to moving to East Aurora, catching up on the classics he missed because he left school in the 10th grade in his hometown of Normal, Illinois, to sell soap for his cousin throughout the Midwest.

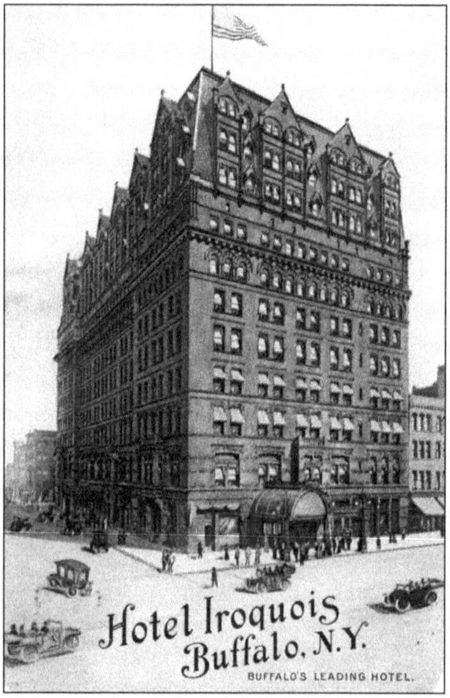


Elbert Hubbard hosted a very famous dinner to promote his magazine, *The Philistine*, with young writer Stephen Crane, just after the publication of the *Red Badge of Courage* in 1895. The dinner was held here at the Iroquois. The dinner's program was published as the first *Roycroft Quarterly* in 1896 and is a rare collectible today. Some correspondence still exists between Elbert and the Crane, giving him letters of introduction to some of his literary friends in London and advice on the proper attire. This was from a man who dressed in a Stetson hat, Oscar Wilde tie, corduroy pants, and western boots!

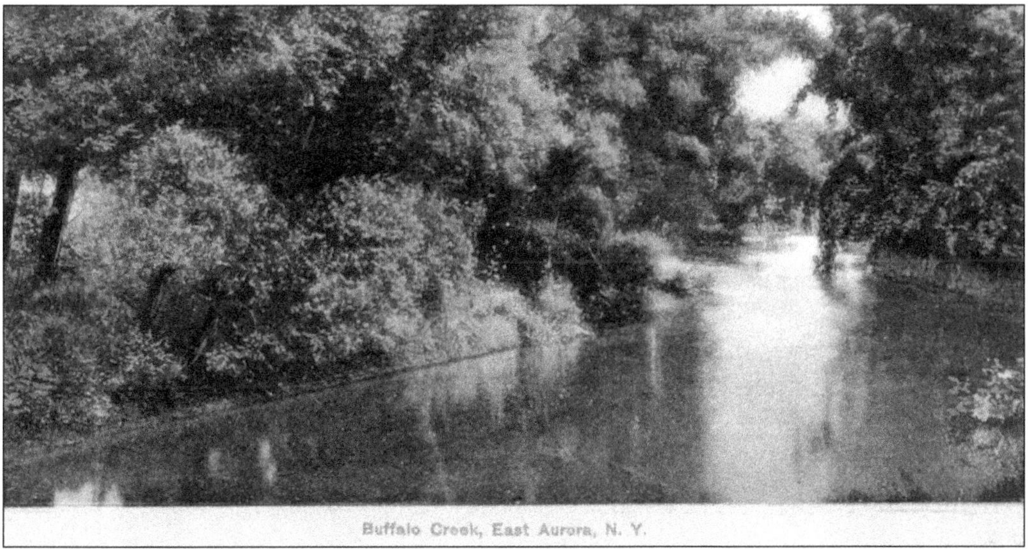


The second water source that flows through the village on the north side is Buffalo Creek. It flows through South Buffalo in an area where the Buffalo Creek Indian Reservation was at the time of Fillmore's administration. The doctor to the Native American inhabitant's was Elbert's father, Dr. Silas Hubbard (1825–1917). The reservation of about 50,000 acres was dissolved by the US government in 1842, the only one of the Seneca tribe reservations in Western New York. Many mills existed on the creek and waterpower was one of the reasons why the village flourished in the early 19th century.

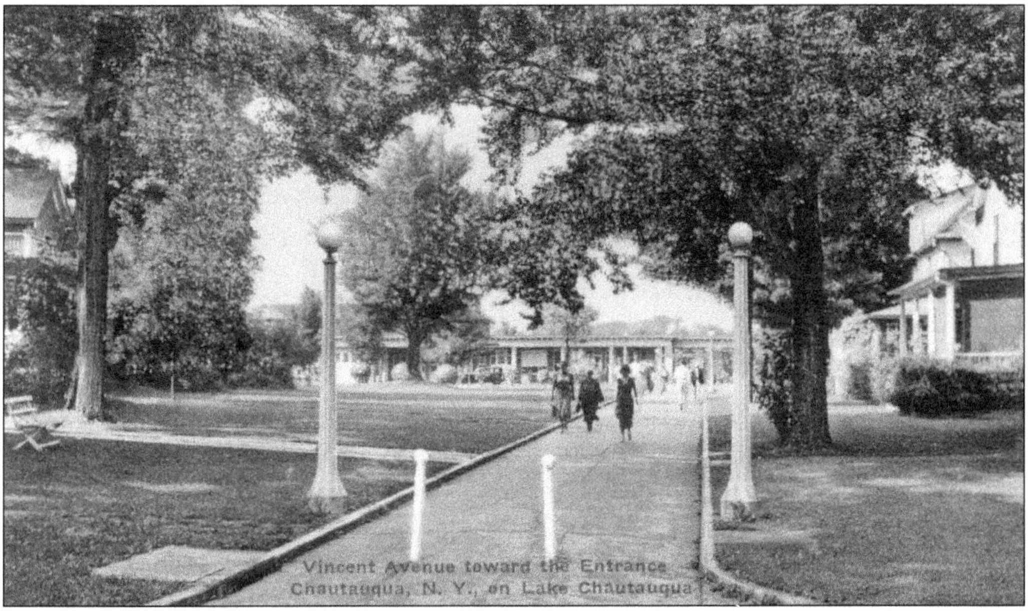


The main plaza at the Chautauqua Institute in southern New York State was a place where Elbert Hubbard lectured frequently until his affair with schoolteacher Alice Moore was known in 1900. He had initially met Alice at a Chautauqua Literary and Scientific Circle meeting held at his home in the 1880s, soon after he and first wife, Bertha Crawford Hubbard (1841–1946), had moved to the village. The Chautauqua movement was at its zenith during Hubbard's days and his doppelganger, William Jennings Bryan (1860–1925), was its most frequent lecturer.

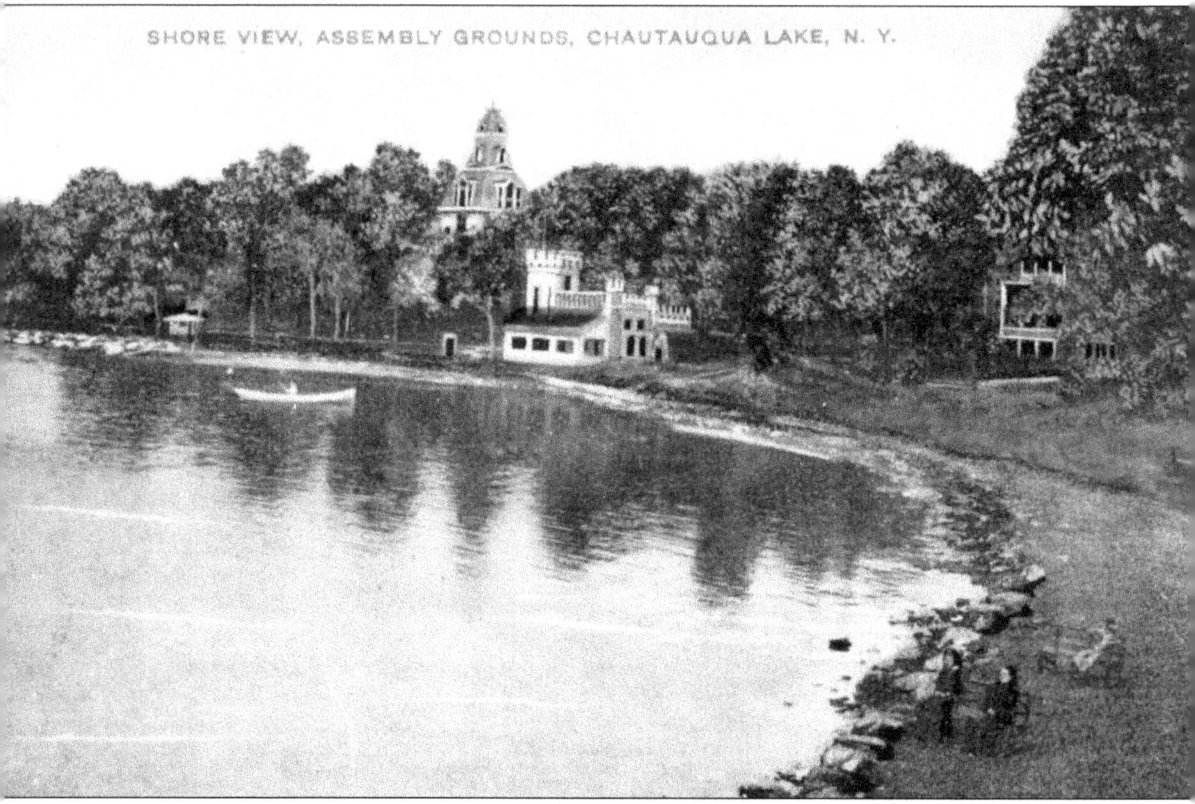


Because the southern shore of Chautauqua Lake was about midway between Buffalo, Pittsburgh, Cleveland, and Rochester, it was the perfect location for the founding of the first Chautauqua Assembly, now the Chautauqua Institute, in 1874. It was founded by Methodist Episcopal bishop John Heyl Vincent (1832–1920) and Lewis Miller (1829–1899), a philanthropist from Cleveland, Ohio. From its inception, the Roycroft's visitor would likely also travel the 70 miles by train to see and hear the many famous orators and authors at Chautauqua between the Fourth of July and early fall.

# *Two*

# Elbert Hubbard
## The Sage of East Aurora

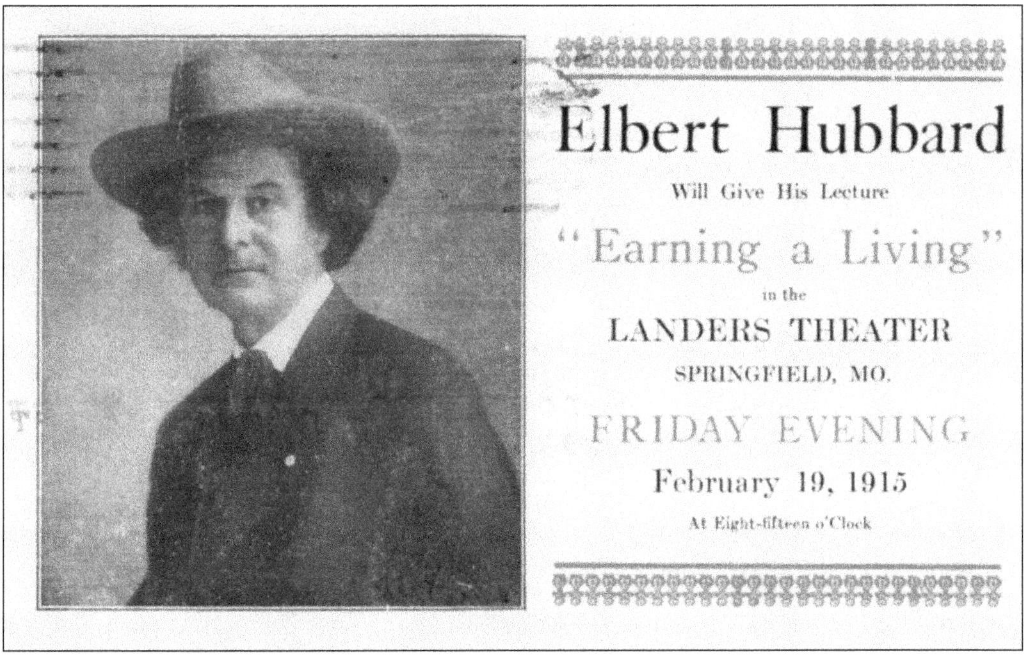


Hubbard was considered a master salesman and one of the founders of modern-day advertising, starting as a young man in Illinois and always sharing his ideas with others, be it in print or his hundreds of lectures, as shown here. (Author's collection.)

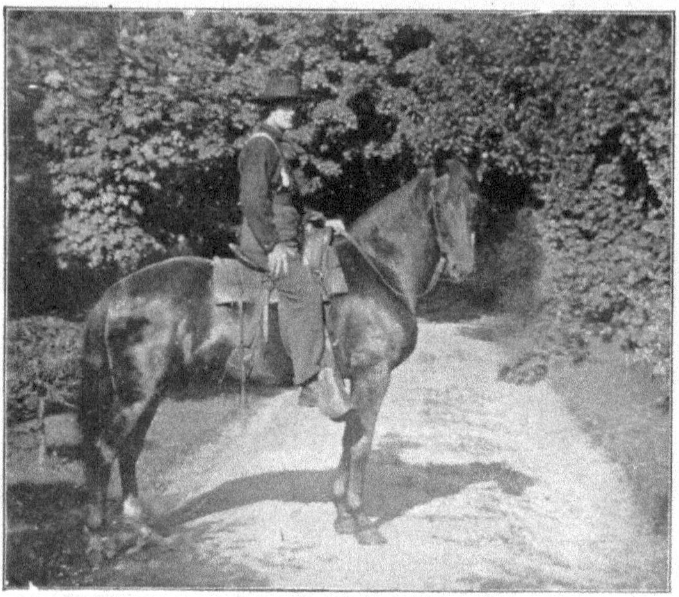


*Fra Elbertus and Garnet*

What brought Elbert Hubbard to the village was its horsiness as much as its New England charm. It had more churches than bars on Main Street and was a good place to raise his boys. He rode his favorite mare named Garnett almost every day after work. Once Roycroft became more than just a press, he would lead rides out into the countryside. In this photograph from around 1900, he has already morphed into his second life as Fra Elbertus, leader of the flock of Roycrofters.

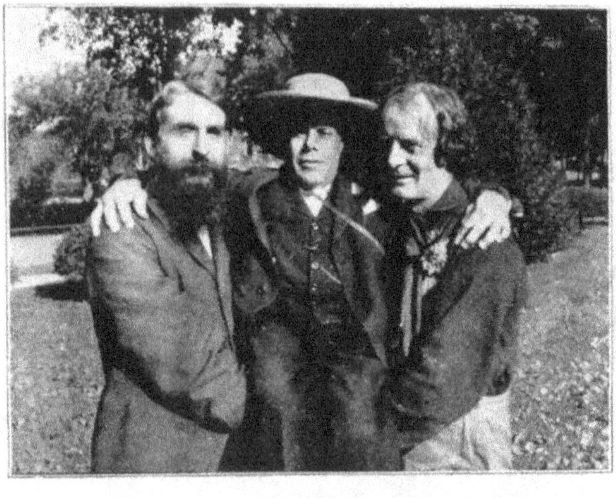


*Honest Roycrofters Three (more or less)*

By 1900, Elbert was already famous, and the already famous celebrities of the day came to visit. Shown here are two that represent two aspects of Hubbard's oeuvre: on the left, Englishman George Wharton James (1858–1923), famous for his writings on the American Indians and a student of John Ruskin, and in their arms the equally famous Marshall P. Wilder (1859–1915), American actor and humorist who also later was the editor of the *Wit and Humor of America*, a 10-volume set published in 1911. Though he suffered with dwarfism and kyphosis, Wilder was a major draw, especially with the royal family in England at this time. Hubbard even produced a special chair in his honor that was named for him and made in the Arts and Crafts style.

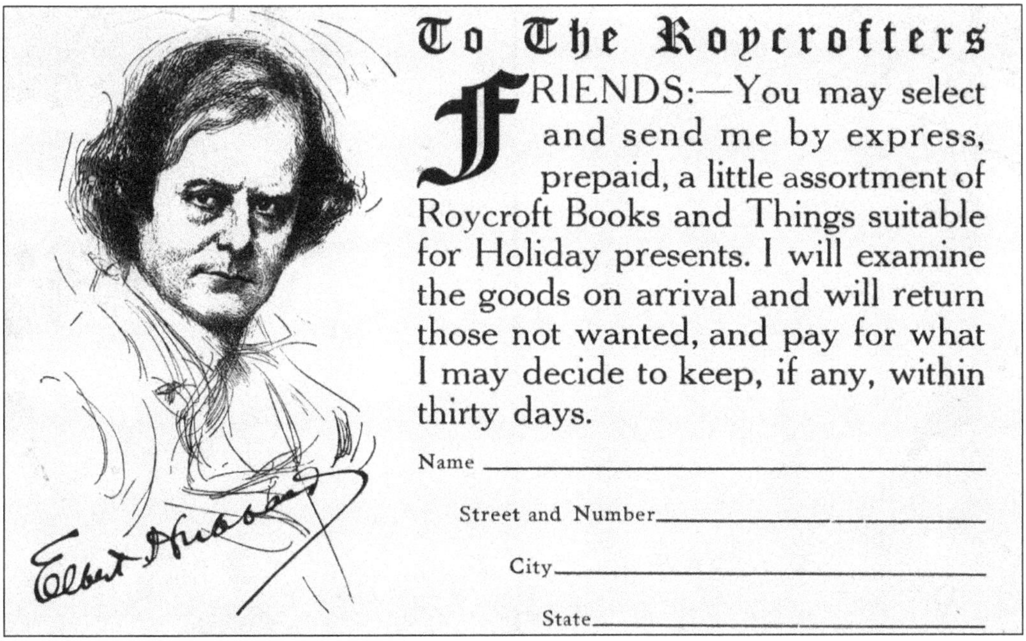


Hubbard was credited as the inventor of endorsement advertising and used his own image to help sell the products of his book artists and craftspeople by postcards sent nationwide. The signature here is printed on the plate, not personally signed.

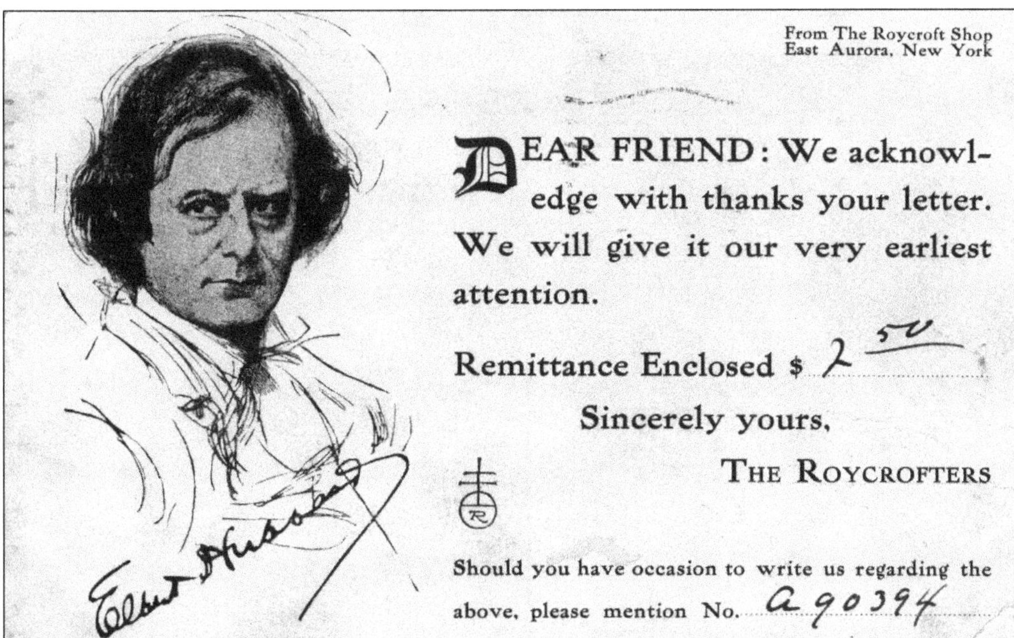


This card, using the same blank, was utilized over and over again for any business correspondence in bulk. Collectors seek out the various differences and especially those sent to famous people of the day. Also, unmailed cards always seem to be more valuable, though this is a fairly common card found throughout the United States.

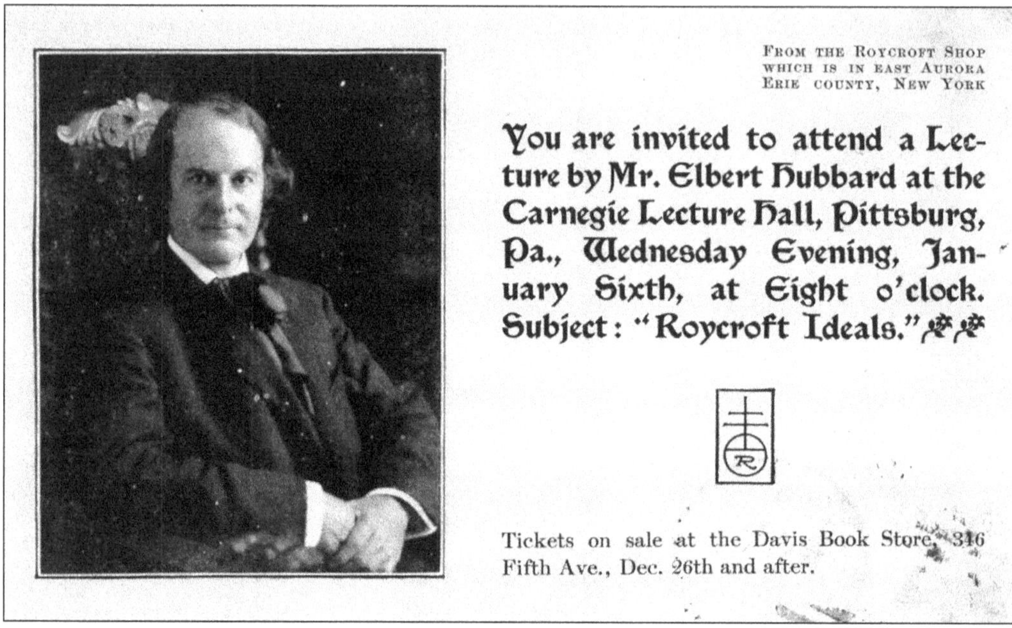


The most heavily collected cards and some of the rarest are those sent out in advance of Elbert's lectures. This one for the other Carnegie Hall in Pittsburgh, Pennsylvania, around 1905, shows him presenting an hour-long sermon on his workers, their products, and the Arts and Crafts philosophy; what today would be called an infomercial!

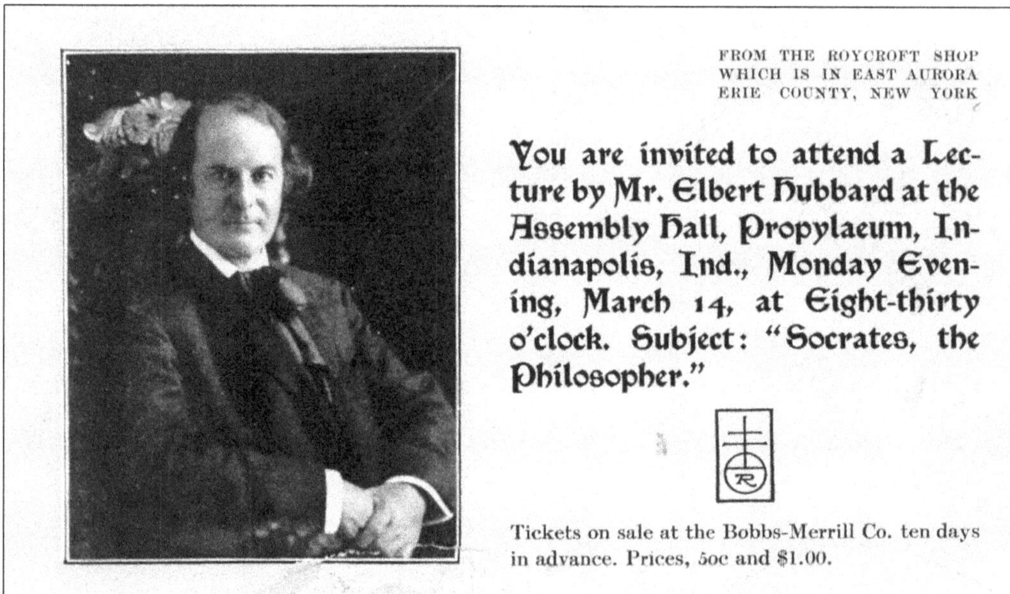


Pictured is an almost identical card to the previous one shown, but this one was for a lecture on Socrates in Hubbard's famous *Little Journeys* series, which was given in Indianapolis in the same year. He had a cadre of over 100 different programs and was on many lecture circuits, the most famous was the Orpheum, which meant appearances away from East Aurora more than three months a year in his heyday from 1900 until his death in 1915.

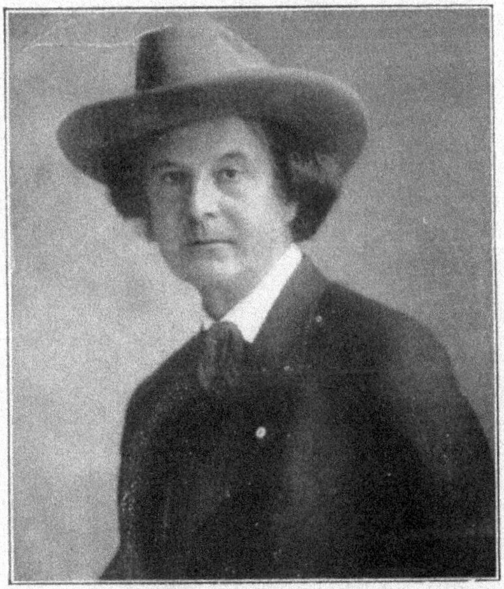

ELBERT HUBBARD

*From*

THE ROYCROFT SHOPS

EAST AURORA, N. Y.

AN educated man is one with a universal sympathy for everything and a certain amount of knowledge about everything that is known, and who still is on the line of evolution and is learning to the end.

—*Fra Elbertus*

This card shows Elbert in his prime. He sat for most of the famous portrait photographers of the day. His favorite seemed to be the Moffet Studios in Chicago. The actual photographs, suitable for framing in Roycroft oak frames, were sold to his followers and hung on the walls of many offices and bungalows throughout the country. Some of these were personally autographed and are the most collectable today.

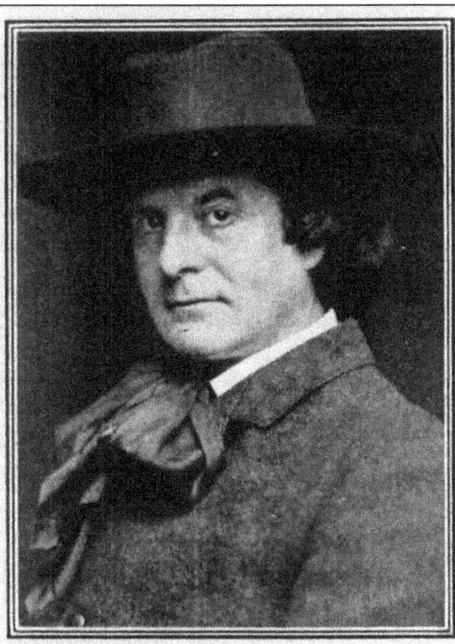

FROM THE ROYCROFT SHOP
WHICH IS IN EAST AURORA
ERIE COUNTY, N. Y., U. S. A.

Being photographed so often by so many helps show today how the stress of all the travel aged him. This image, when compared to the previous one, shows the bags under his eyes and an almost weary look. Taken in late 1913 or early 1914, it was only months before he was to board the *Lusitania* for his last voyage.

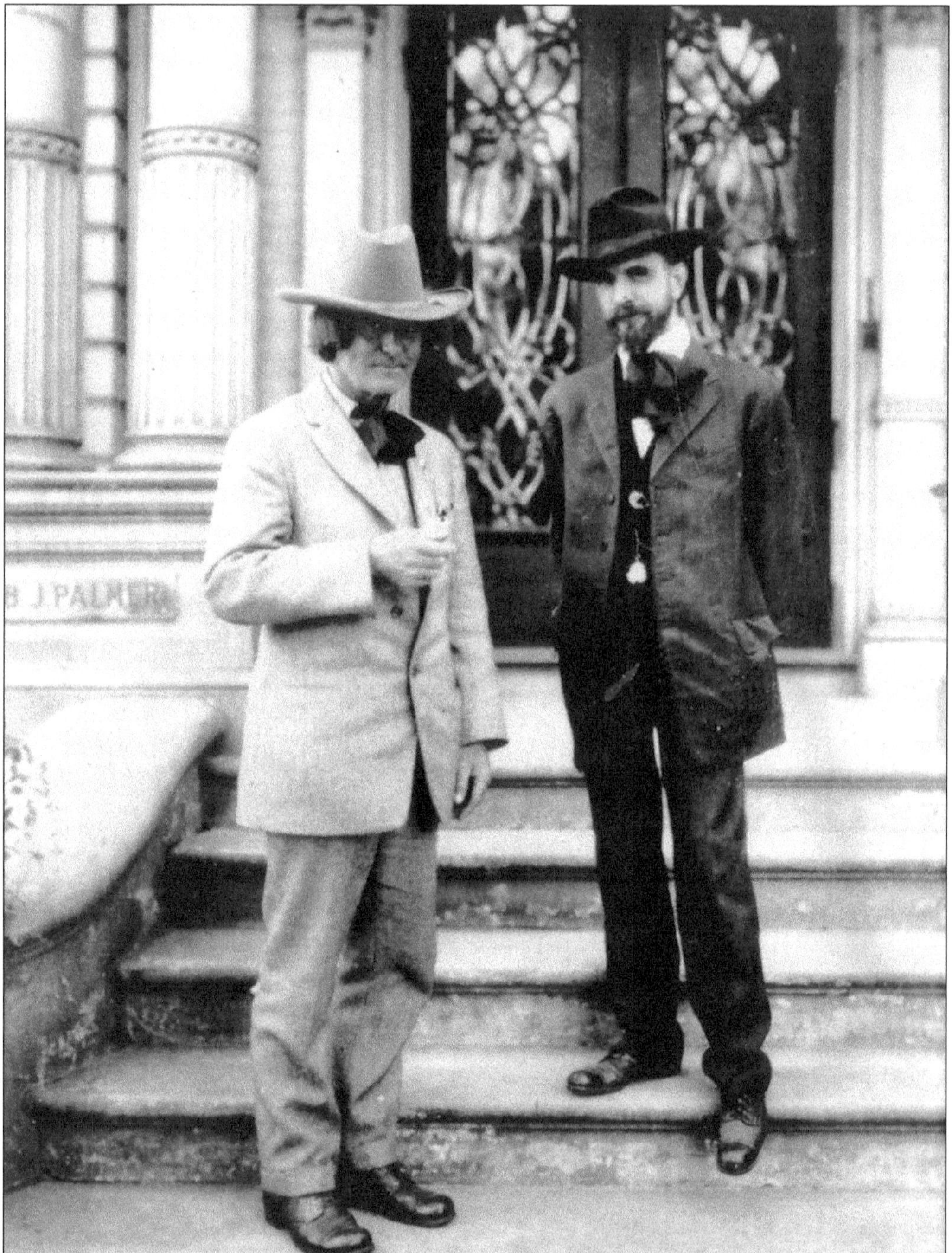


This rare and real-photo postcard (RPC) shows Elbert with one of his good friends, B.J. Palmer (1862–1961), on the steps of Palmer's home in Davenport, Iowa, around 1905. Hubbard fully endorsed Palmer's Chiropractic Medicine in his magazines with full-page advertisements, using this photograph in *The Fra*. His father, Dr. Silas Hubbard, MD, though also a phrenologist, did not agree with his son. He was known to be very vocal in his opposition during Hubbard's Sunday lectures from the platform in the inn's music salon.

Almost as good-looking as his much more famous father, Elbert Green(e) Hubbard II was his father's favorite son. Bert, as he was known especially after his father's death, ran the Roycroft Enterprises until 1938 and a business selling the Roycroft books, as the House of Hubbard, until his death. He lived in a large English Tudor Revival house up the hill just north of the campus named Hubbard Hill. It was built in 1929 just as the Depression was to end many of the aspects of the American Arts and Crafts Movement.

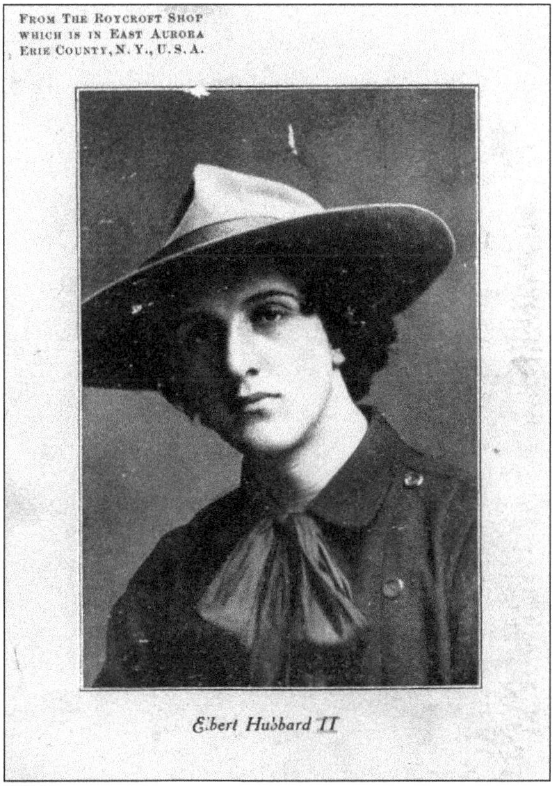


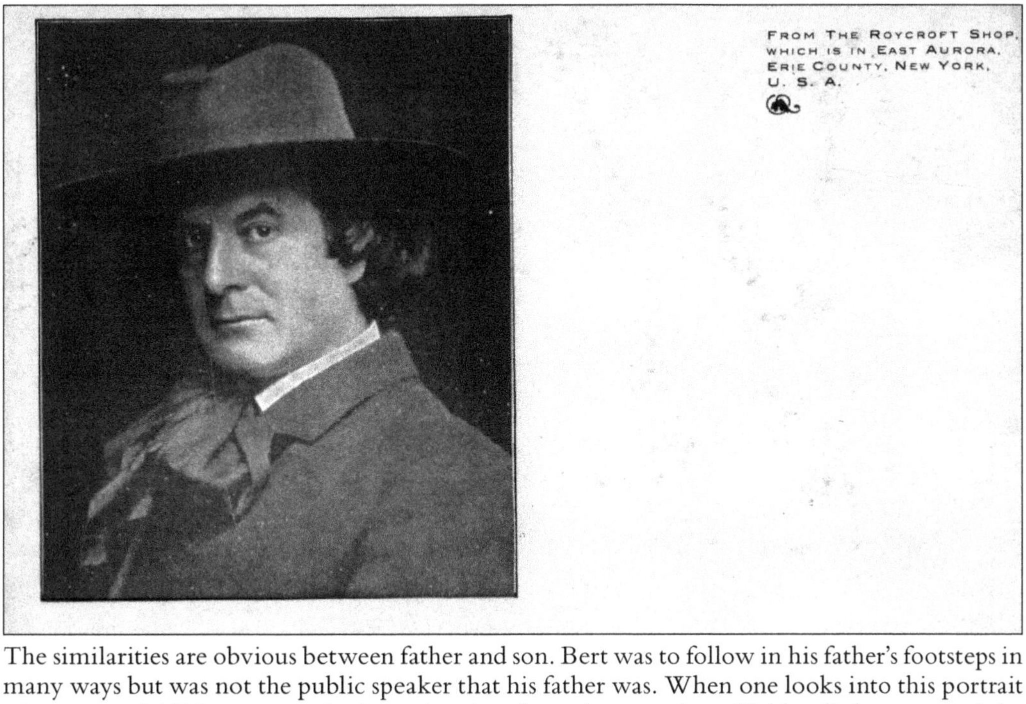


The similarities are obvious between father and son. Bert was to follow in his father's footsteps in many ways but was not the public speaker that his father was. When one looks into this portrait taken around 1910, one sees the intensity that drew the crowds to Hubbard's lectures and the thousands to visit East Aurora and the campus to see the man himself and his workers.

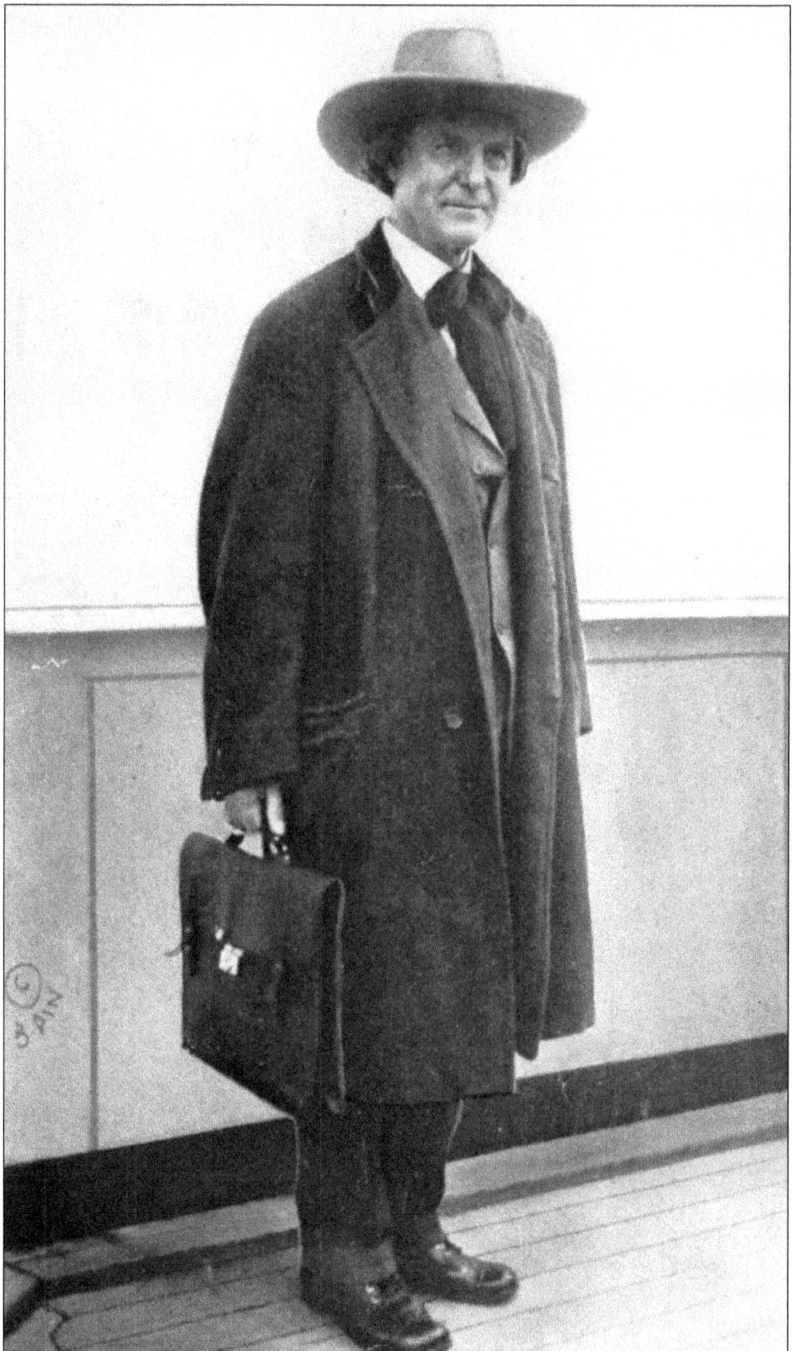

This image taken of Elbert Hubbard on board the RMS *Lusitania* on May 1, 1915, in New York Harbor by press photographer Bain was issued as a memorial postcard. It was published in hundreds of newspapers after the ship was torpedoed in the Irish Sea by a German submarine six days later, on May 7. Elbert and second wife, Alice, were on their way to Europe on their first visit there together. Elbert had told the press he would attempt to meet the Kaiser and keep the United States out of the World War I, or the Great War as it was known then.

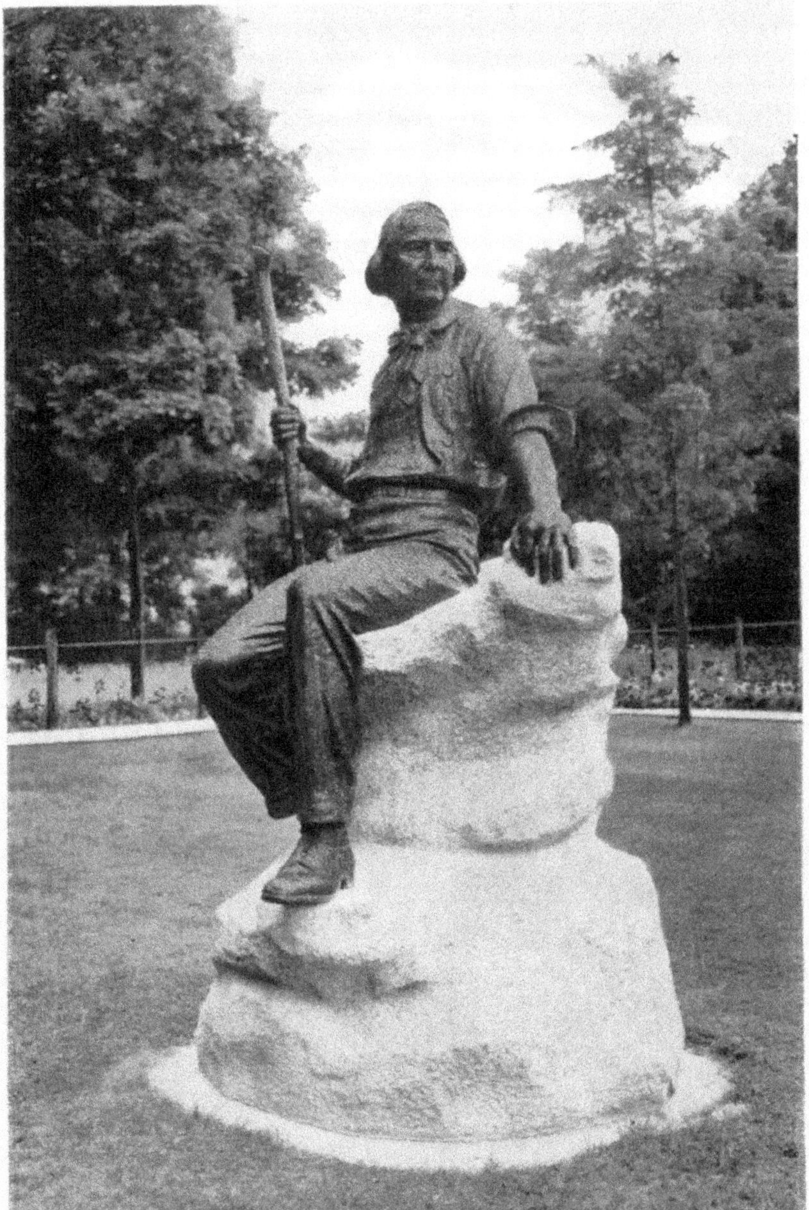

BRONZE STATUE (HEROIC SIZE) OF ELBERT HUBBARD ERECTED ON THE ROYCROFT CAMPUS, EAST AURORA, N. Y., JUNE 19TH, 1930 HIS 74TH BIRTHDAY. ST. JEROME CONNOR, SCULPTOR

On Elbert's birthday, June 19, 1930, this large, bronze, heroic sculpture of Hubbard as leader of his flock was unveiled to hundreds. The sculpture was created in the Dublin, Ireland, studio of original Roycroft artist and designer Jerome Connor (1874–1943). The more than life-size depiction sat on the lawn of the Print Shop, across from the inn, from 1930 through the late 1950s, when the need for a parking lot almost forced its destruction. Moved across Main Street to the Aurora Middle School lawn, today it looks across at the campus he founded more than 100 years ago.

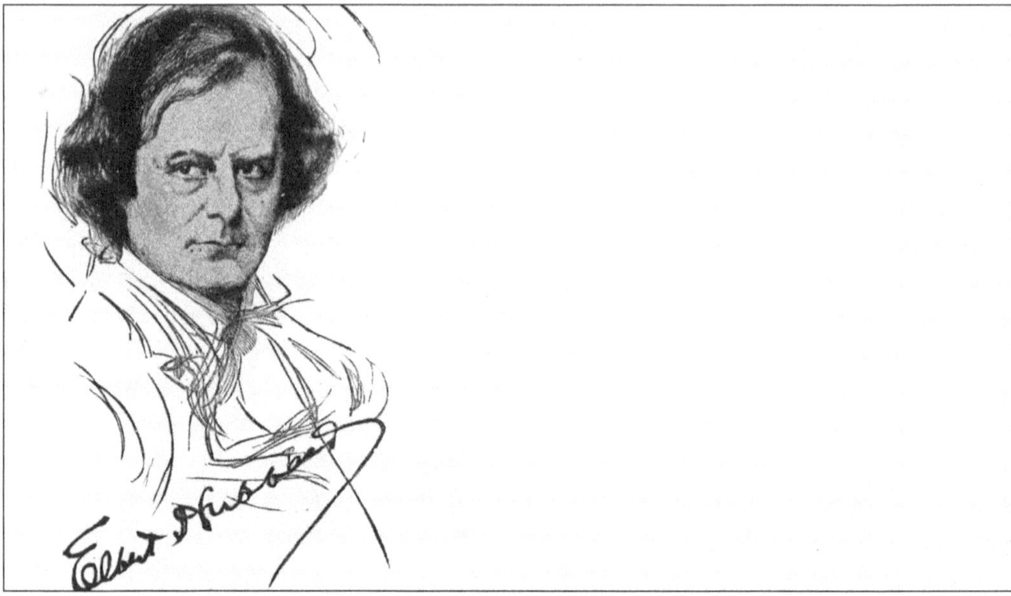

This blank card is one of the most common of the portrait cards found today. The original ink sketch was done by Roycroft artist Otto J. Schneider (1875–1946). He was most well-known for his illustrations used as the frontispieces of the individual monthly *Little Journeys*, once they began to be issued by the Roycroft Press in 1902, rather than G.P. Putnam and Sons in New York, the original publisher.

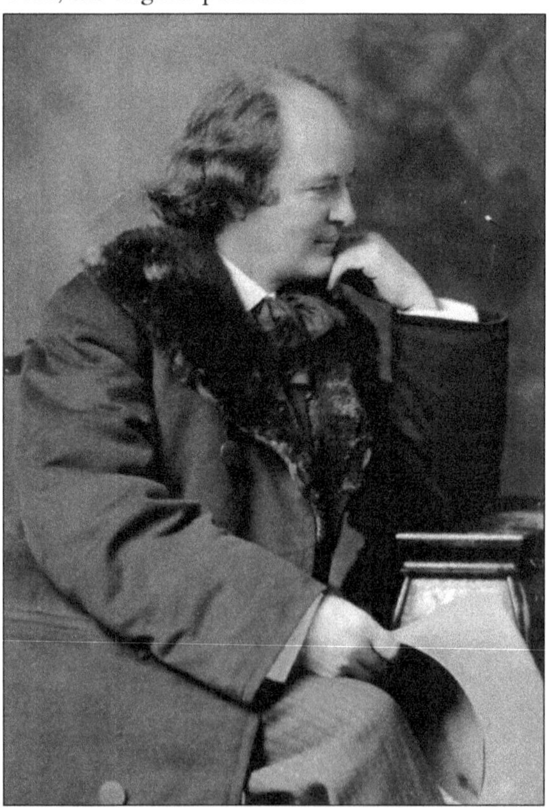

Elbert traveled to nearby Canada as well, and in Ottawa he posed for this card, which would be given out or sold to lecture attendees. This image dates from about 1913.

# *Three*

# From the Phalanstery into an Inn 1898–1938

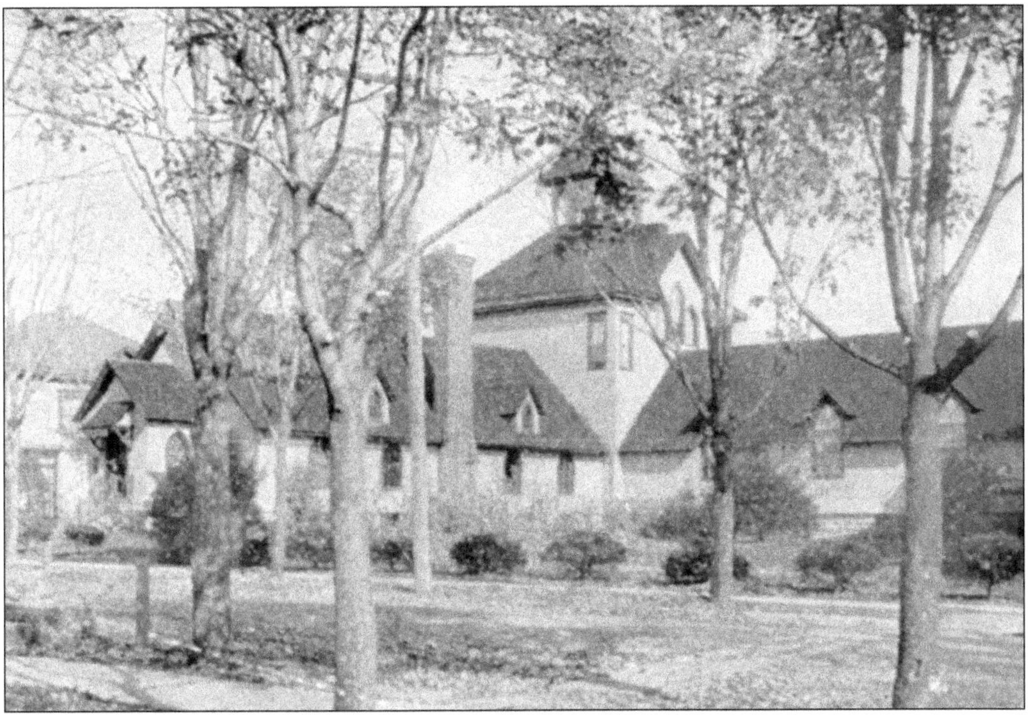

This is the only image of the first shop on a postcard from the first series issued in 1899 and 1900. The structure was then known as the Roycroft Print Shop and Phalanstery. This title was only used for about five years, when major additions were made connecting Hubbard's own home, just off this photograph to the left, and his neighbor's house, to the far left, with a long porch structure. By 1905, when the inn was completed, the visitors to the campus did not recognize this church-like wooden building.

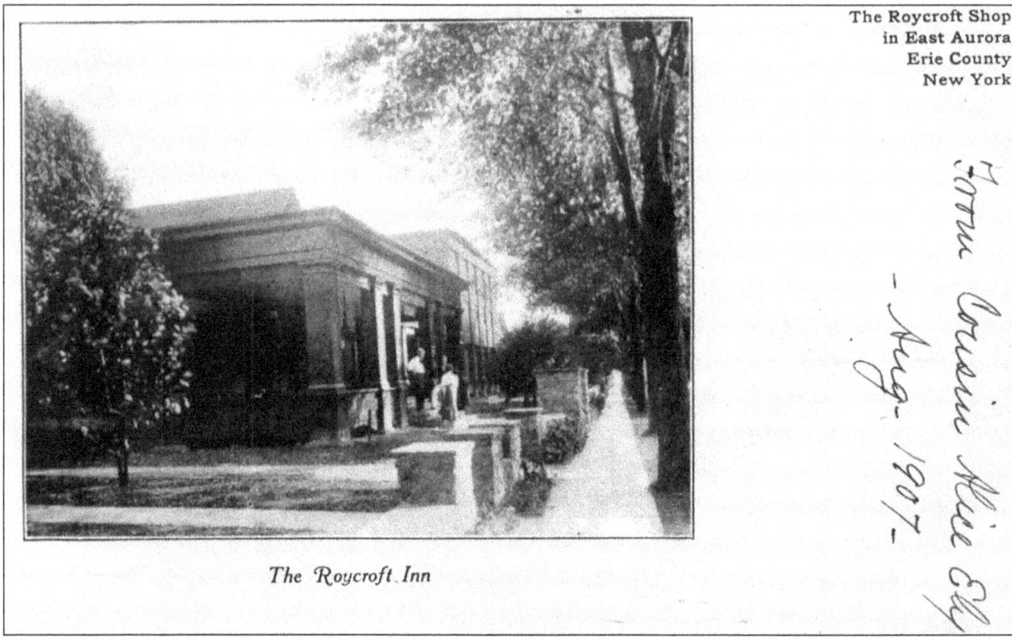


This card sent in 1907 looks down the east side of South Grove Street at the completed Roycroft Inn. What is especially significant of this image is that on the steps of the inn are Elbert Hubbard and soon to be famous Arts and Crafts designer Dard Hunter (1883–1966) from Chillicothe, Ohio. Hunter designed the most notable of the Roycroft Press's books starting in 1904 and 1905. His designs were used for the life of the press, though he was only on the campus until 1909.

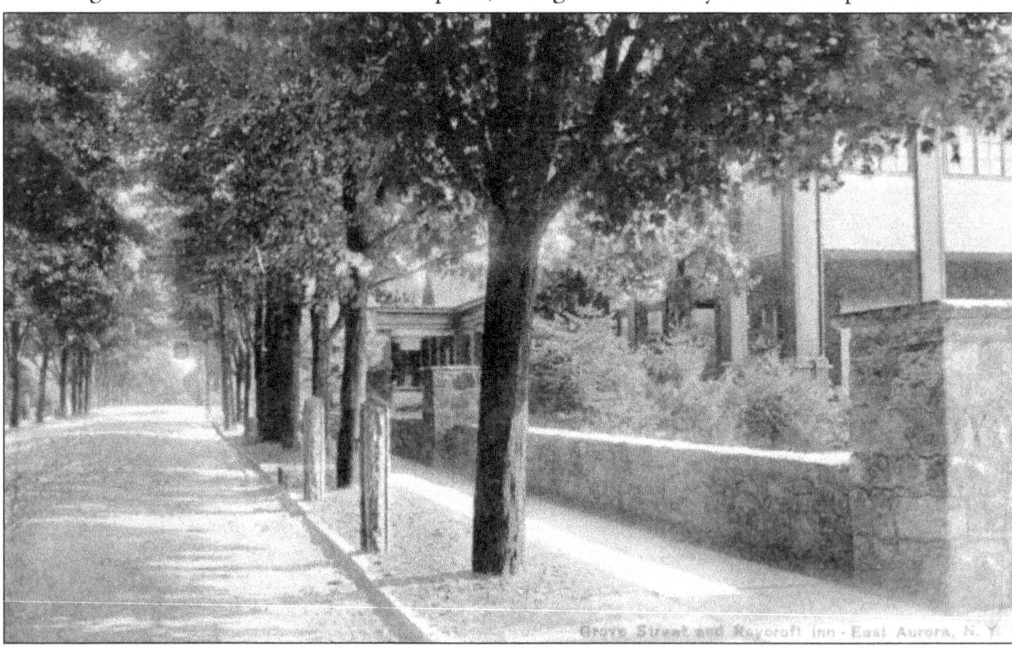


Made at the same time as the previous card, this view shows the original hitching posts that were left during the 1905 renovation. The original Hubbard House was incorporated into the new hotel structure and contained the living quarters for Elbert Hubbard and his new wife, Alice, and their 10-year-old daughter, Miriam Elberta Hubbard (1894–1985).

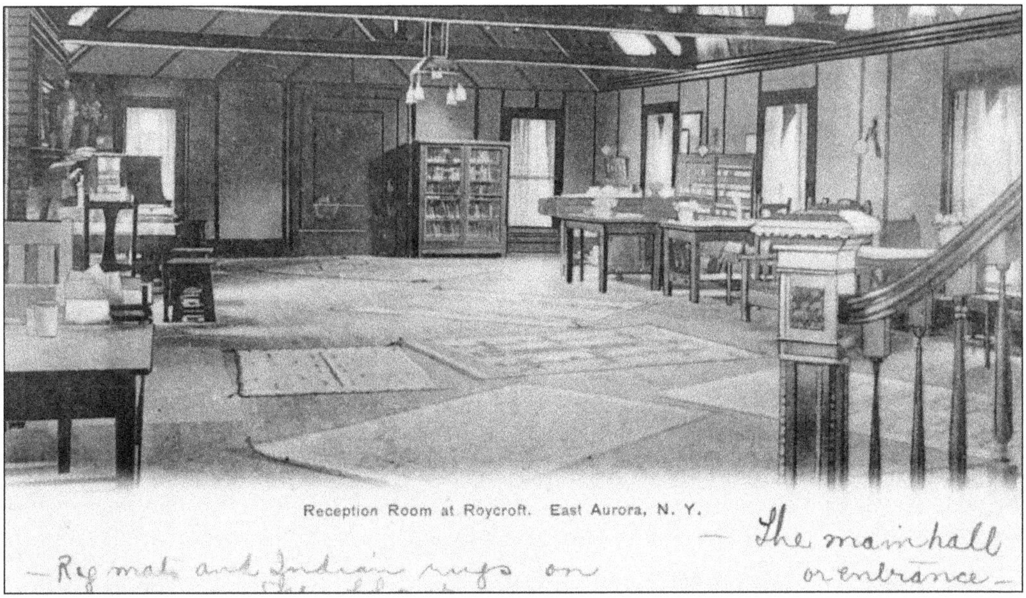


Inside the renovated Print Shop and Phalanstery, one saw a room filled with newly made Roycroft furniture, signed with the name and the now famous orb and cross logo. As written on this card, it also had rag mats and Indian rugs on the floor. All the furniture was also marked with an inventory mark with building location and style number, so the guests could order some to have shipped to their homes. The copper and glass hanging fixtures were designed by Dard Hunter in the Voysey style with heart cutouts; some of these still exist elsewhere and appear at auctions occasionally.

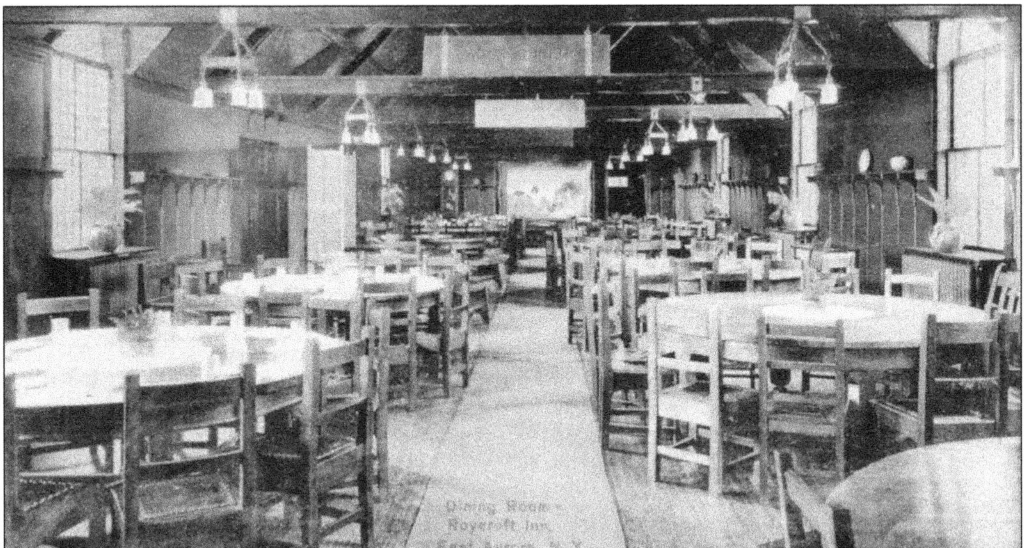


Also around 1905 and 1906, this shot shows the first incarnation of the dining room of the Roycroft Inn with Alexis Jean Fournier's large painting *Entrance to the Grand Canal, Venice 1901.* Hubbard had met Fournier at the 1893 Columbian Exposition; it is believed they also met at the 1901 Pan American Exposition in nearby Buffalo. He convinced Alex, who replaced Samuel Warner as art director of the Roycrofters in 1902, to bring this large artwork with him. It is presently on view at the Burchfield-Penney Art Center in Buffalo, New York.

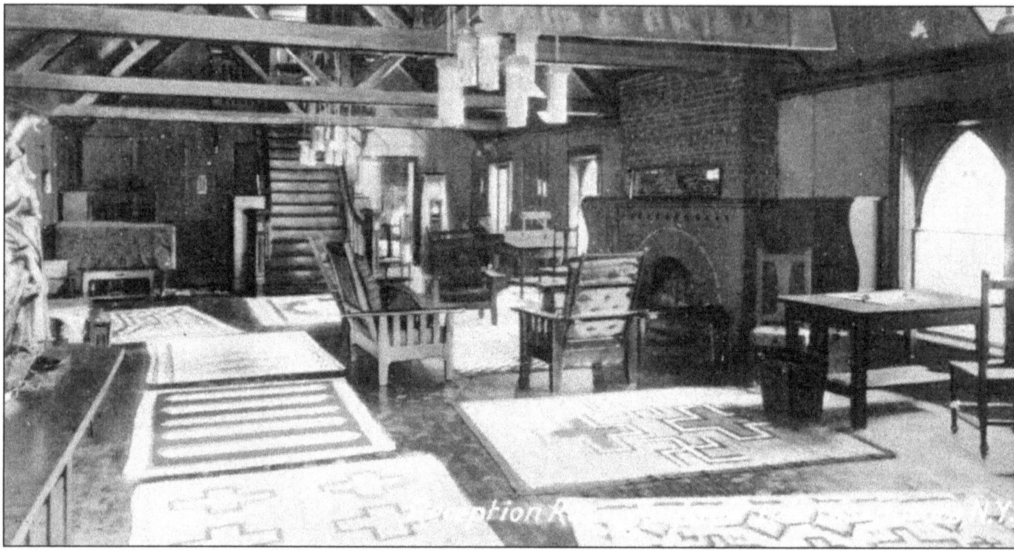

Compare this to the earlier image of the reception room and lobby of the inn and one sees many improvements. Exquisite art glass chandeliers in the new Secessionist style from Austria were designed and installed by Dard Hunter in 1910. These originals were removed in the 1950s, but exact reproductions were made in 1995 and were ready for the reopening of the inn after being closed for almost eight years. Newer styles of morris chairs and a one-of-a-kind oak tall case clock were installed, which can be seen in the background on the right. It would be a major discovery if its location were found today.

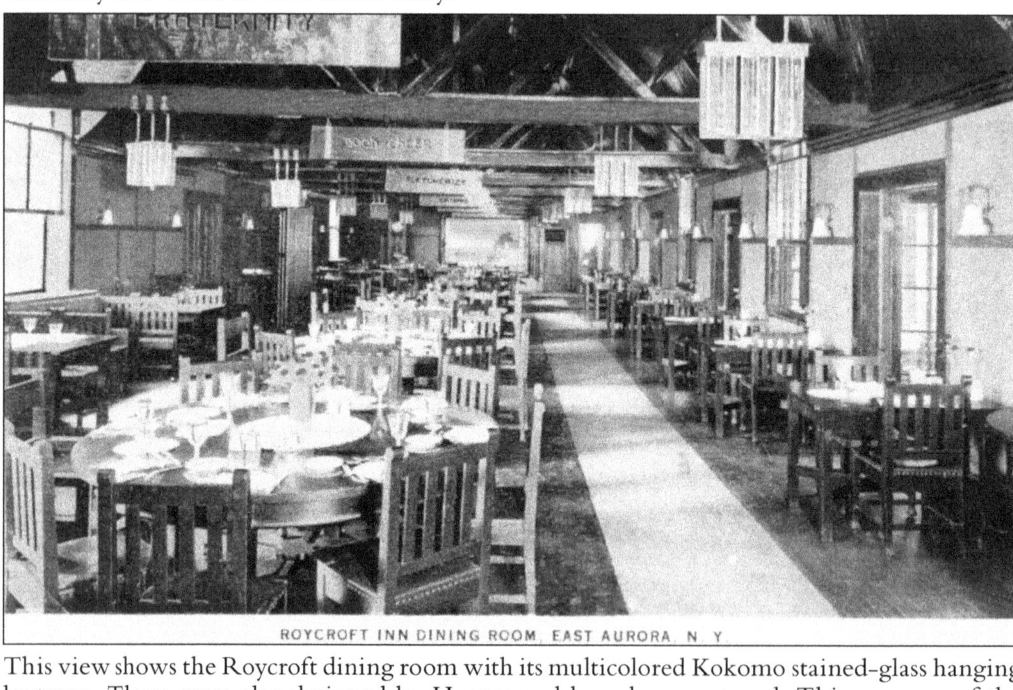


This view shows the Roycroft dining room with its multicolored Kokomo stained-glass hanging lanterns. These were also designed by Hunter and have been restored. This was one of the most elegant rooms in the Arts and Crafts style in America at the time. It was unfortunately divided up by owners in the late 1950s and only since 1995 have guests been able to experience a somewhat similar space.

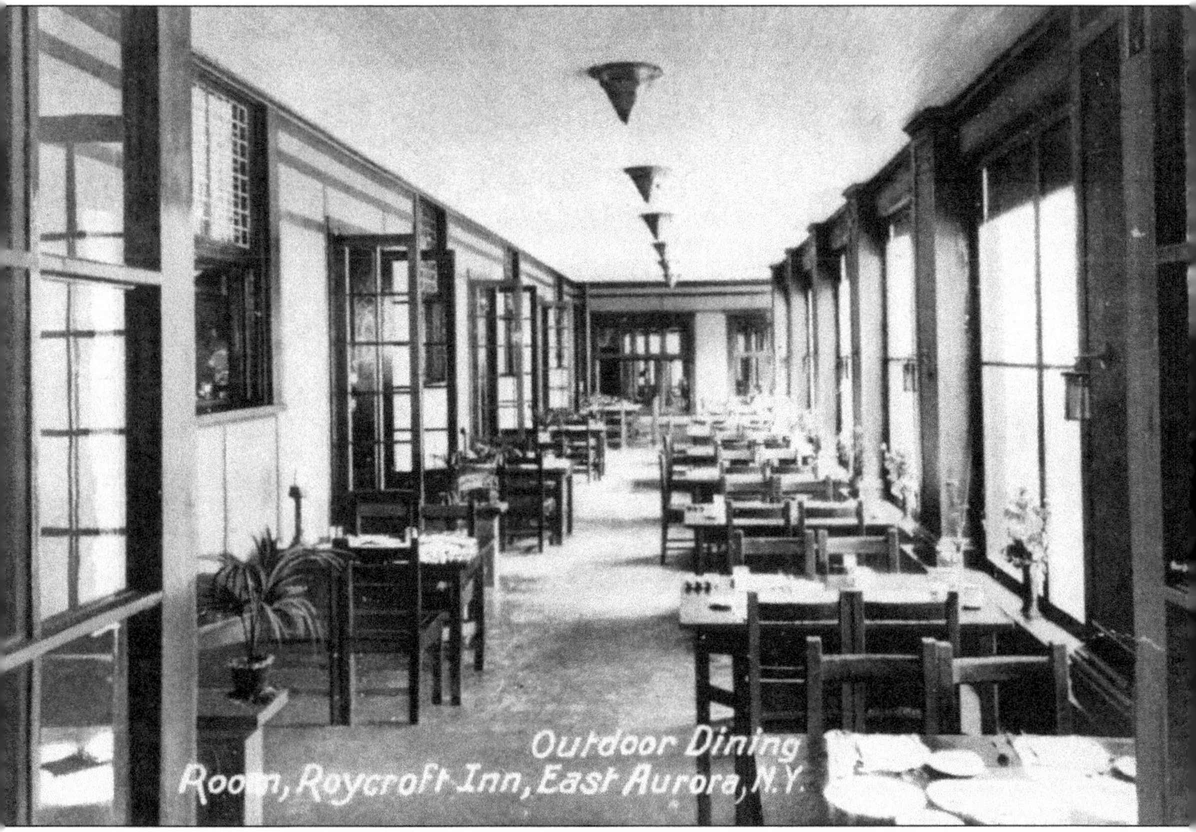


Turning right and down three stairs from the reception room, one enters the outdoor dining room that was open for the summers starting around 1910. One will notice the tables fully set, and if one could see back in time, it would be Roycroft's own house china pattern made by the Buffalo china division of Larkin Soap Company. It is said to have been designed by Dard Hunter.

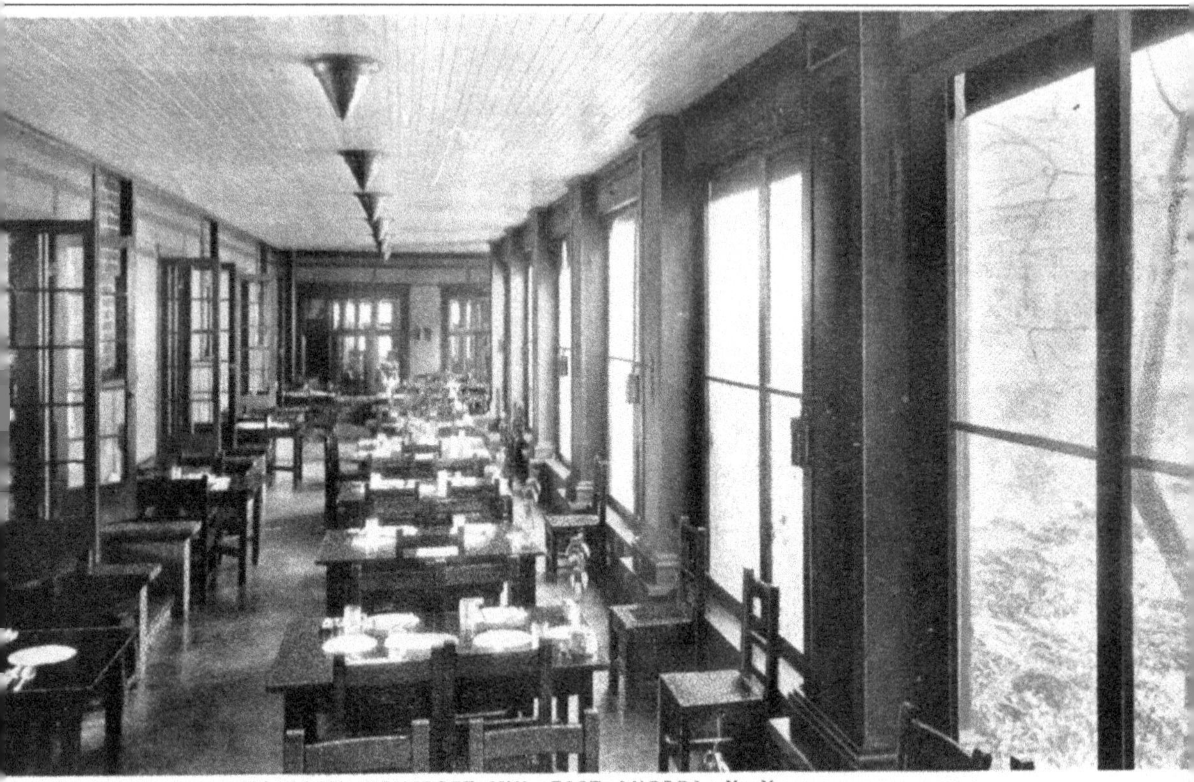

OUTDOOR DINING ROOM, ROYCROFT INN, EAST AURORA, N. Y.

This photograph, taken about 10 years later, shows a different table setting and by this time full glass covered the windows and heat was sent across the street from the new powerhouse in the form of hot water. Missing on close inspection are the very rare copper and glass table lamps seen in the earlier view. These lamps, also designed by Hunter, are almost unknown to collectors today.

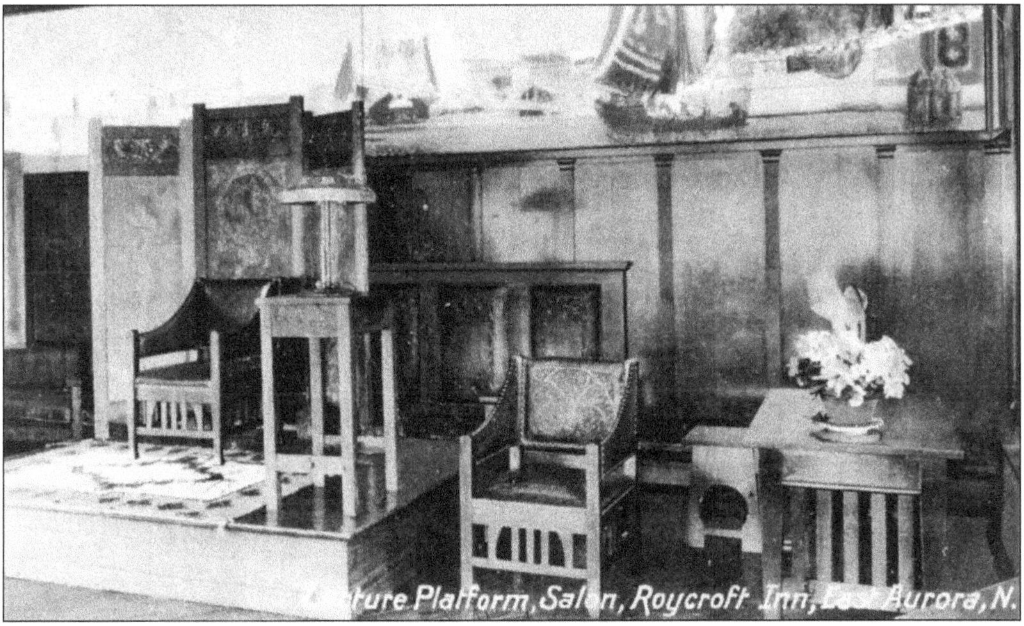


The largest and most beautiful room was the music salon. An undertaking of Alice Hubbard, Alexis Fournier, and James Santiago Cadzow (whose names were emblazoned on a bronze plaque), this multiuse room was a delight to visitors and locals alike. The murals by Fournier, the *Eight Wonders of the World*, were painted in his studio on Walnut Street and delivered to the inn in a procession of Roycrofters in 1905. The eighth wonder was of course the Roycroft Campus, shown in a time-line style from Indian village to modern day in 1905.

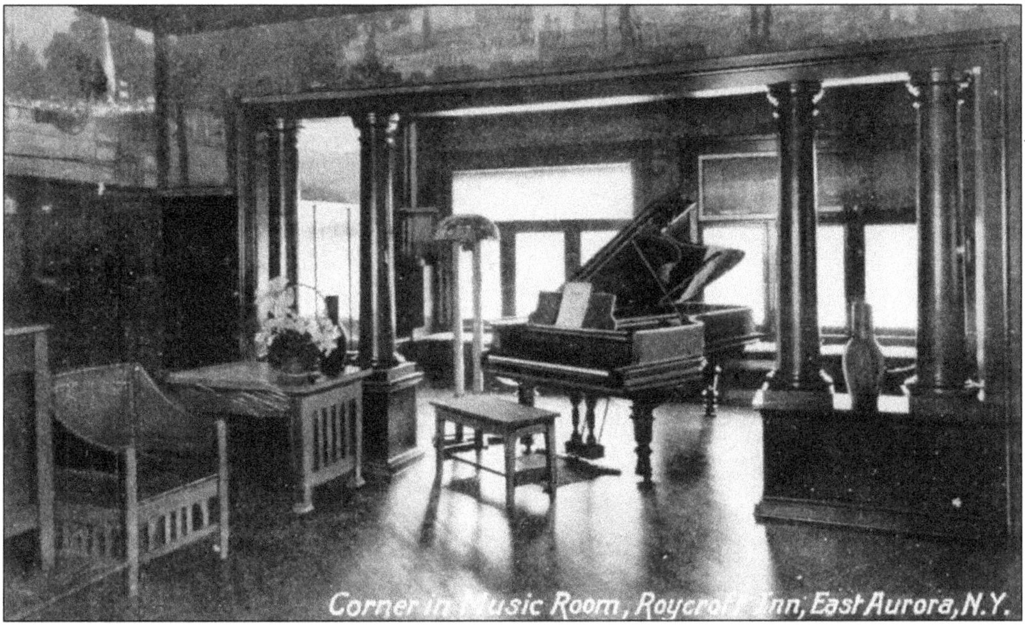


This view looks to the southeast through the salon to the gardens beyond. Featured are one of a dozen pianos scattered throughout the campus buildings, including some Steinways, and the special furnishings designed for this room by Dard Hunter and the modeled leather department in the Furniture Shop across the street.

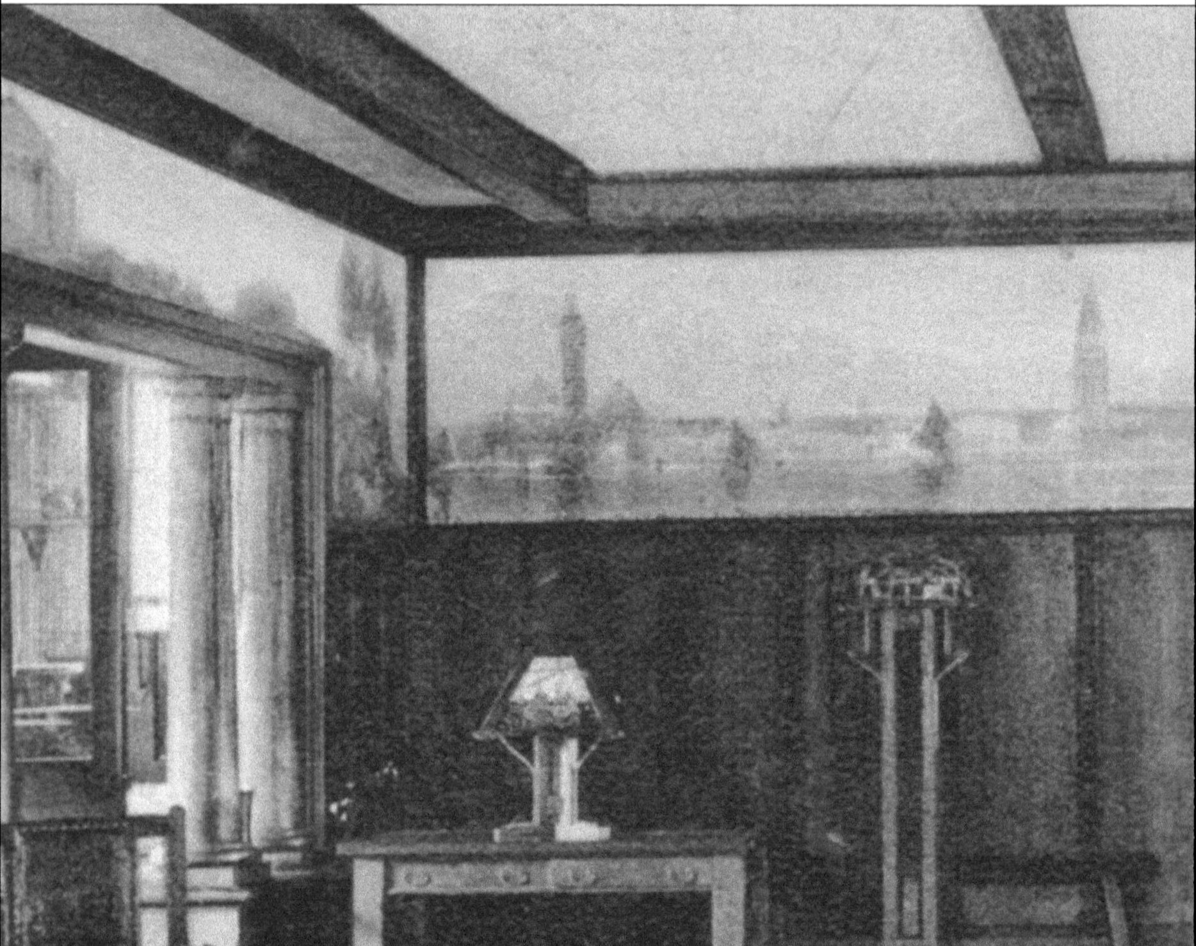


Looking towards the east with the lecture platform removed, two fabulous leaded and stained-glass lamps by Hunter can be seen. The table lamp on the left features a sailing ship, and the floor

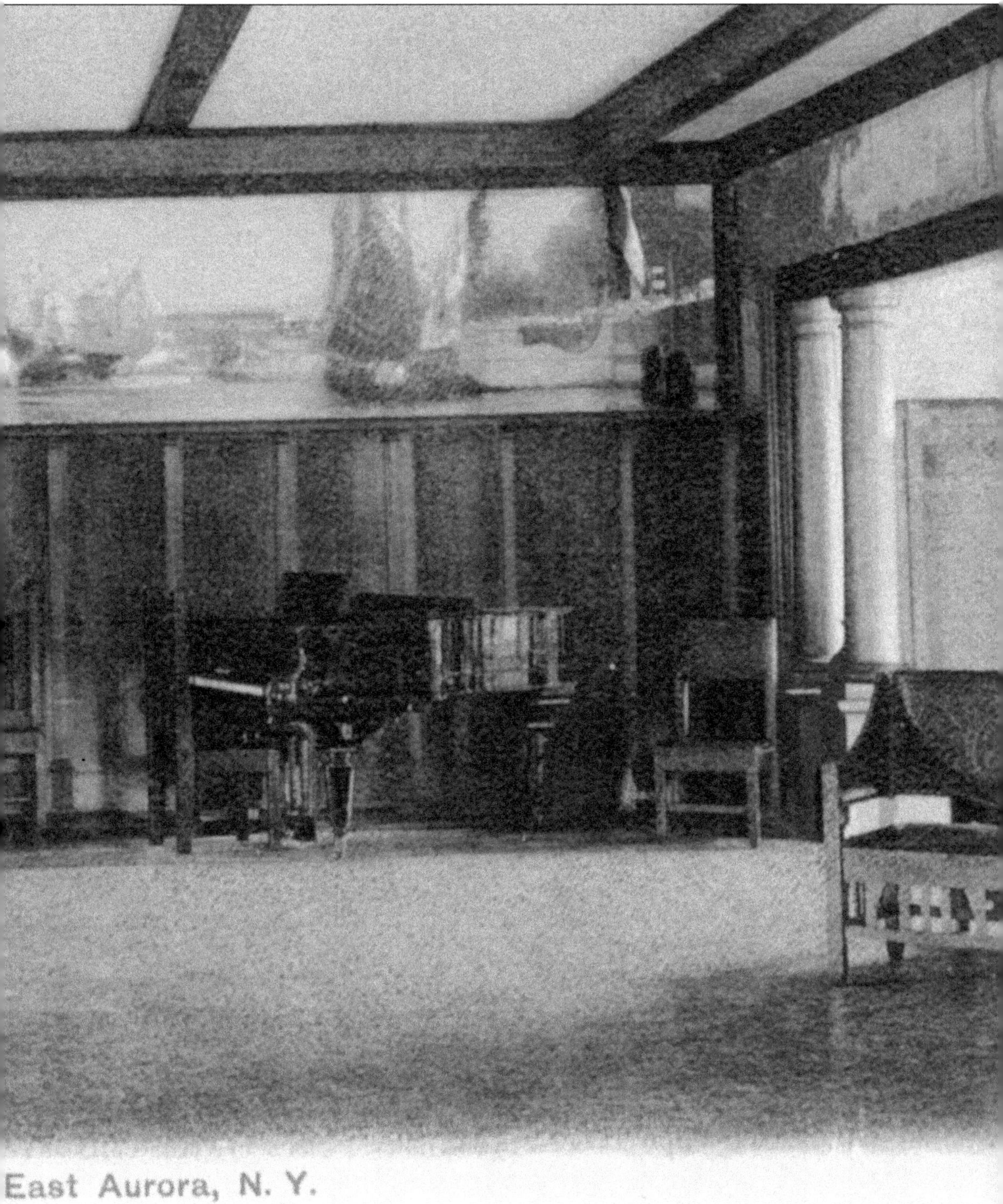


lamp in oak and leaded glass features a dragonfly pattern in gold and green. The whereabouts of both of these masterpieces of design and execution are unknown to the author.

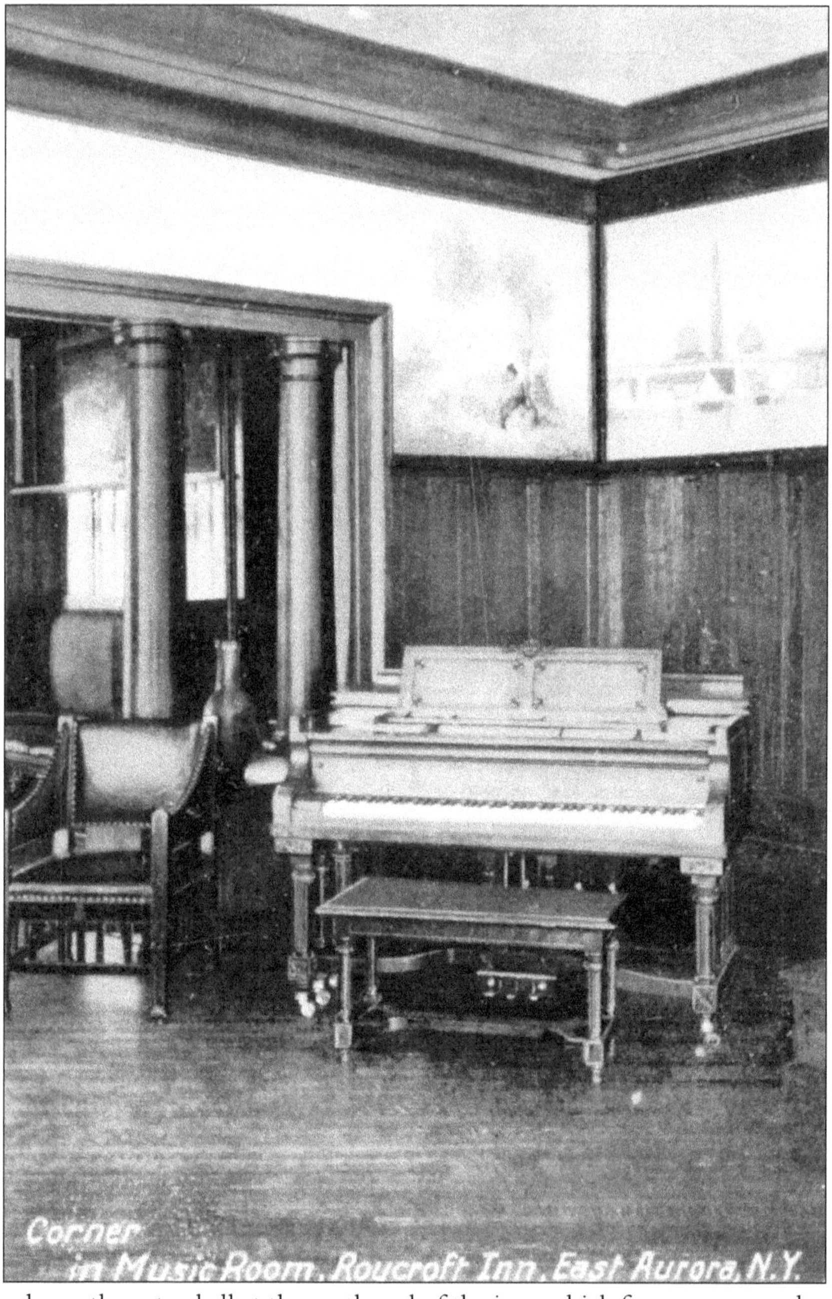


This view shows the entry hall at the south end of the inn, which features a second set of four murals by Fournier, depicting the *Four Seasons*. They were painted on stretched canvas and restored in the late 1990s by the Keck Conservation School of Buffalo State University College at Buffalo. The special leather and oak armchair is one of two used on the dais for Hubbard and his special guests, who were invited to speak here. These lecturers included Clarence Darrow, Henry Ford, Carl Sandburg, Margaret Sangster, Susan B. Anthony, and Elbert and Alice Hubbard. Musical performances were held weekly and directed by Rudolph von Liebiech, the music director. One of the performers who used the piano was Edith Cornell, destined to be Mrs. Dard Hunter in 1908.

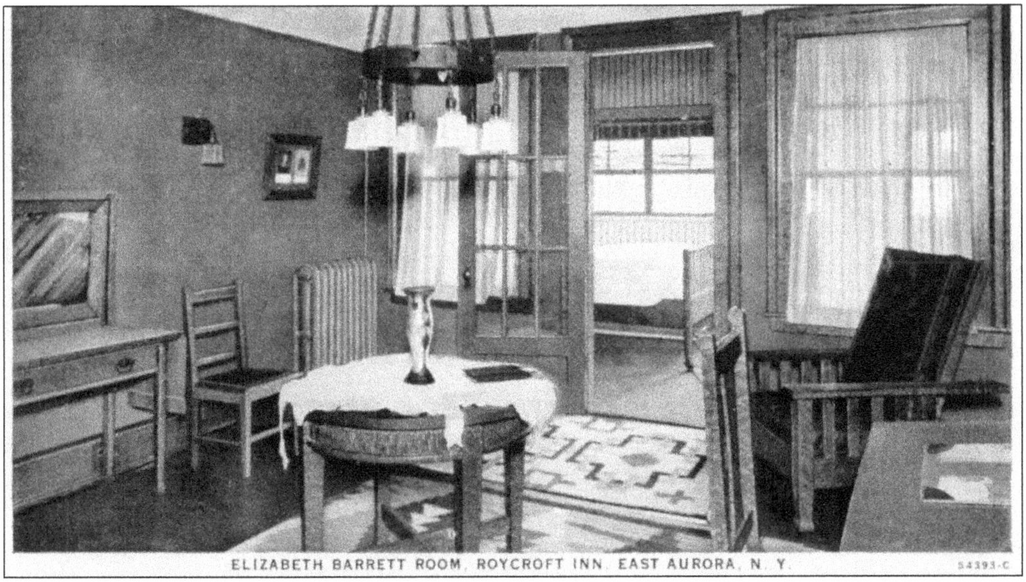


All of the inn's rooms were named after famous personages that Hubbard had featured in his *Little Journeys* series. The second and third floors featured three- and four-room suites with outside sleeping rooms, unheated for healthy sleeping. They featured various furnishings in special woods, including bird's-eye maple, cherry, mahogany, chestnut, and ash. The Barrett Room was done in maple and had Navajo rugs throughout the suite. Note also the early heart cutout copper chandelier. When the inn opened, it featured electricity throughout.

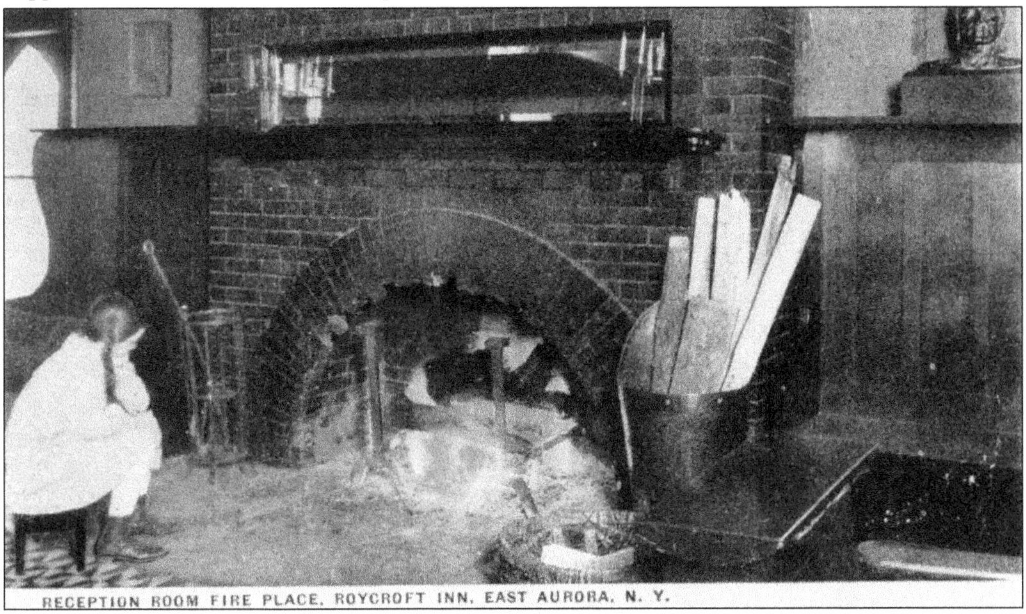


A later view of the lobby features one of Hubbard's granddaughters and shows the two large settles flanking the hearth. One of these still exists with a reproduction on the other side. The original was rescued by the author from destruction at a local Boy Scout camp in the early 1980s. Its mate had been chopped up for firewood only the year before. Two rare copper candleholders designed by Karl Kipp (1881–1954) appear on the mantel. One fine example has brought over $100,000 at auction recently.

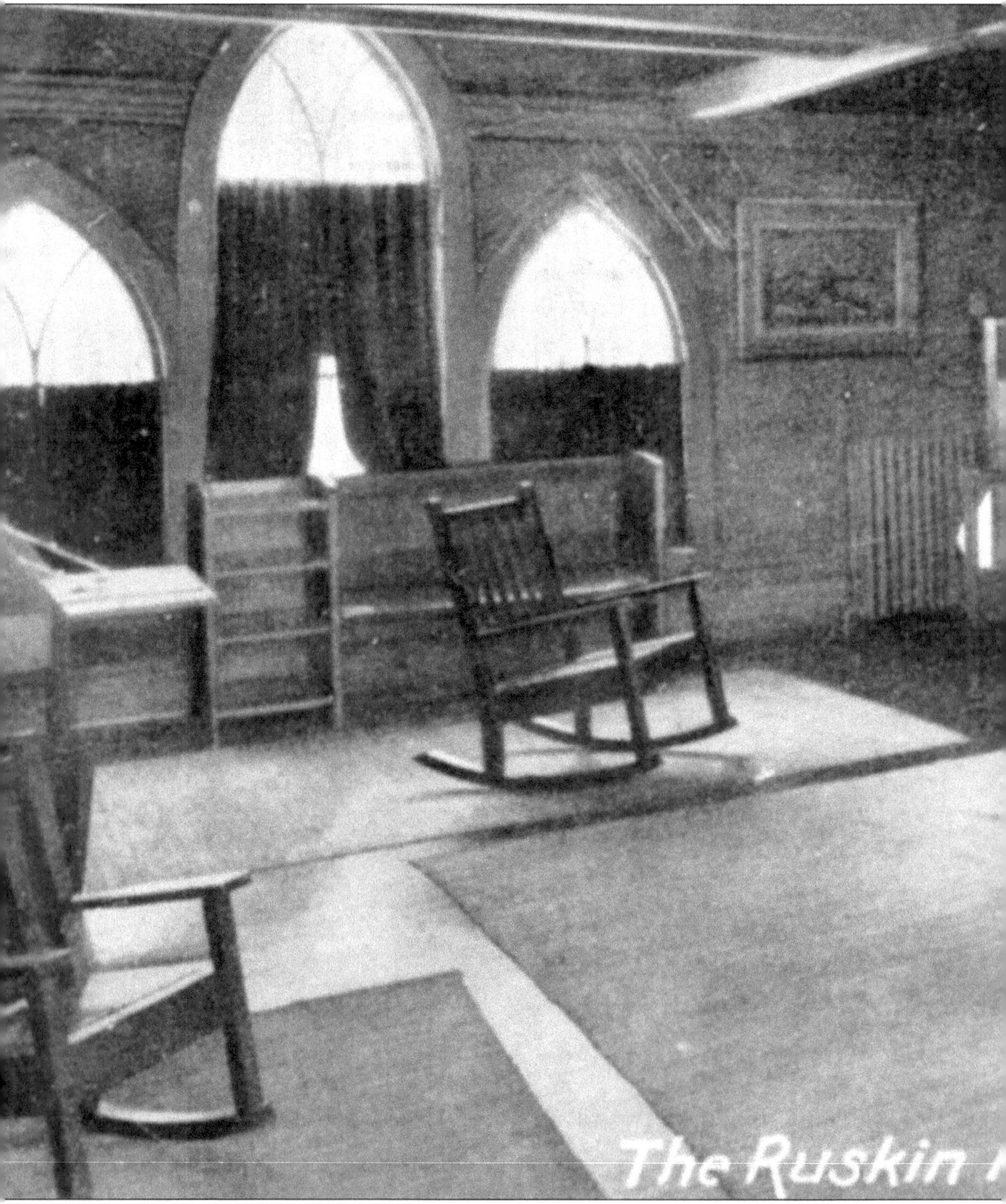


The top floor of the original Phalanstery, originally a studio for the book illuminators, became the premier suite at the inn. Named after John Ruskin (1819–1900), the man Hubbard credited as a mentor and father of the Arts and Crafts Movement, it had many fine Mission oak pieces of Roycroft furniture. It also had a fireplace that held W.W. Denslow (1856–1915) -designed sea

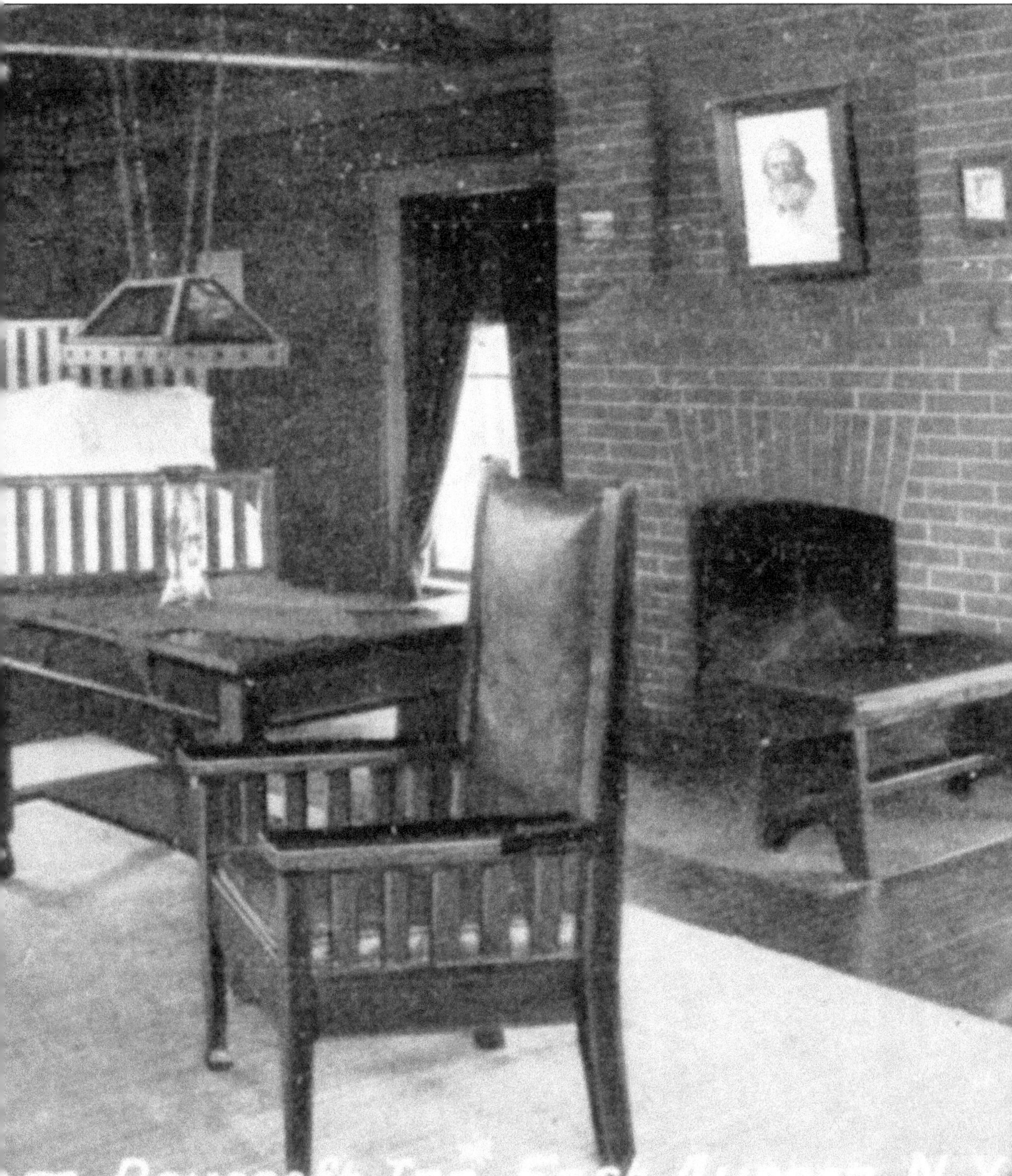


horse handwrought andirons, made in the Blacksmith Shop across the street around 1899. These are much sought after today by collectors. Special large and long oak bookcase settles were made for this room and are still in the inn's collection of original furnishings. John Ruskin's portrait by Schneider is framed above the mantel.

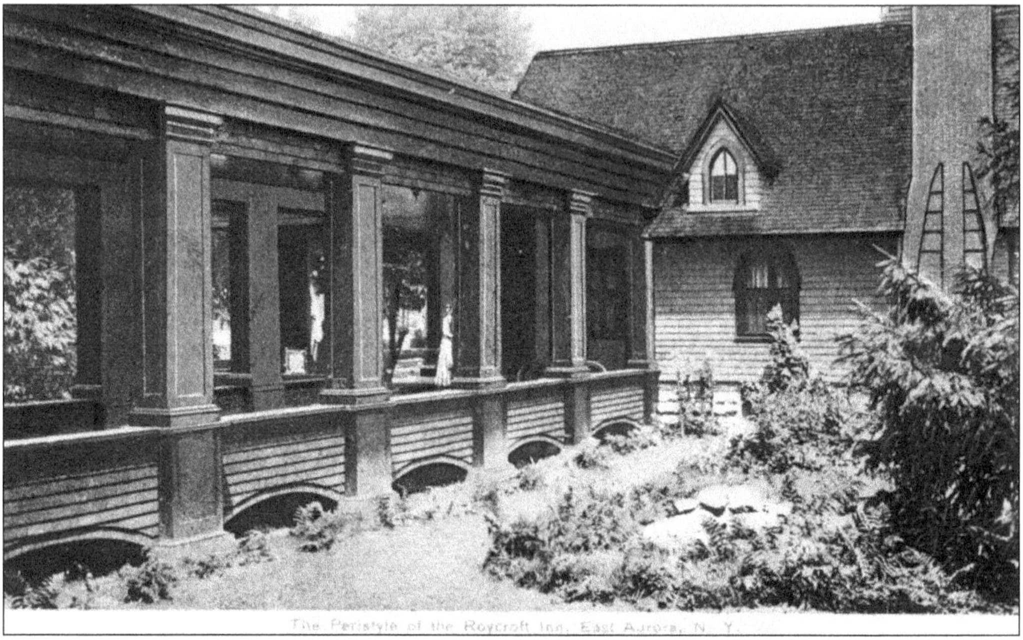


The connector porch that gave the final building its modern look was dubbed the Peristyle by Hubbard, after the Romans. Looking across the garden, vestiges of the first Print Shop can be seen in the Gothic arched windows before they were replaced by leaded glass, designed by Dard Hunter.

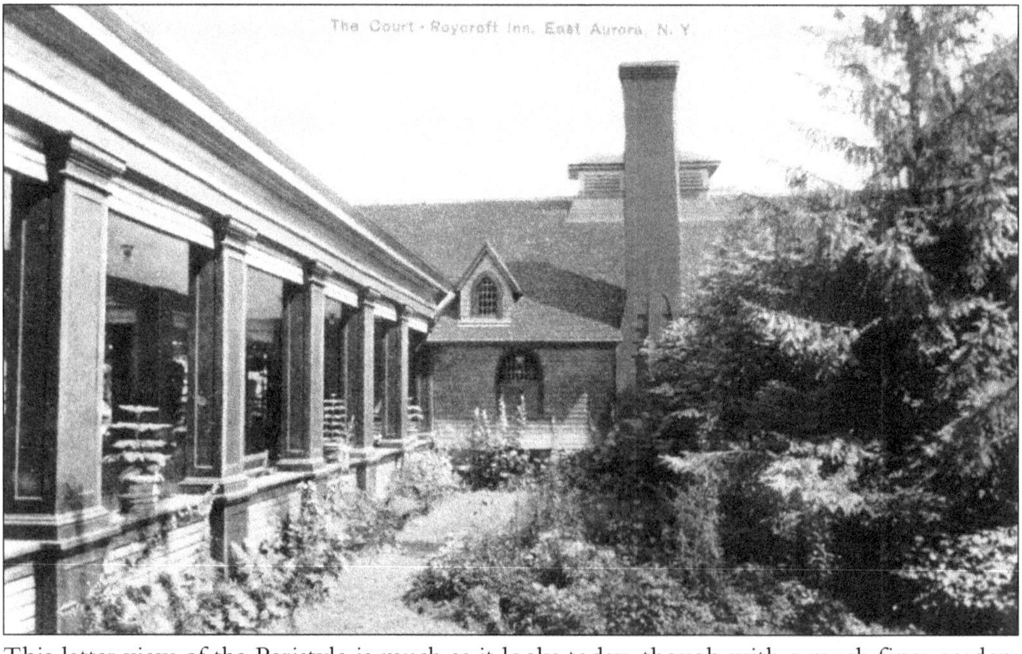


This latter view of the Peristyle is much as it looks today, though with a much finer garden. The Hubbards were not much for formal gardens and used local trees and bushes with ferns for their plantings.

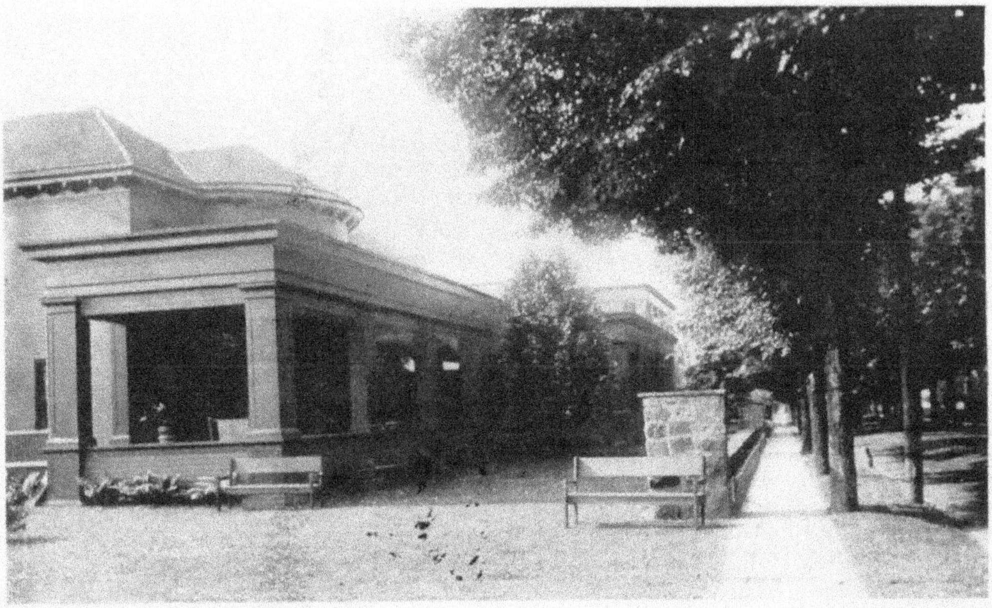

Peristyle of The Inn

The Roycroft Shop
East Aurora, N. Y.

The two postcards on this page show in the foreground the early benches that could be seen throughout the campus between 1906 and 1910. The advent of the automobile was soon to change the look of South Grove Street again. The building at the north end of the Peristyle, Hubbard's neighbor's home, was christened Monticello. It became the special guesthouse, where families traveling together could have the whole house to themselves but still be connected to all the inn's services. Part of the Peristyle was removed to create a driveway to allow access for large trucks delivering supplies to the kitchen in the early 1940s.

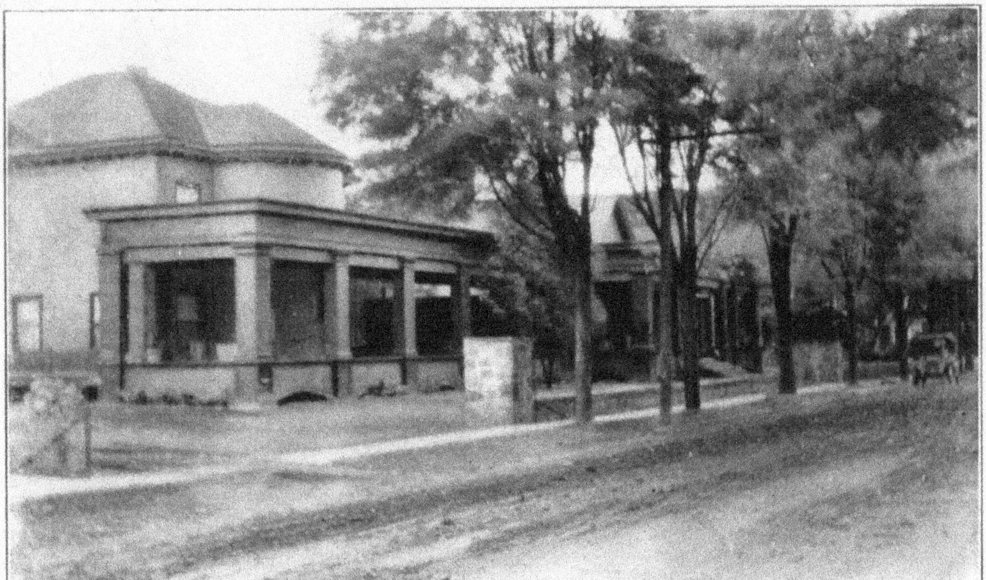

The Roycroft Inn, East Aurora, New York

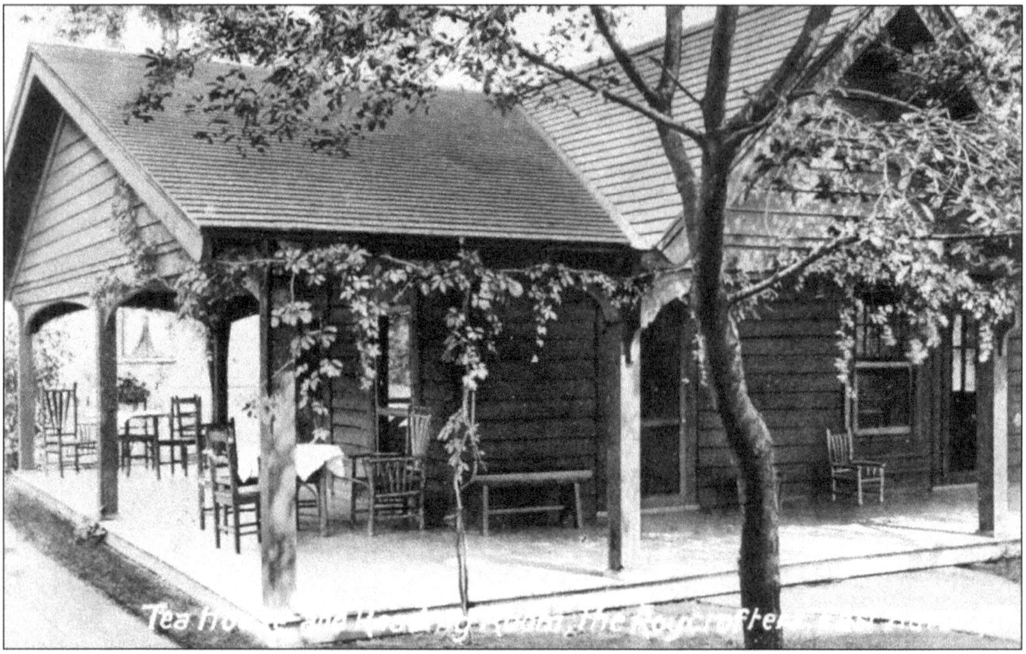

One of the buildings missing from today's campus is the teahouse, which was named Twill-do. It featured leisurely afternoon teas and lunches and was located just east of the gardens, at the south side of the inn. It was a favorite of guests until the 1930s.

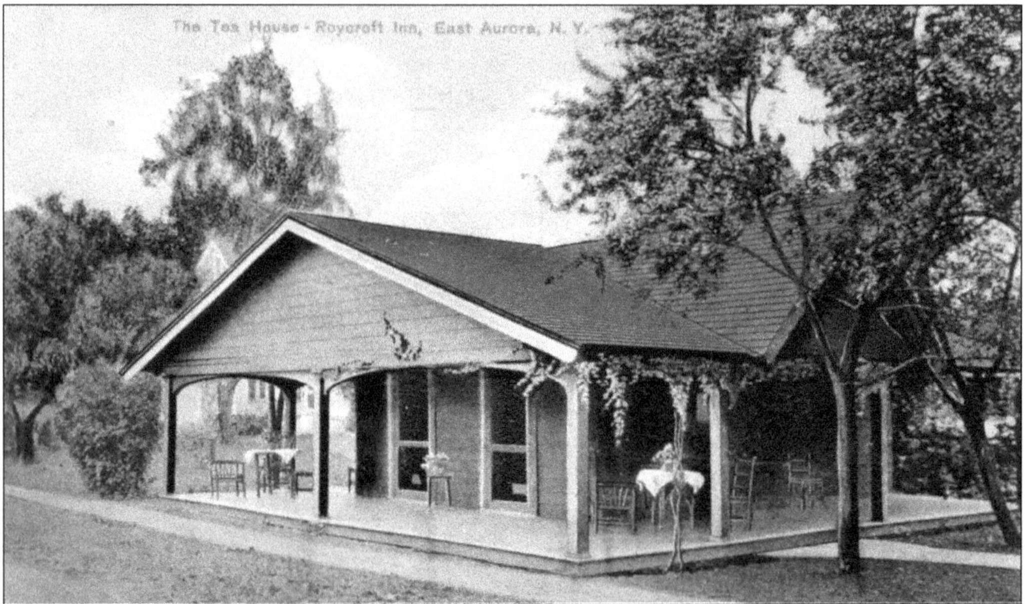


On the last postcard to feature the teahouse, one can see its setting among apple trees and large sycamores. The arrival of automobile travelers in the 1920s in throngs necessitated a parking lot, and this building and most of the trees were victims. Only the copper hand-hammered sign from the door and one of the largest sycamore trees in East Aurora still exist.

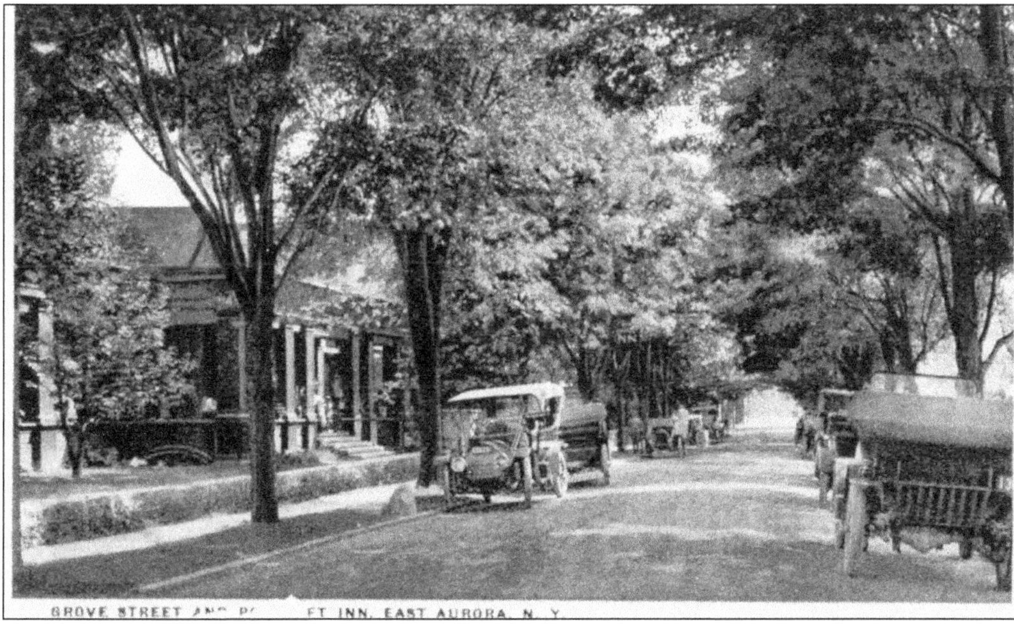


The Western New York community embraced the automobile early on. A great day journey from Buffalo or Rochester to the campus was a must for the owners of early cars. By the 1910s, as pictured here, the trees had grown almost across the street. The local Automobile Club headquartered in Clarence, New York, about 15 miles north of the village, was the largest of its type in the United States in 1905.

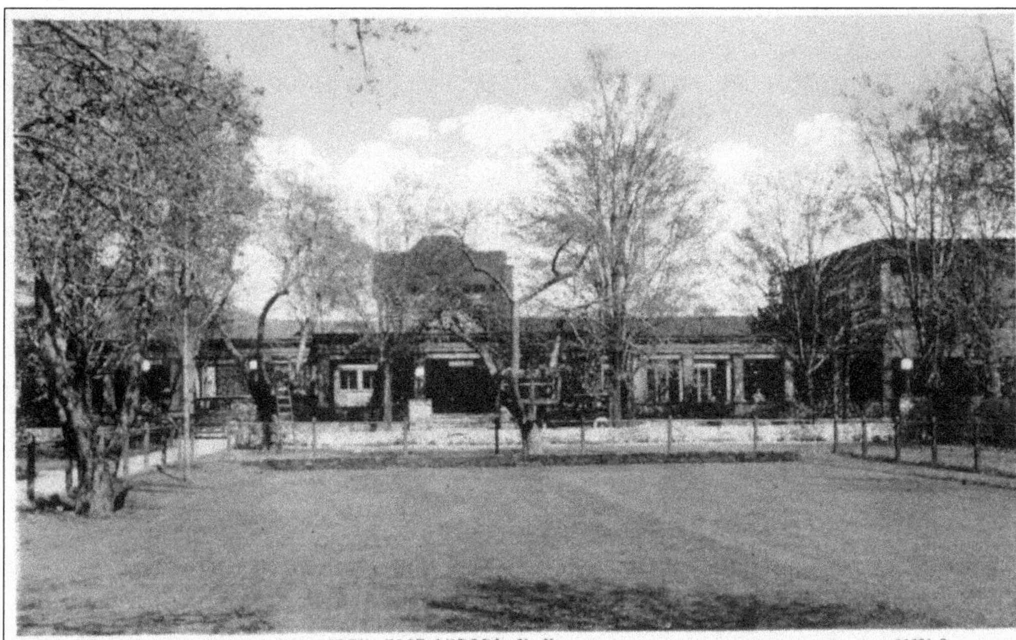


This view from around 1925 shows the inn from end to end and the large lawns that existed at that time for the guests and workers to enjoy. Hubbard believed in physical exercise everyday and gave his employees time off to play ball and other sports. Of course, they were using baseballs and medicine balls made in the shops and offered by catalog to the world.

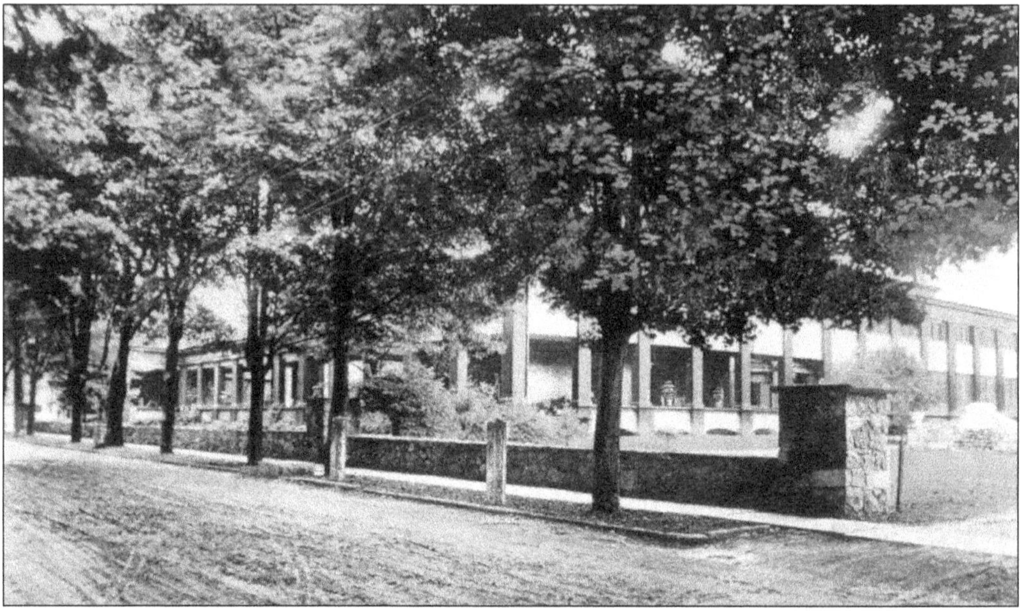

Shown on this card c. 1912 are the gardens at the south end of the sleeping rooms. The fountain contained a sculpture (at far right) by English suffragette Katherine Emma Maltwood (1878–1961). It was named *Magna Mater*, in the celebration of womanhood. Maltwood was a correspondent of Alice Hubbard's, and she was first recognized internationally for this bas-relief, still in existence today in two examples. Her original mold, made of copper, rests in the museum named after her at the University of Victoria, BC. The remaining cement, center fragment, is located around the corner from the present inn in the gardens of the ScheideMantel House at 363 Oakwood Avenue. It was found in the 1990s in a local villager's garden as an ornament.

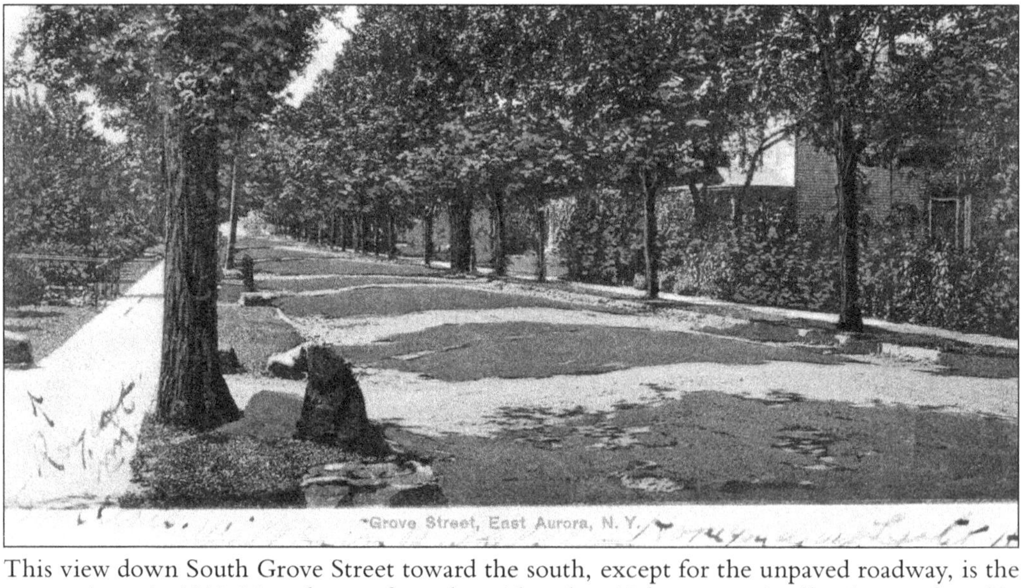


This view down South Grove Street toward the south, except for the unpaved roadway, is the same as it was in 1910. Many houses from the mid- to late 19th century, in all styles, are found in the next few blocks. Many of these single-family wood homes have been lovingly restored and are sought after because of their beauty. In 1910, most were owned by workers and craftspeople from the Roycroft Shops. It was only a short stroll to work.

*Four*

# The Campus Grows
## An Arts and Crafts Mecca

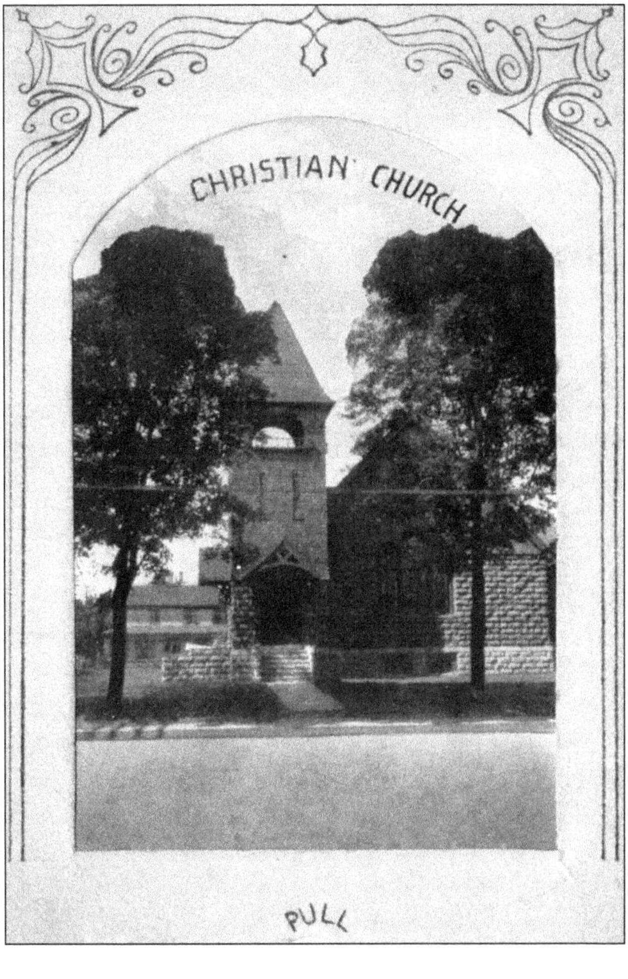


Though hard to show with one image, this card is a very rare pullout of six images, of which two are churches and all the others are buildings on the Roycroft Campus. The photographs are from before 1905. Unfortunately, the producer thought the Christian Church to be the village's most appealing building. (Courtesy of the library of Jack Walsdorf.)

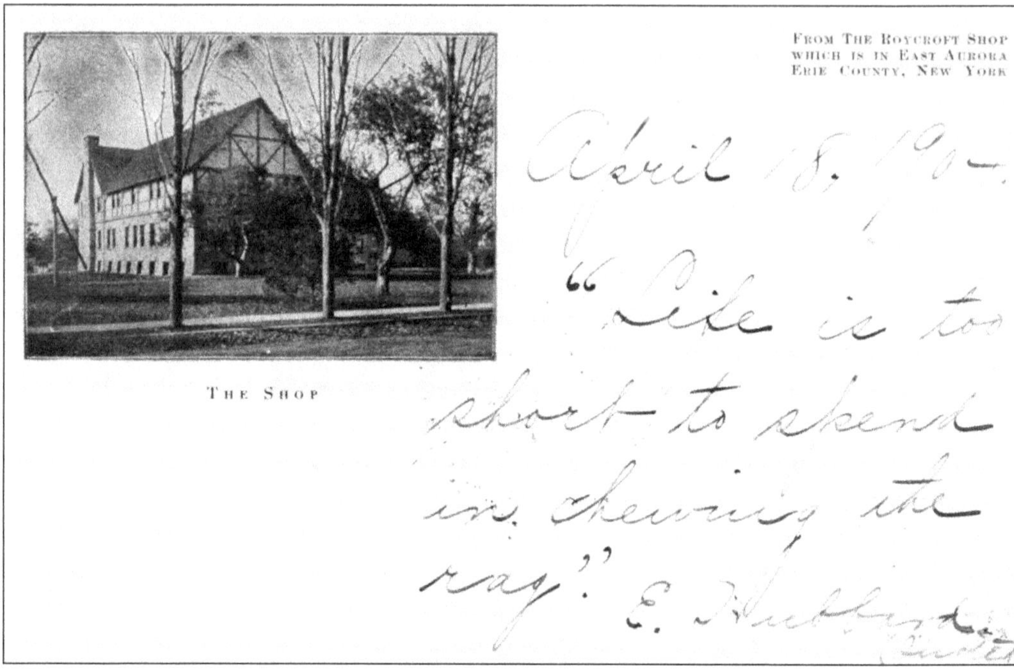


The shop, built in 1901 and 1902 to meet the demand for Roycroft periodicals and fine handmade books, was constructed of local stone from Farmers field. Western New York is a glacial remains area with many large rounded boulders found just below the earth, a major problem for the farmer's plows! The publication of the second or third millionth copy of *A Message to Garcia*, Elbert's most famous piece of literature, fostered the need for new, better, and bigger presses and a building to house them and the additional offices and meeting rooms. The owner of this card wrote one of Elbert Hubbard's more famous epigrams attributed to Ali Baba, his handyman and alter ego.

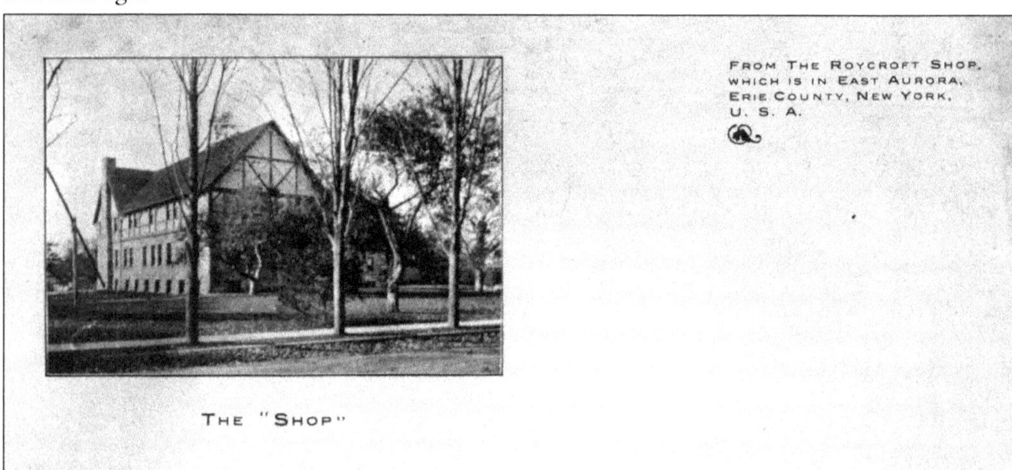


The printing operation moving across the street from its original location, north of Hubbard's home, gave space for the expansion into the Roycroft Inn, gradually starting in 1903. This building was known in the village as the "shop" for many years, as it employed more families than all the other businesses combined.

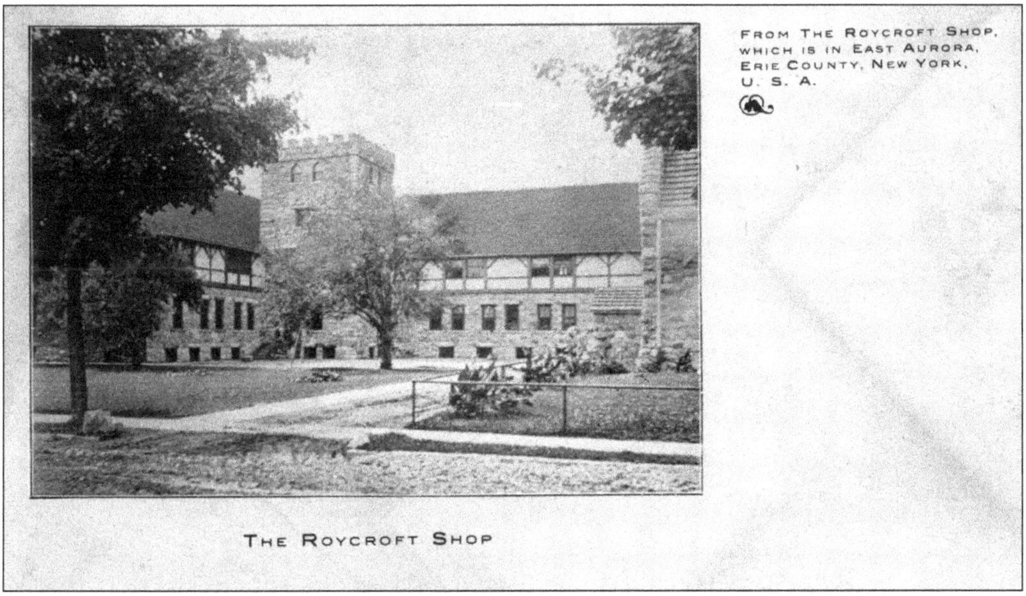


The Print Shop has a very British look, intended by the Roycrofters to link them to the Arts and Crafts Movement and its beginnings in England. The crenellated stone tower, very castle-like, housed Elbert and Alice's office. For a time between 1906 and 1909, it housed the studio of Dard Hunter, the commune's main artist and designer who was given a space overlooking the campus grounds, which showed his importance within the community.

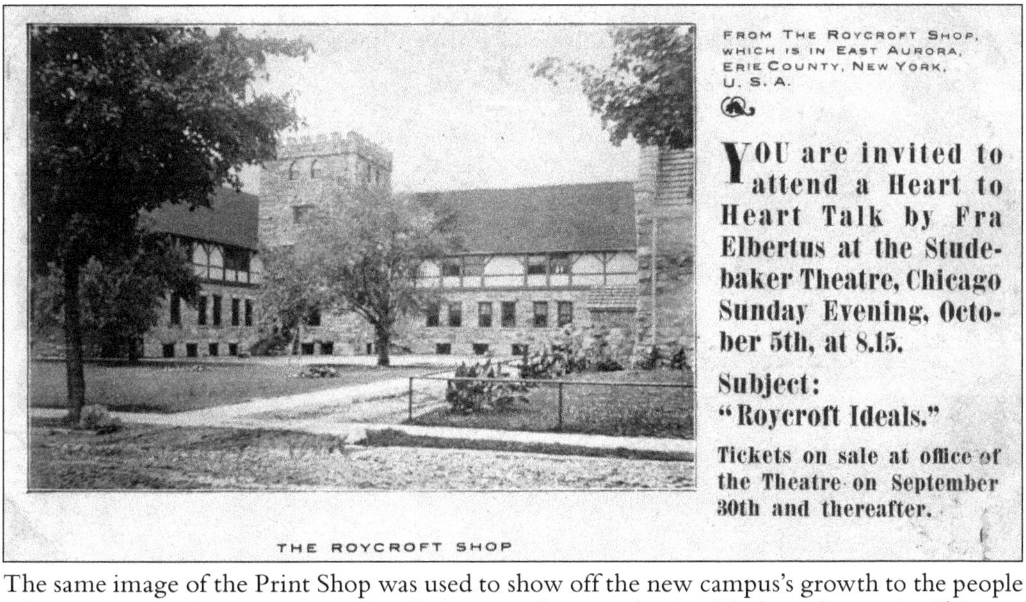


The same image of the Print Shop was used to show off the new campus's growth to the people who were invited to attend Hubbard's lectures, here at the Studebaker Theater in Chicago. Hubbard advertised his campus of joyful workers and produced his books and magazines, and subscribers and the curious came in droves. He was known to fill auditoriums of 4,000 people and more at Chautauquas nationwide.

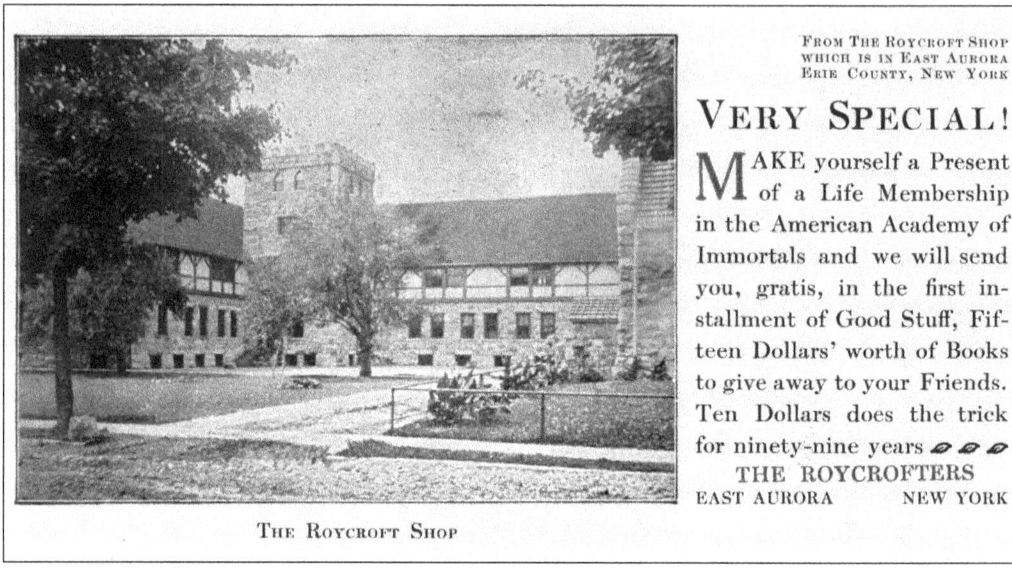


The Academy of the Immortals was an advertising idea of Hubbard's to fuel the presses and keep his employees printing books and magazines. For a fee, which changed later, one would receive a copy of every title that the Roycrofters published for 99 years. He was so successful in this endeavor that his son had to buy out its members after his father's death with an offer of a bookcase and some choice expensive full-leather books still in inventory.

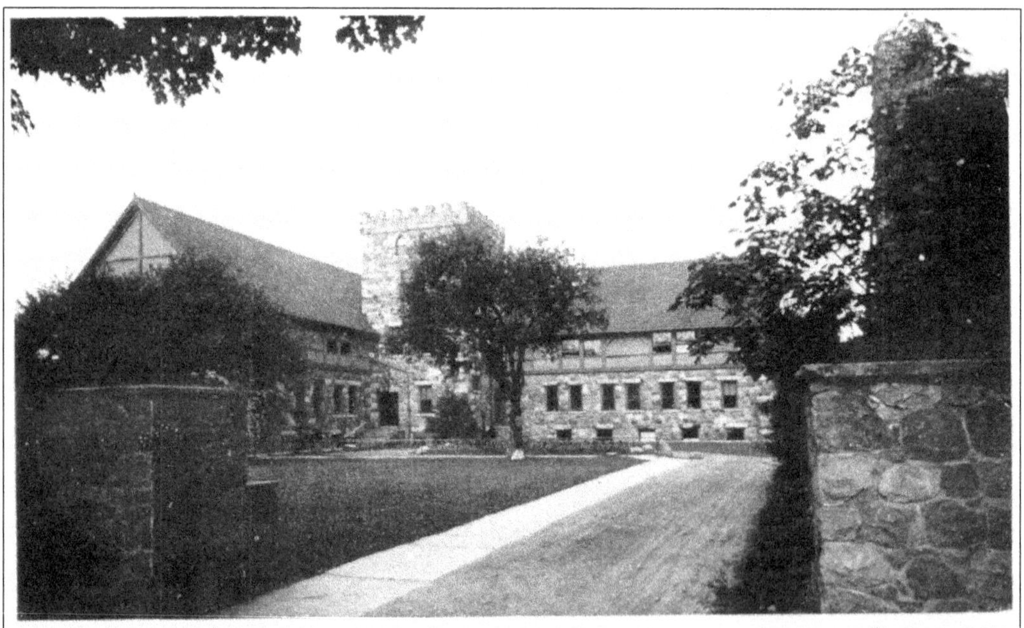


This view of the Print Shop is how it looked for only about a span of five years between 1905 and 1910. Many changes were made to the street and the lawns in front of the shop. These lawns were used for large gatherings during the yearly Roycroft Conventions, held from 1903 until the mid-1930s.

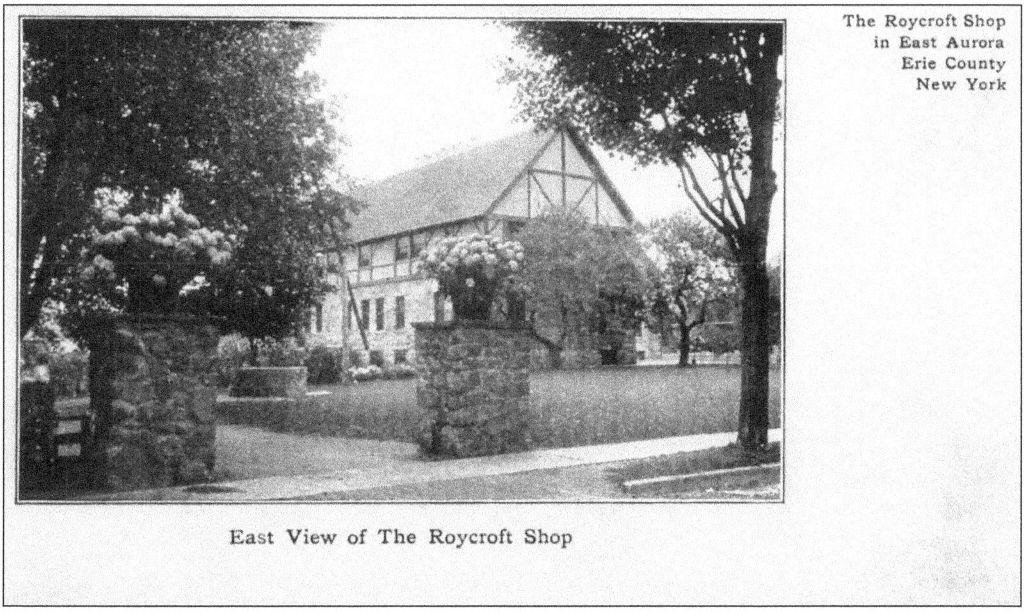


Surprisingly, the shop, or the building holding the presses, is the most varied and also the most common card. Hubbard wanted to promote the Arts and Crafts aesthetic and what better way than with a building that looked like a medieval castle. This image from around 1904 was printed in black and white.

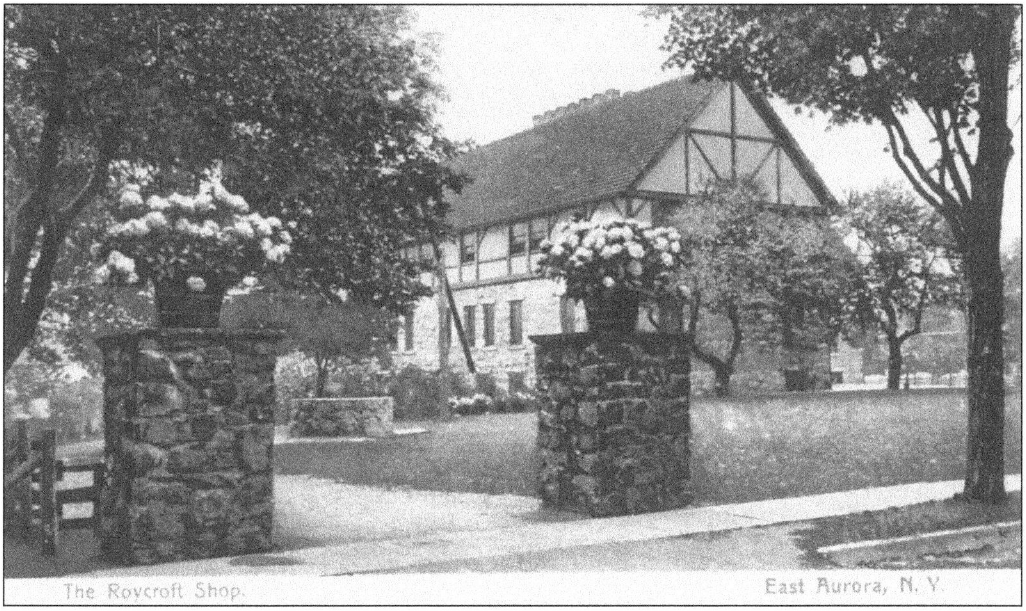


This almost identical shot of the previous image is a hand-colored lithograph produced in Germany. This may be from a series of images photographed by 17-year-old Paul Fournier, son of artist Alexis, Roycroft's court painter. Paul became a famous pictorialist photographer in the early 20th century. Notably, in 1905, his work was included in the first-ever exhibition of photography in a fine art museum, at the Albright Art Gallery in Buffalo. He also later exhibited internationally in London and Paris.

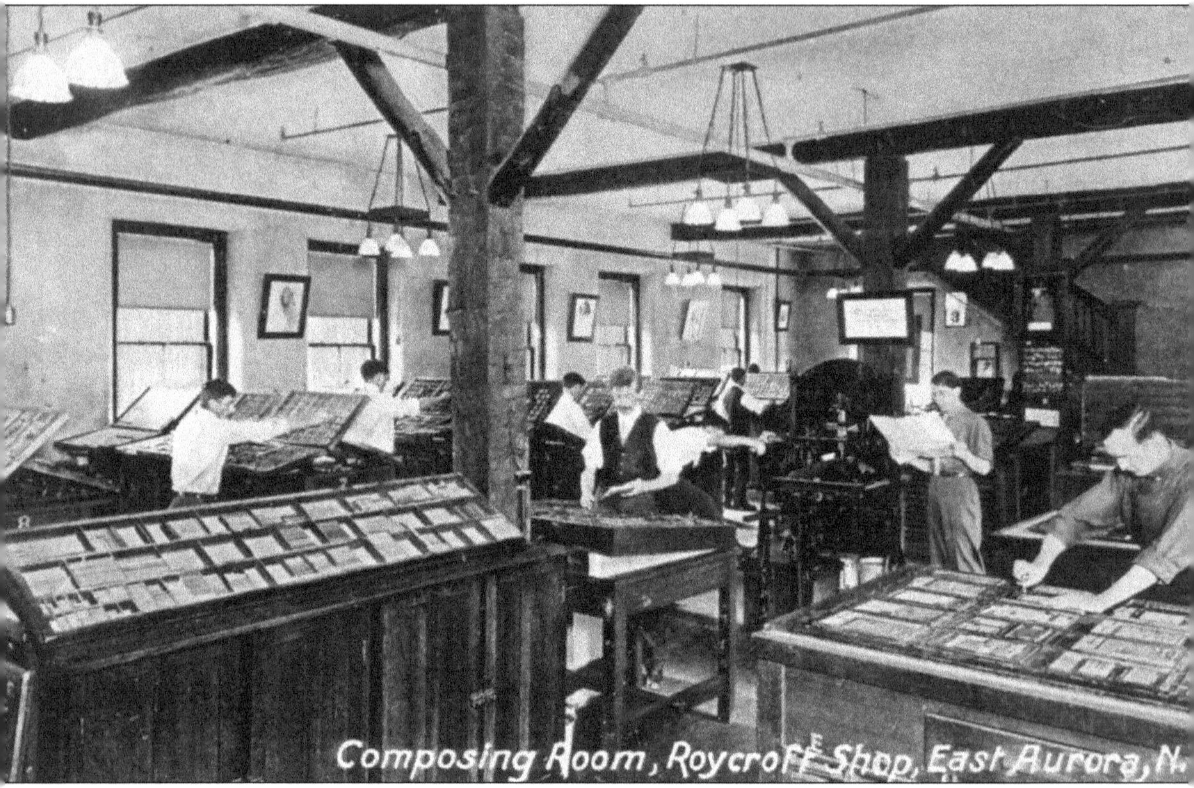


This rare card is one of the very few that shows Roycrofters at work. The composing room, where the type was handset, was located on the first floor of the Print Shop in the north-facing wing. The presses original and first Washington handpress that moved from Main Street, where the *Philistine* was first printed in 1895, to the first Print Shop in 1897 to the location here was a reminder to the workers of where it all began. The original card is colored, one of the first issued around 1905.

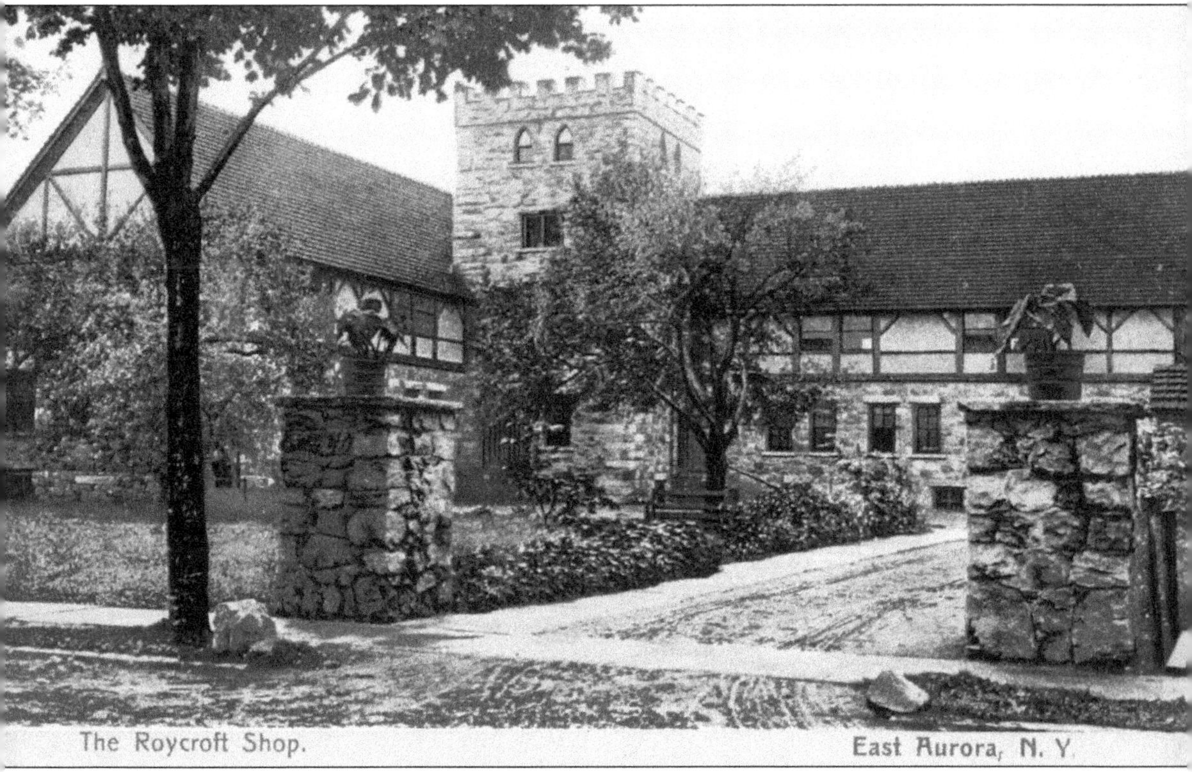


More variants exist of postcards featuring the shop, even more than the famous Roycroft Inn. The next four pages will show the collectors some of the many different cards available. Postcard collectors and ephemera collectors alike want to have all the many variants in their complete collection. It seems that there are always new ones found, which makes the hunt all the more interesting.

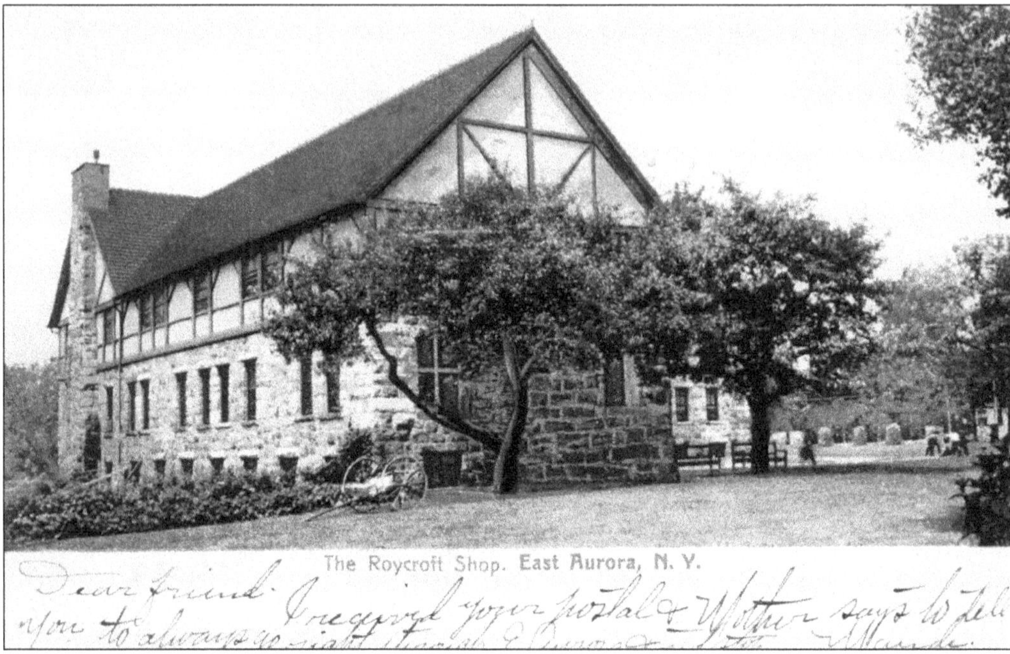


This view printed in Germany and sold by the Roycrofters dates from before they had their own lithography department. They began producing their own card in the 1910s. It is available in black and white and also colored.

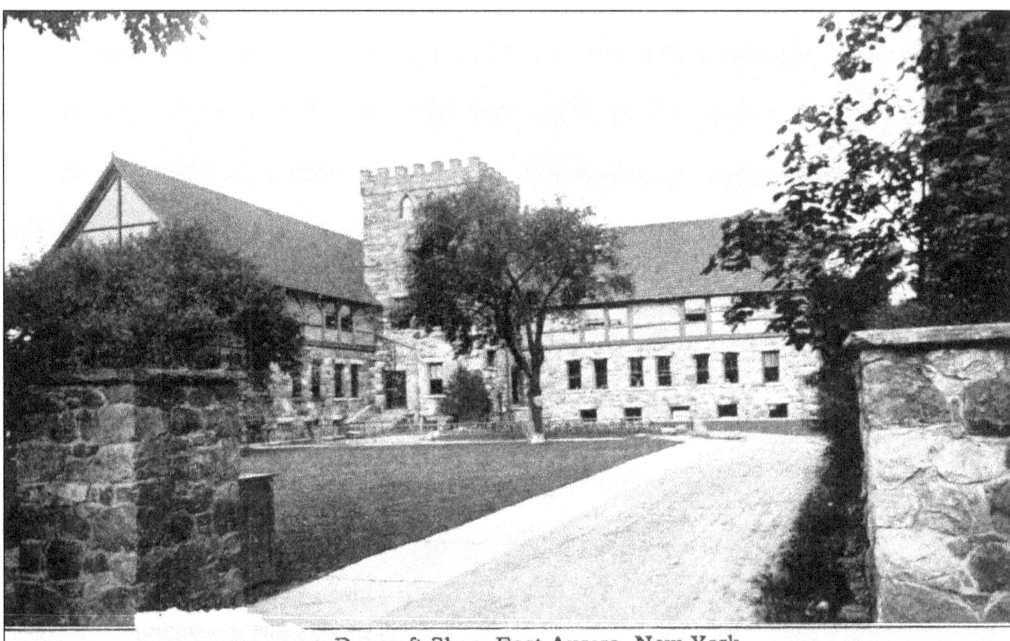


The Roycrofters added paved walkways on the campus around 1905, and the drive was to accommodate the carriages and horse-drawn dray wagons with paper and other supplies. This view is looking west from South Grove Street. This area is presently all paved over with asphalt and a parking lot.

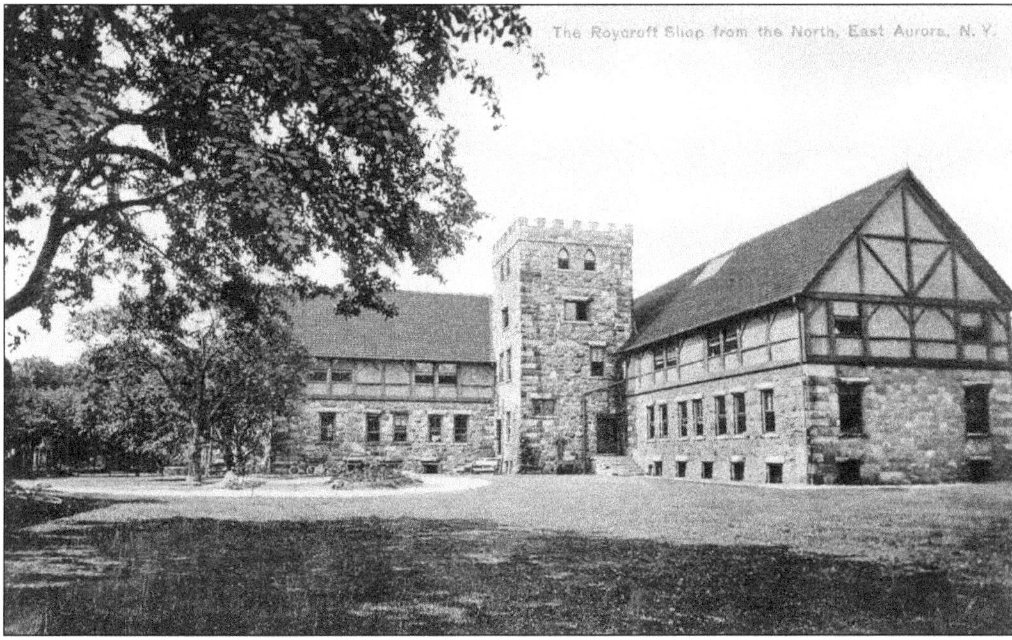


Looking south from Main Street, this is the most picturesque view of the Roycroft Shops. When the lawns were in place, it gave a very good impression to visitors of the village. It really was a very pleasant environment to work in for the craftspeople. Many thought it was or is a college campus, and it is believed it was intended as such. This building is the same today from this view, though many trees and plantings have changed.

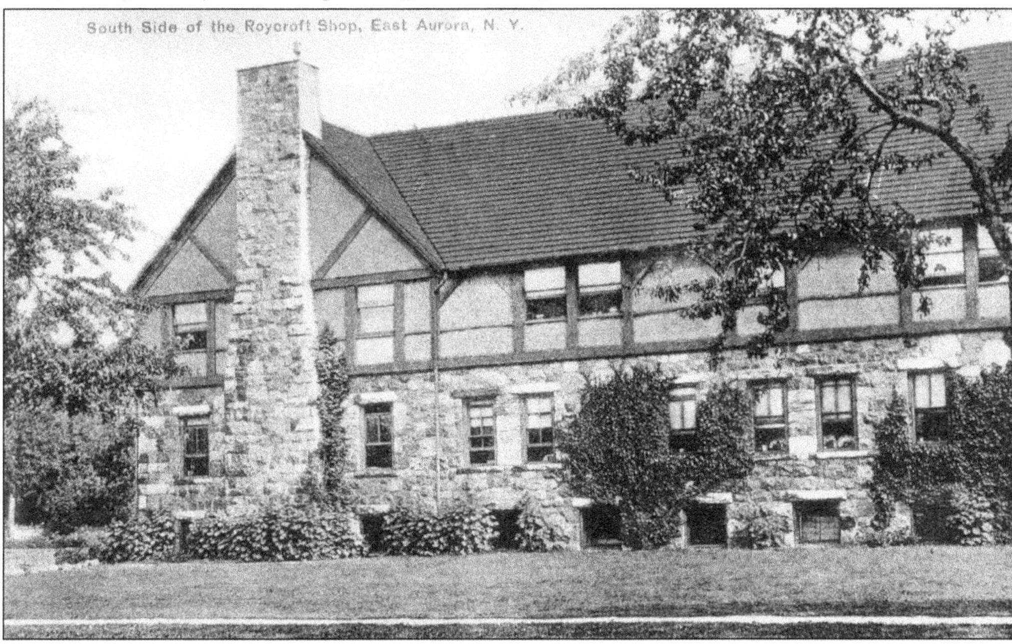


Facing north when walking across from the inn, this colored view dates from around 1910. Over 500 people were working among the seven main campus buildings at that time. Today, the lawns have been replaced by asphalt and will hopefully be restored when the revitalization is fully realized.

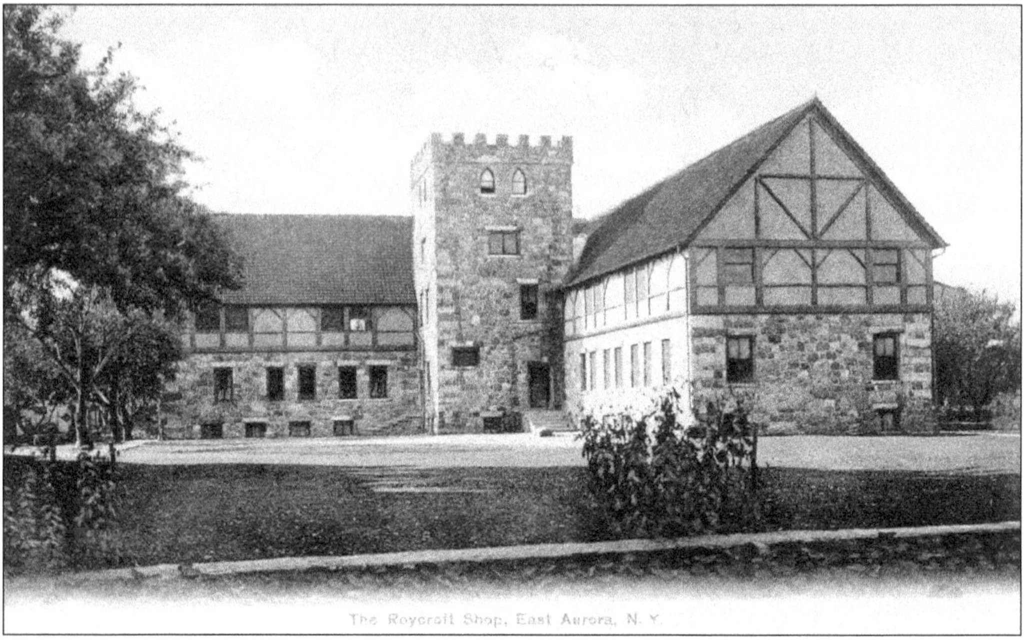

This is the image that one would see while standing on the sidewalk on Main Street looking south. This image in colored and uncolored versions has added clouds for extra interest.

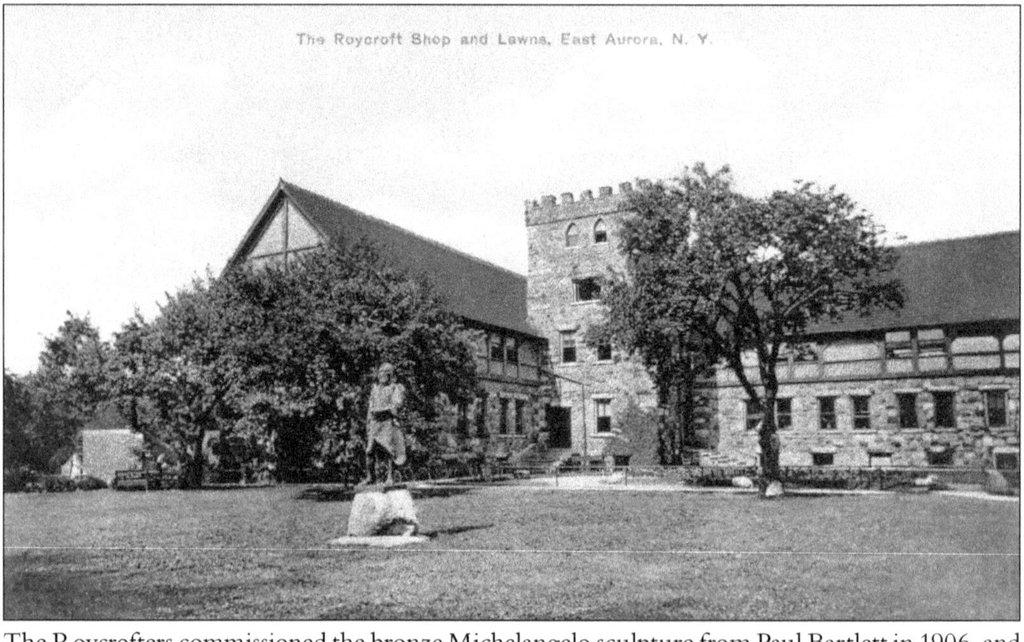

The Roycrofters commissioned the bronze Michelangelo sculpture from Paul Bartlett in 1906, and it was installed on the lawn in 1909. Hubbard was impatient and hounded the artist for the work. Paul Bartlett sent a bronze turtle instead with a note attached stating, "Fine art takes time."

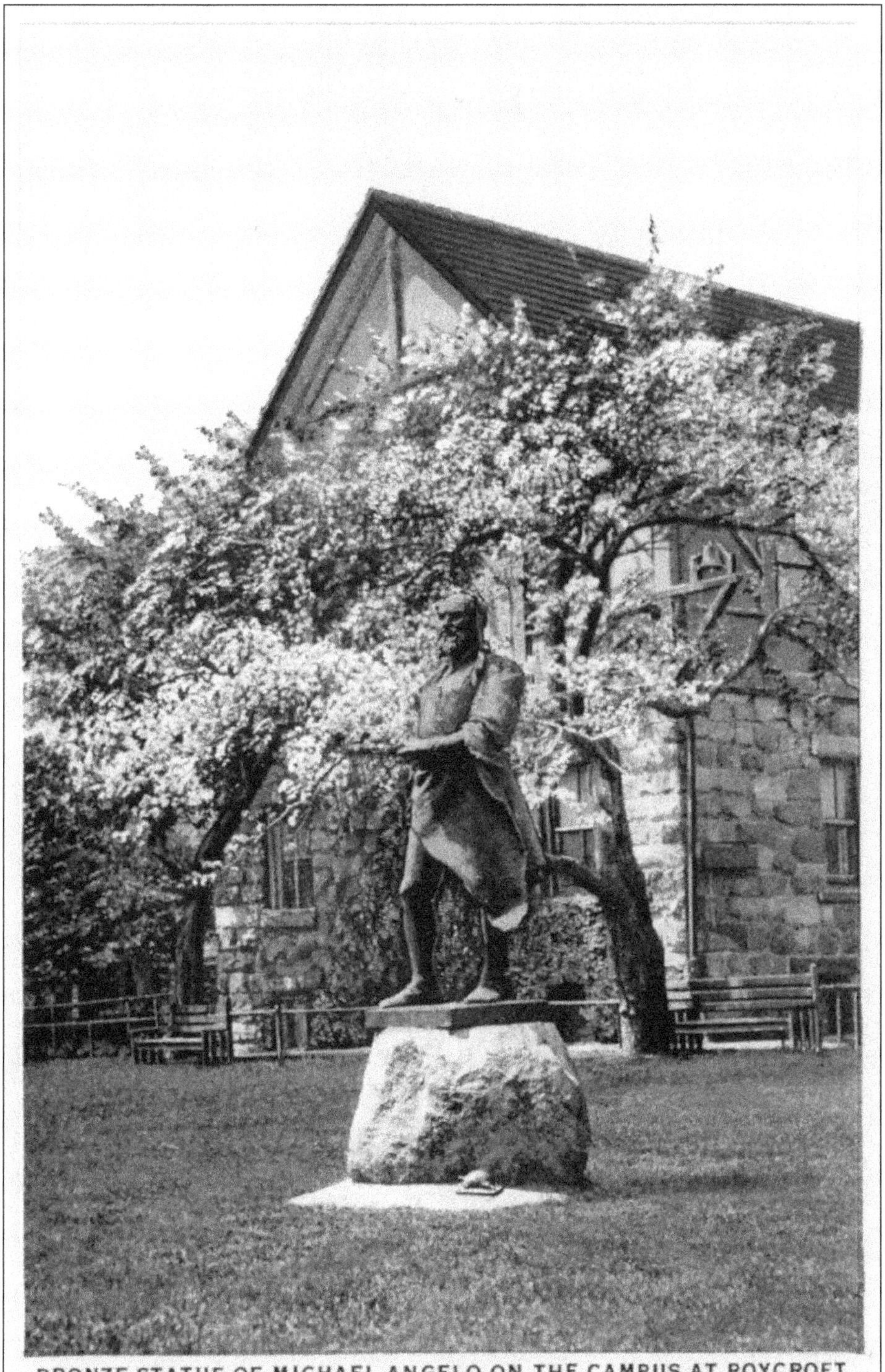

A series of cards were issued in the 1920s that featured the campus in the spring with the apple trees in full bloom. Alex Fournier also produced oil paintings of the campus at the same time. Note the benches for the workers on their breaks to enjoy the setting.

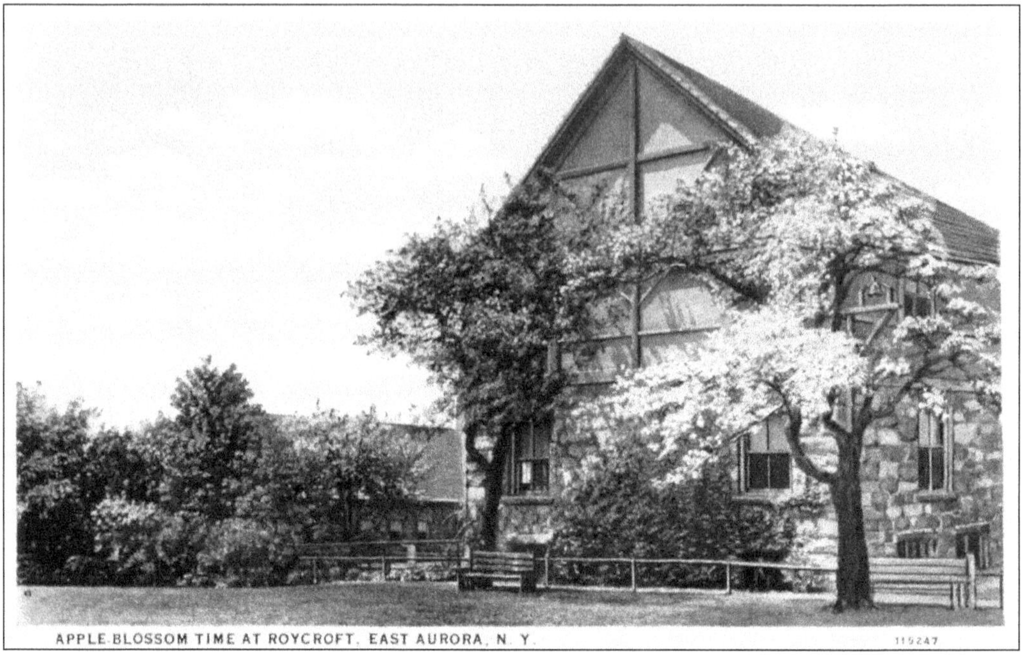


Another view when the apples were in full bloom gave the impression of the orchards that existed behind all of the original houses that were on Main Street. Hubbard bought these homes and moved them farther south a few blocks and sold them. In some instances, he gave them to favored artists and craftsmen.

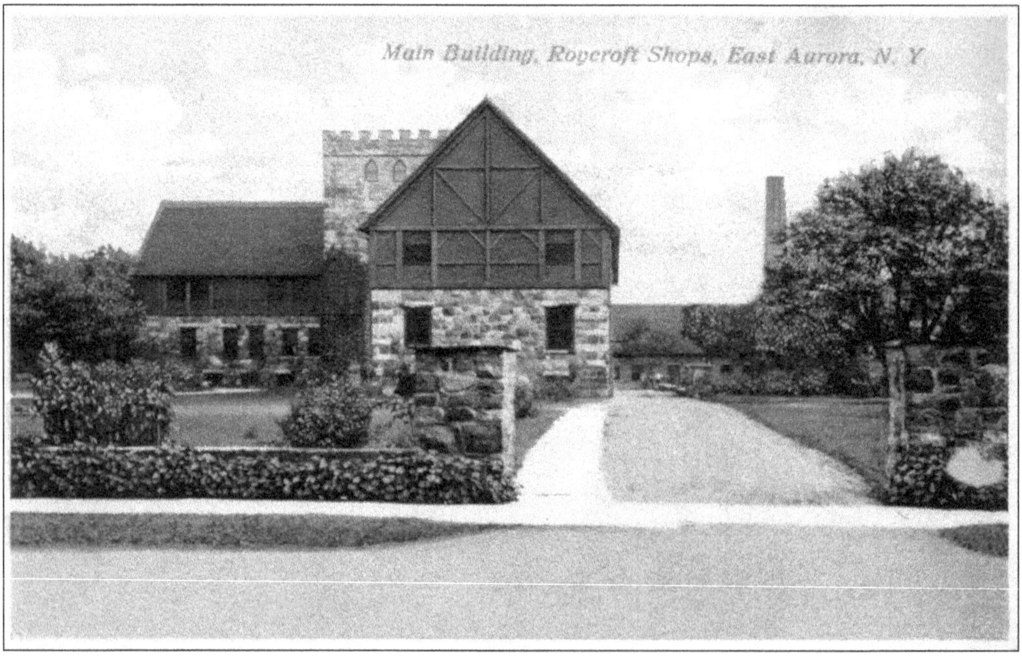


This was the drive for deliveries to the rear of the shop from Main Street after 1911. The very tall chimney in the background is the new powerhouse, which provided the campus with both heat and light from steam boilers powered by coal.

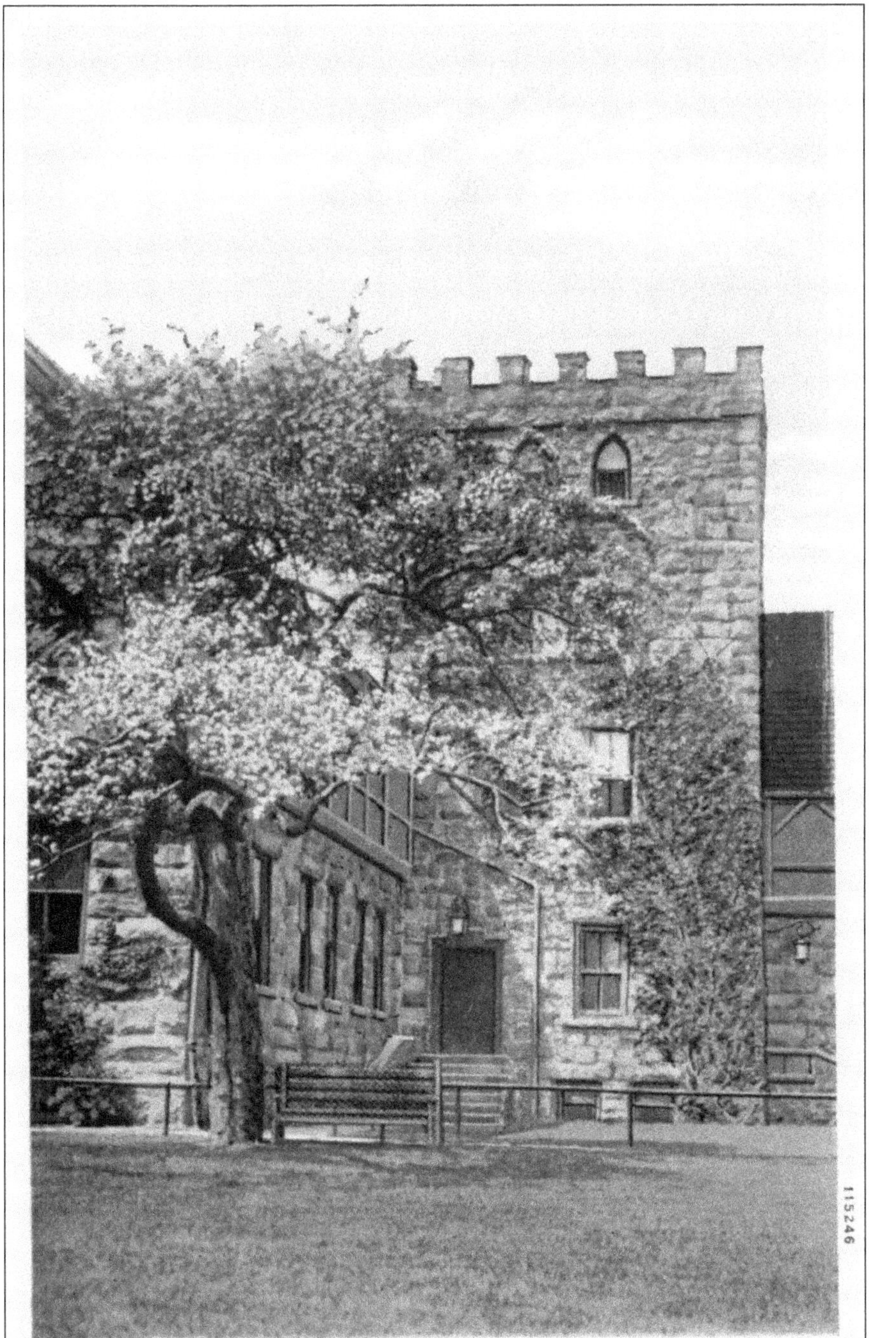


The main entrance of the Print Shop around 1920 shows the large door carved with a motto to inspire the workers. Hanging on the corner behind the tree in the foreground was the company bell, which was rung instead of a siren for breaks for exercise or to hear a visiting speaker. Bert Hubbard removed the bell in 1938 when the shops were sold in bankruptcy. He returned it when the farm and home center took over the building in the 1950s, as he felt a meeting hall for farmers and the cooperative extension were a proper use for the structure again.

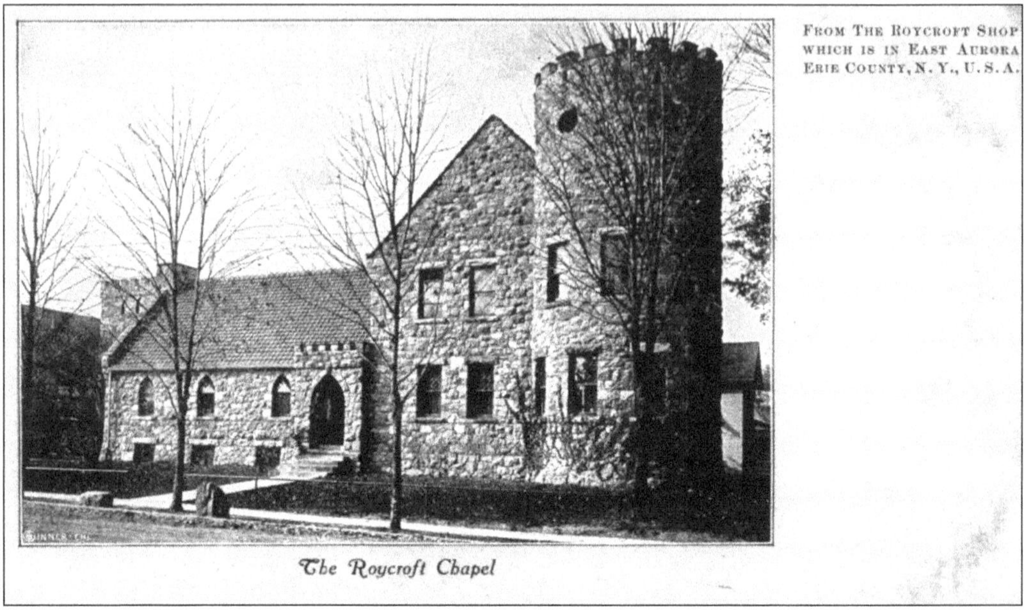


The southwest corner of South Grove Street at Main Street was the entrance for visitors, and the chapel was their first sight of the campus beyond. Hubbard used the chapel as a meeting place for the printers, not in a religious sense. This card is from the first series issued as a Private Mailing Card in 1899 and 1900, soon after the building was finished.

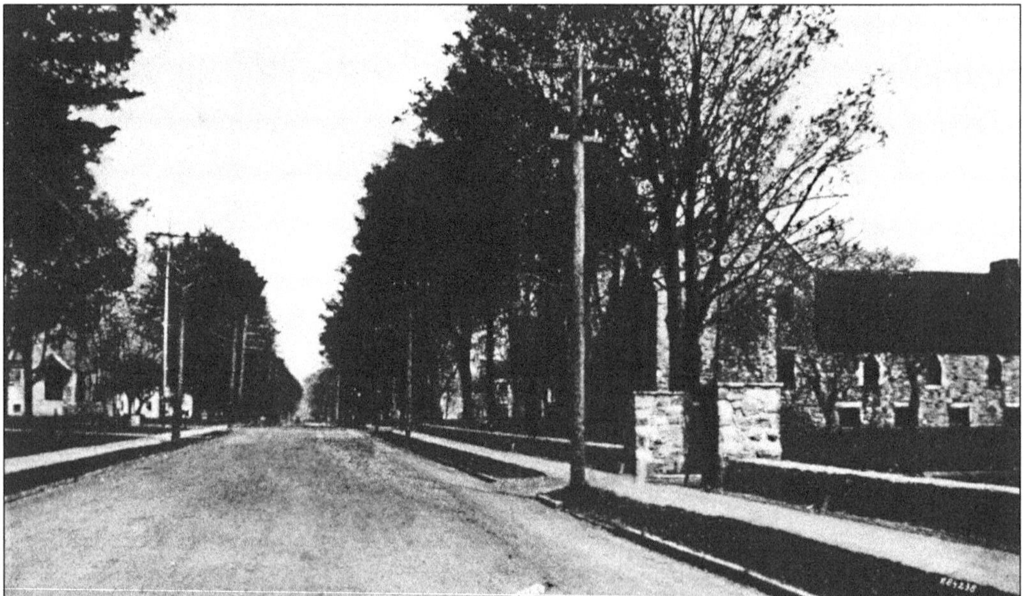


This is an early view along Main Street toward the village's downtown, about six blocks farther east. The far left shows one the many churches along the street, so people at first sight believed the stone edifice to be one as well. Many accused Hubbard of starting his own religion, as one with his surname did a few generations later.

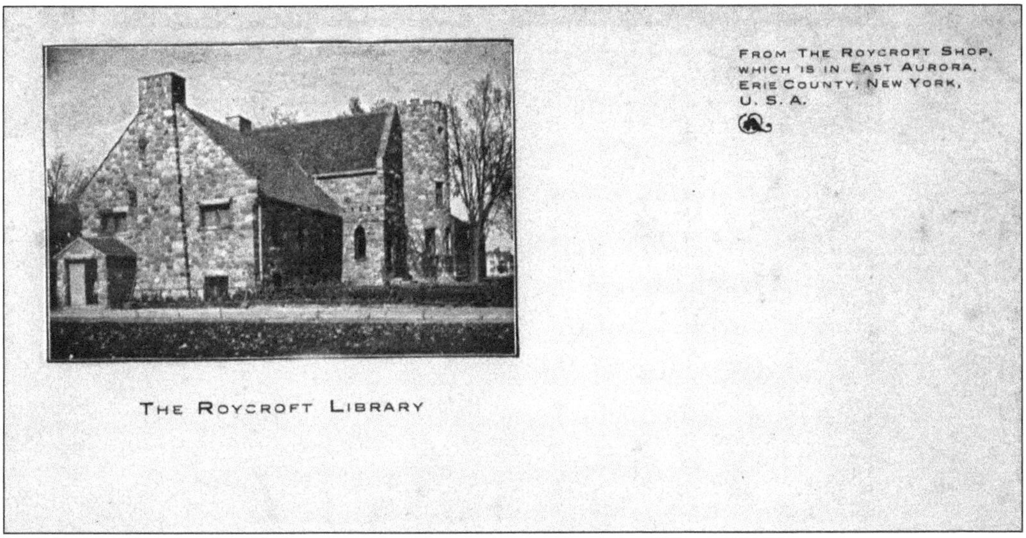


One of the earliest and rarest cards is this image titled "The Roycroft Library," which was one of the chapel's many incarnations. Hubbard moved his extensive library into the main floor and offices before the Print Shop was completed. The first Blacksmith Shop, a wooden attachment on this south end of the chapel, was where many of the early hinges and metal furniture parts were made by Peter Robarge, head blacksmith, and Jerome Conner, artist and blacksmith.

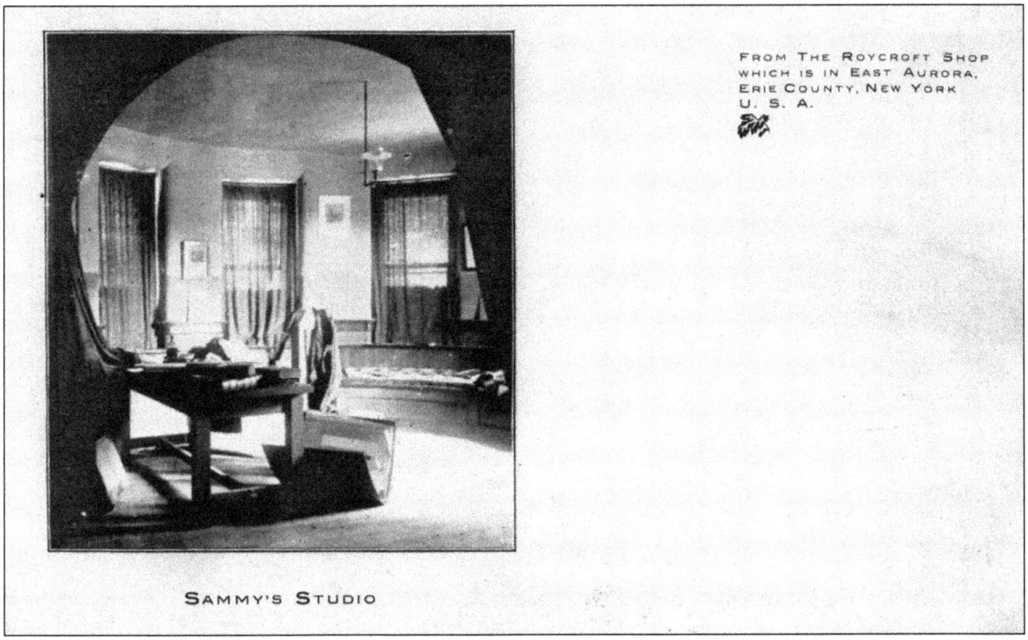


Art director Samuel Warner was given the premier studio on the upper floor of the round tower facing Main Street. Warner held this position designing many books for the Roycroft Press from 1898 to 1902. Note the very early oak table and the many fine, large, leather-bound books from the library on the lower level.

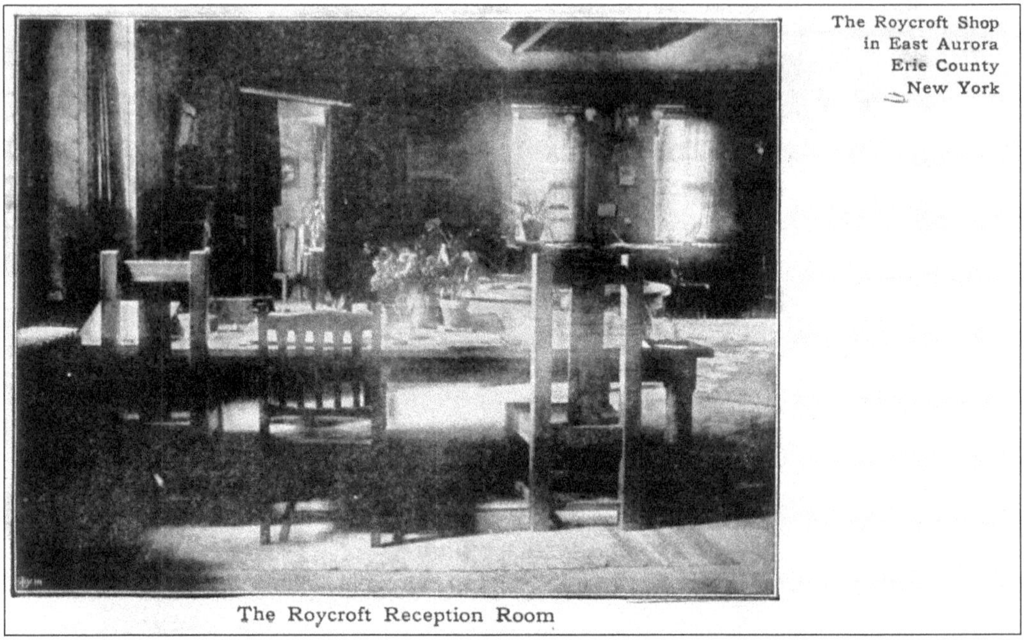


This reception room was located just inside the entrance to the chapel. It existed in this state for only about two years. The hall chairs shown here were massive heavy, fitting for the medieval setting of the campus buildings. An example can be seen today at the Roycroft Museum on Oakwood Avenue.

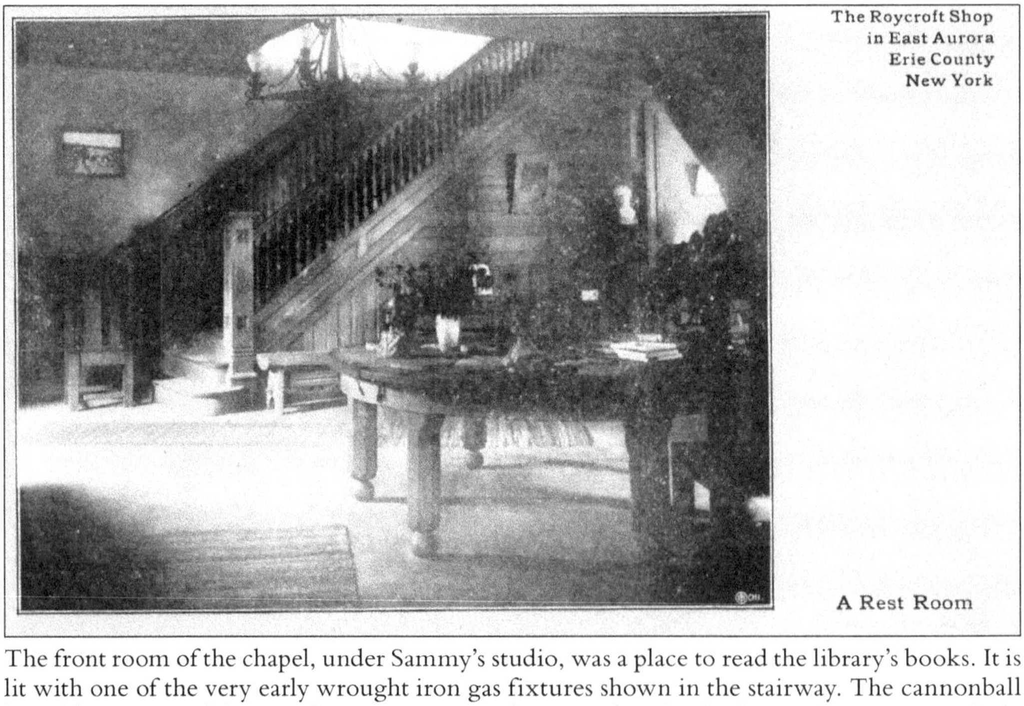


The front room of the chapel, under Sammy's studio, was a place to read the library's books. It is lit with one of the very early wrought iron gas fixtures shown in the stairway. The cannonball leg table was one of the very first items ever made in numbers by the Roycroft carpenters. Only a very few exist today.

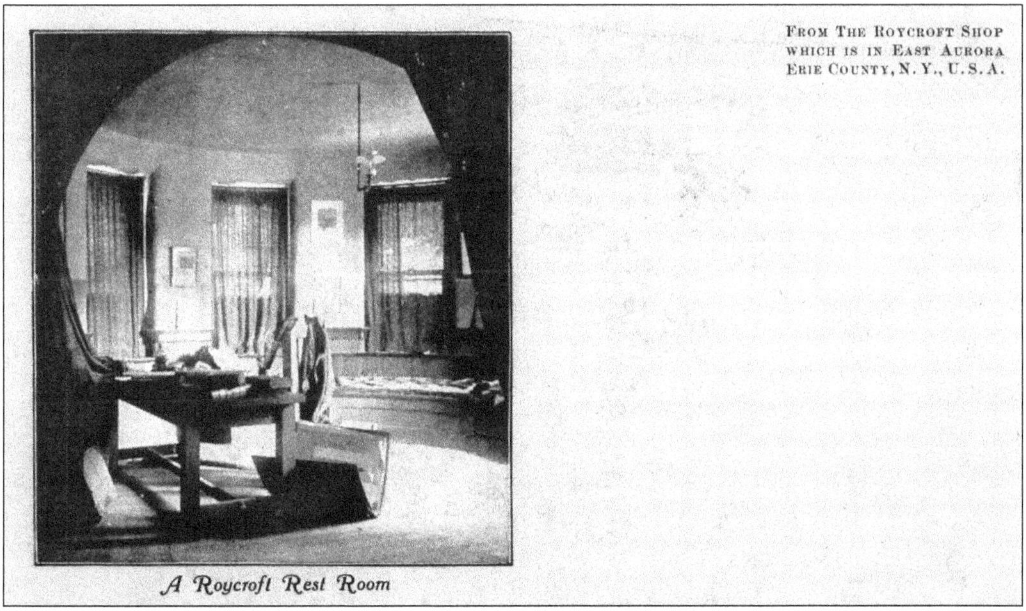


The same view as shown in the card on page 61 is seen here, but it is reset with a new title after Samuel Warner had left the campus and moved back to Massachusetts in 1902. Warner became an art teacher in the public schools there and never returned to Roycroft. His son mounted an exhibition of his father's artwork on the campus during one of the first Roycrofters-at-Large Summer Conventions in the late 1970s.

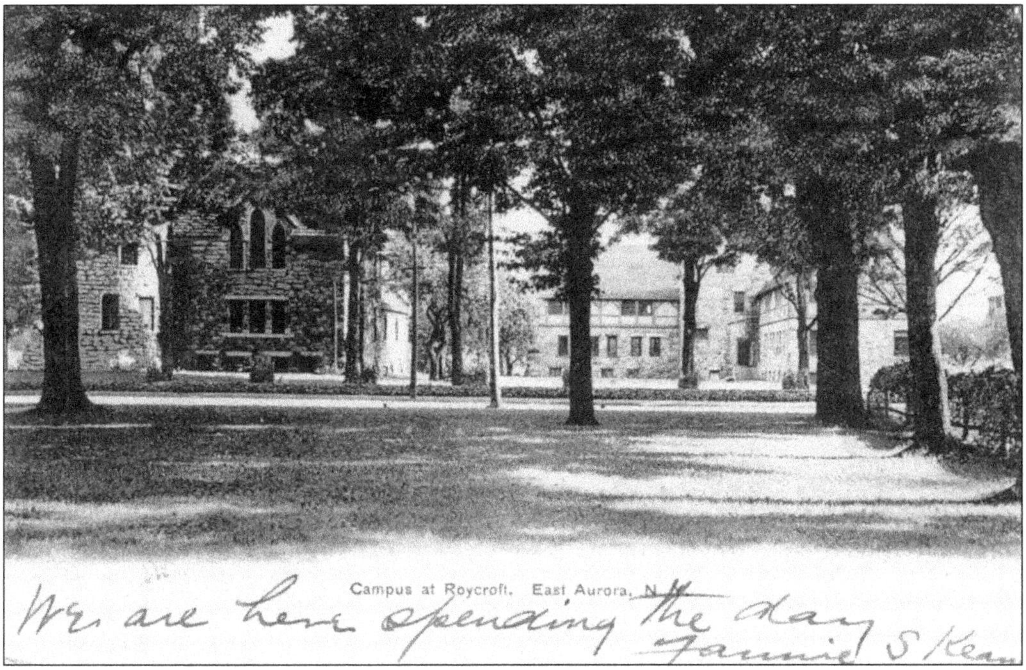


In a view almost never seen by visitors, the photographer of this image was standing on the doorsteps of the Aurora Union Free School, opposite the campus on the north side of Main Street. All of the Hubbard children attended this school, yet, as their father, not all finished high school.

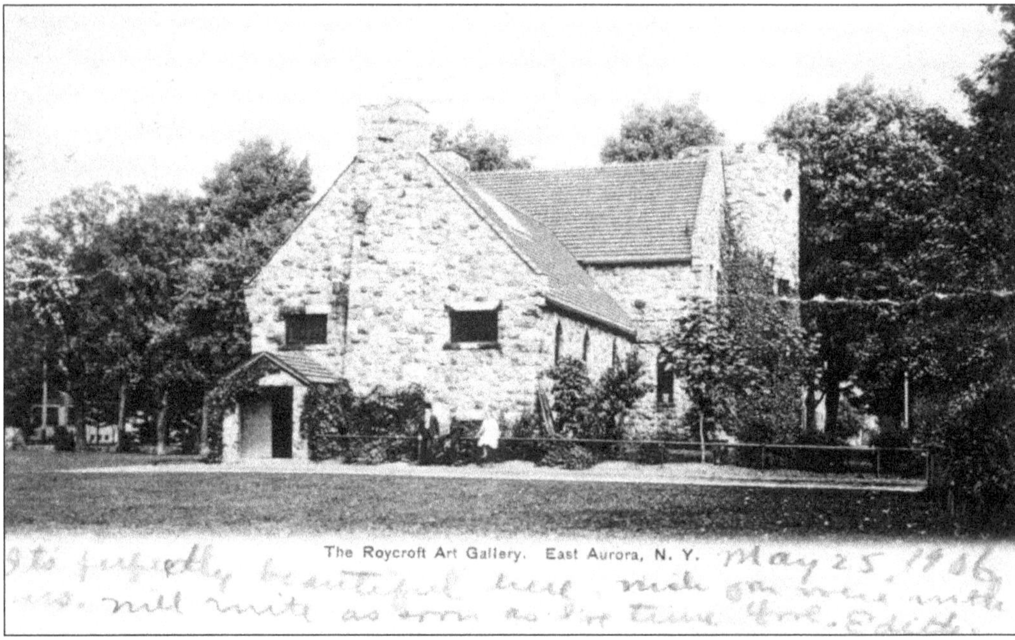


The chapel's main room became the campus's new art gallery with the hiring of the Roycroft's first art director, Samuel Warner, in 1899. He was hired to train the illuminators and also as a designer of the presses title pages and decorations. He brought along Irish sculptor Jerome Connor (1865–1943), who would exhibit his work here in 1900.

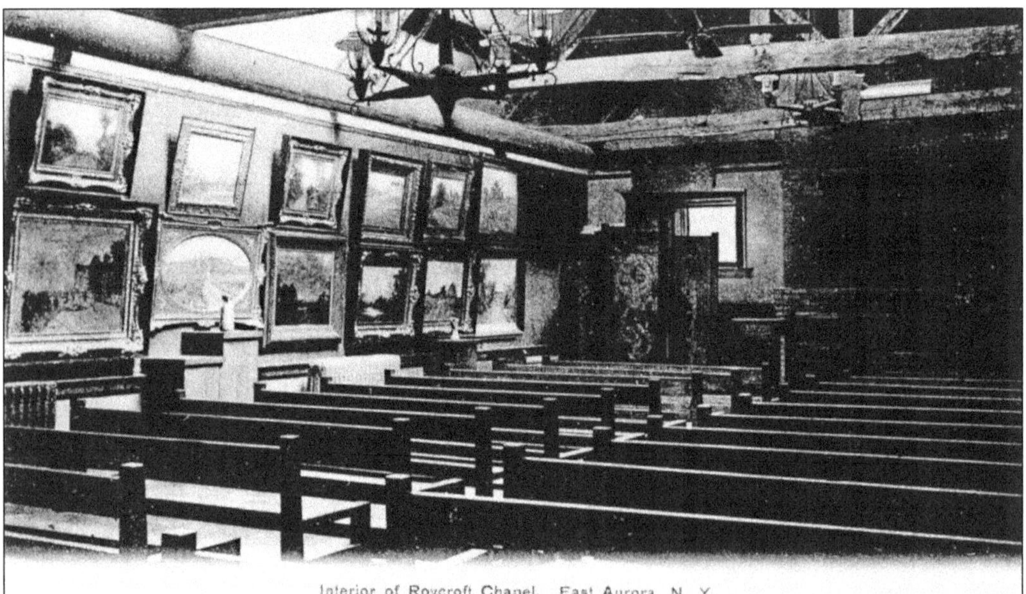


Hired in 1903 as art director of the Roycrofters, Alexis Jean Fournier mounted many exhibitions in the gallery space in the chapel. This exhibition showed his own work, many from his European travels and studios. Having trained at Academy Julian in Paris beginning in the 1880s, he became enamored by the Barbizons and became friends with many of their families. A large number of his paintings still turn up in East Aurora, as he was known to pay his debts with fine artwork. Elbert even authorized the press to print a catalog with prices for this 1904 exhibit.

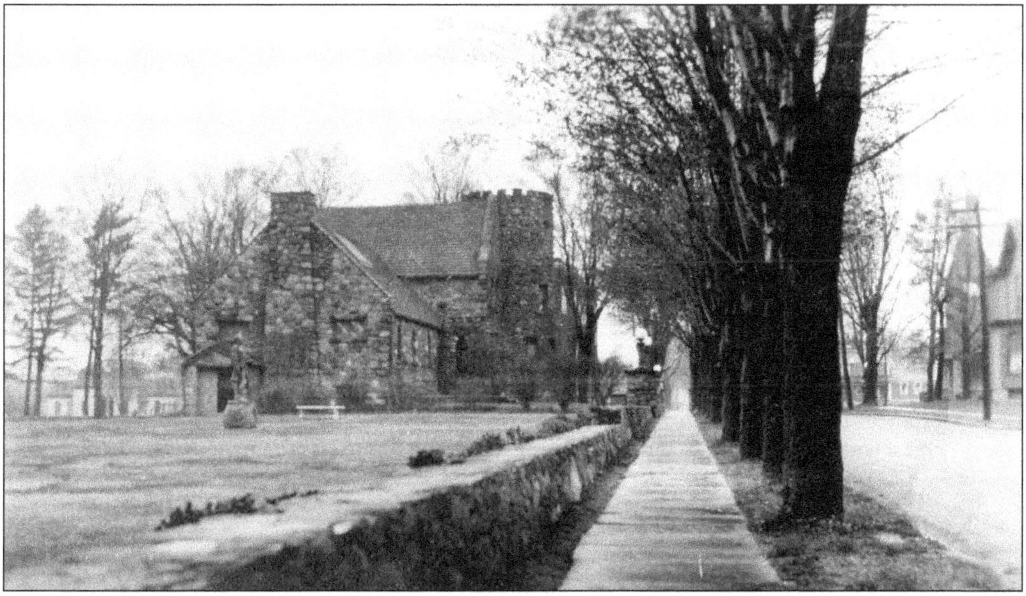

This photograph was made from a real-photo postcard in September 1914. It gives one an idea of a very early morning on the campus, before the workmen and women arrive. It was taken by a visitor from Toronto, Ontario, Canada, who had arrived by train from Buffalo the evening before. At this time, the chapel was both a large living room and library and a gift shop for the campus.

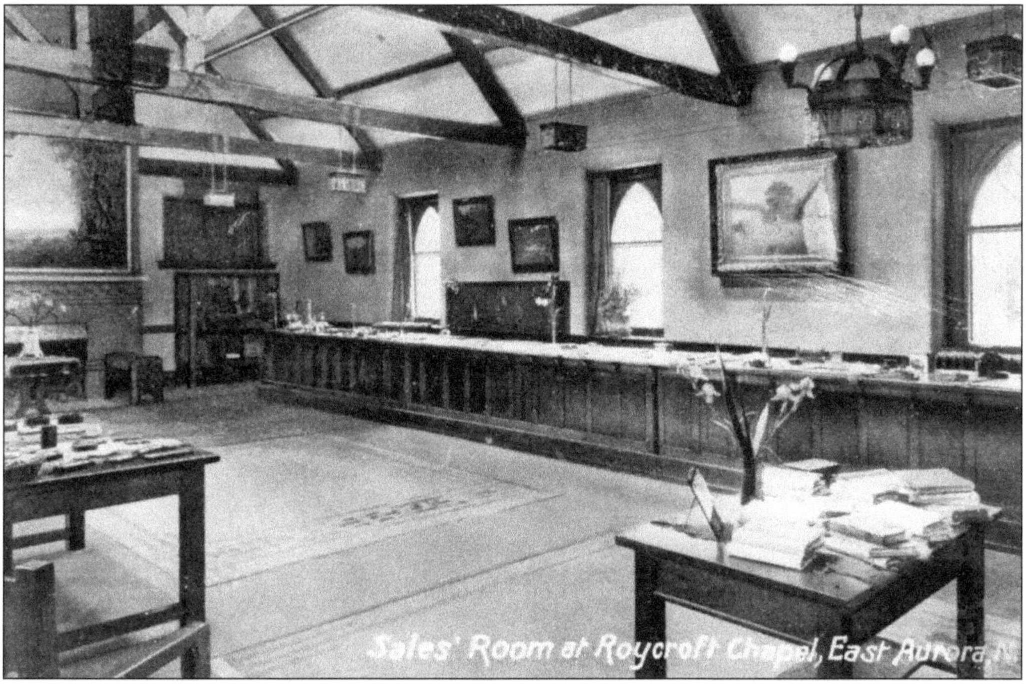


The Gift Shop, located in the largest of the chapel's rooms called the sales room by the Roycrofters, offered visitors the chance to see and order the finest books, copperware, pottery, and even modeled leather items made in the nearby shop buildings. Note also that there are both Alexis Fournier oil paintings and Dard Hunter–designed glass lanterns on the walls and ceiling, respectively.

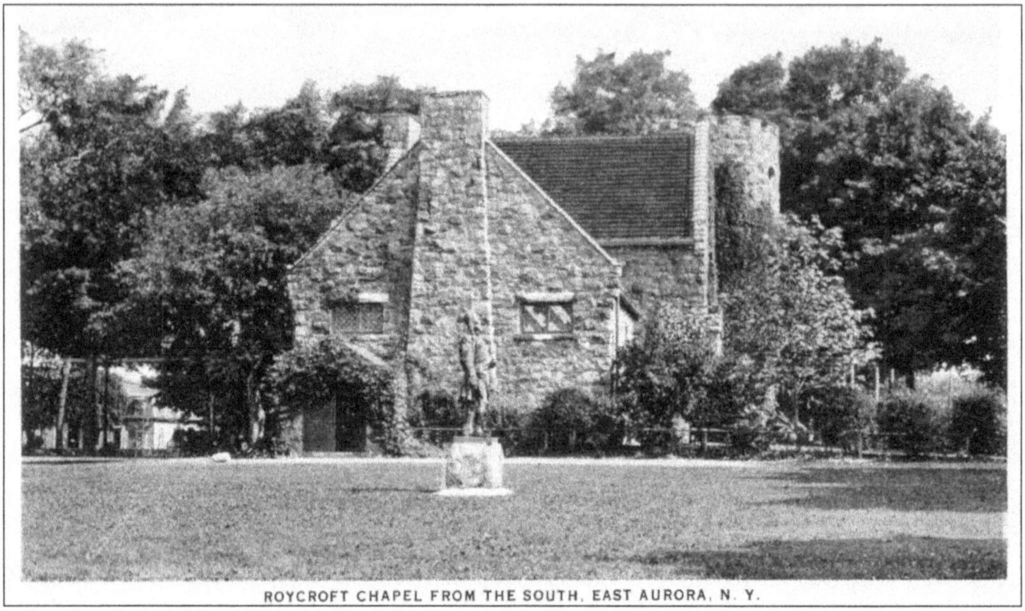


Looking directly north from the Appian Way across from the inn, the original location of Bartlett's sculpture can be seen. This monumental work is now about 500 feet farther north on the grounds of today's Aurora Middle School, formerly the only Aurora School building. Also if one looks closely to the far left, a mansard-roofed, Victorian-era home that was moved off Main Street to accommodate the expansion of the school in the 1920s can be seen.

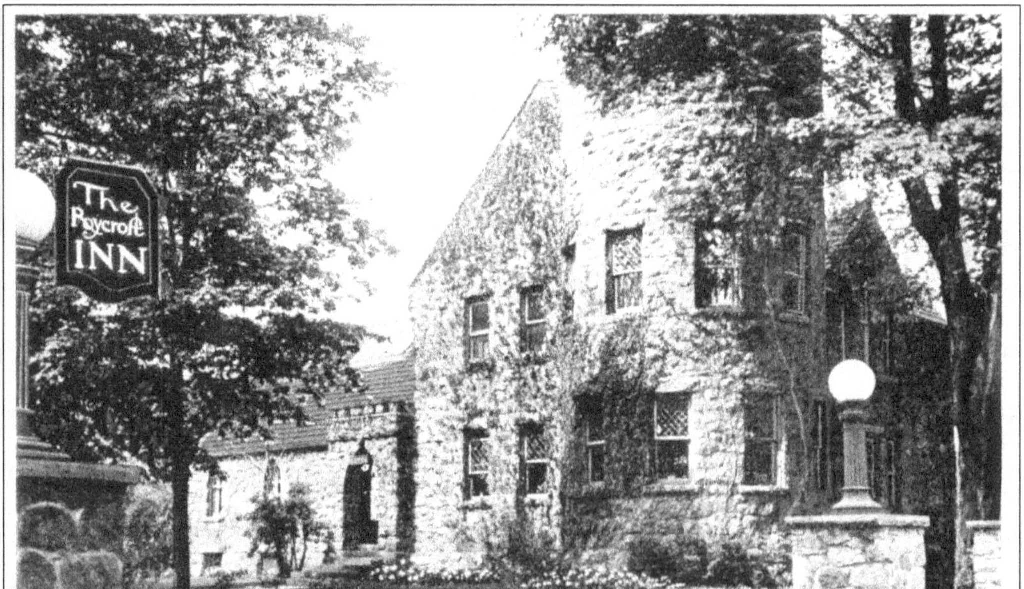


Here is a late-1920s or early-1930s view of the entrance to the campus. The Roycroft Inn's welcome sign could be seen by all those traveling through the village. The sign hung out over South Grove Street and was flanked by the electric globe lamps on the stone walls. These have all been restored since 2000.

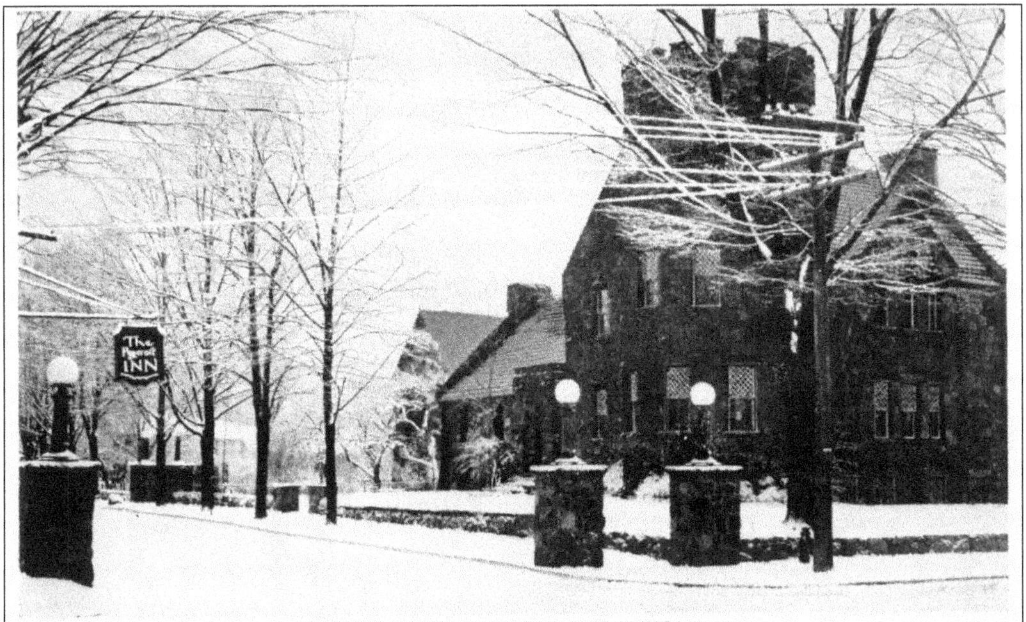

ROYCROFT CHAPEL IN WINTER, EAST AURORA, N. Y. 60344-C

Though not a welcoming sight to some, snow is enjoyed by many Western New Yorkers. There were and are many winter activities in and around the village and town. Skiing, sledding, and ice-skating in Hamlin Park, just three blocks down the street, were all enjoyed by workers and visitors. The sign remained into the 1960s.

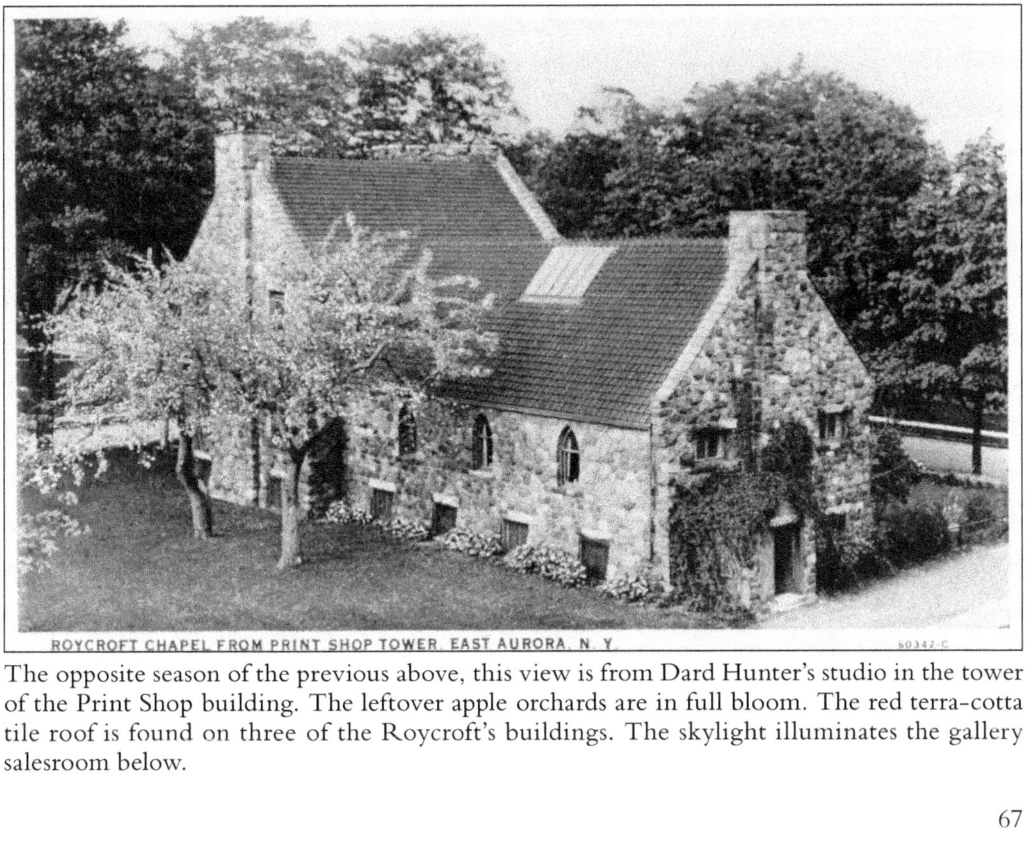
ROYCROFT CHAPEL FROM PRINT SHOP TOWER, EAST AURORA, N. Y. 60342-C

The opposite season of the previous above, this view is from Dard Hunter's studio in the tower of the Print Shop building. The leftover apple orchards are in full bloom. The red terra-cotta tile roof is found on three of the Roycroft's buildings. The skylight illuminates the gallery salesroom below.

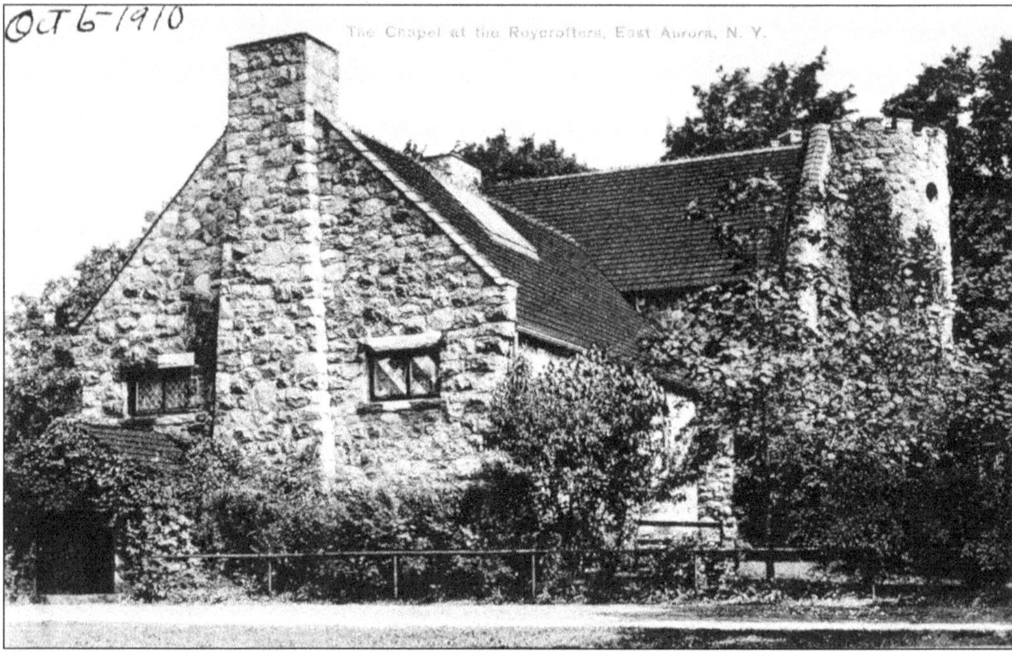


Though no postcard exists of this building before 1899, this location was where the first Blacksmith Shop of Roycrofters was located in 1898-1900, when the new shop was built. Of note are the diamond glass leaded windows. These were never updated, like those of the Roycroft Inn. Dard Hunter and Karl Kipp had designed and built indoor lighting for this building but never changed the original windows.

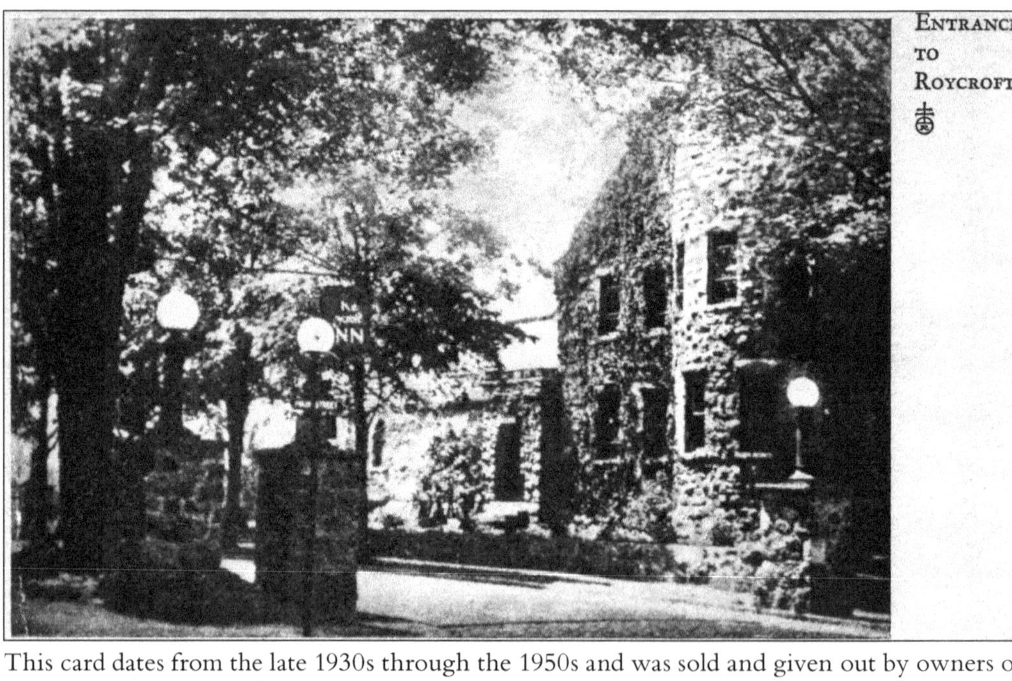


This card dates from the late 1930s through the 1950s and was sold and given out by owners of the Roycroft Inn until the early 1960s. The Roycroft printed hundreds of these cards; so many were leftover after the corporation's bankruptcy in 1938.

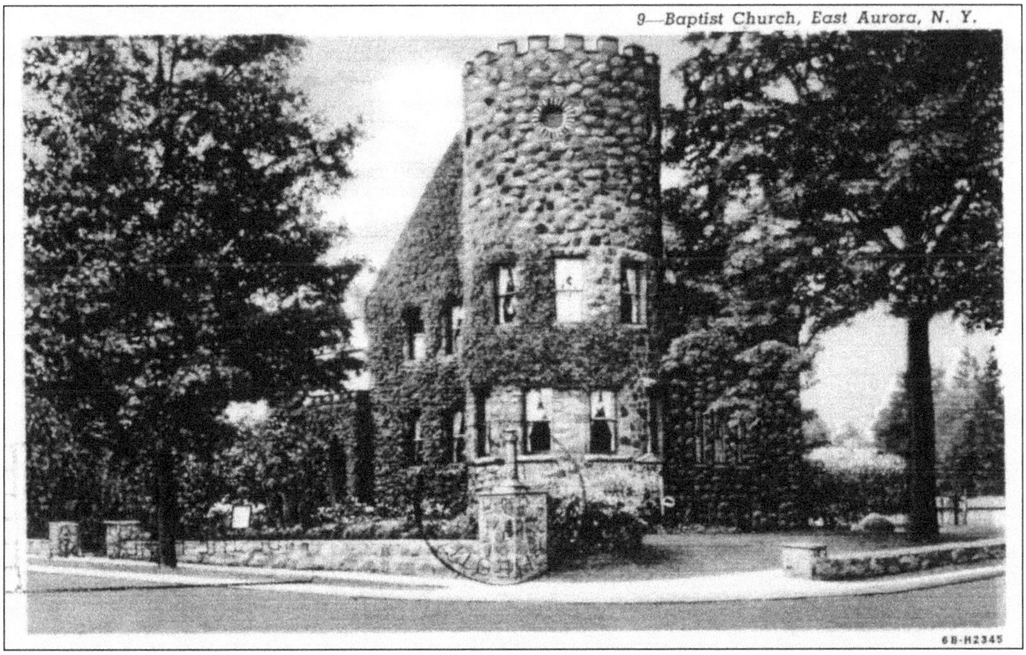


For a short time beginning in 1939, the chapel was owned by Samuel Guard's printing offices. The short-lived predecessor to the Roycrofters, Inc., also went into bankruptcy in a few short years. The structure then became the First Baptist Church of East Aurora in the 1940s until their new building was constructed just outside the village. In 2010, the congregation celebrated their 200th anniversary.

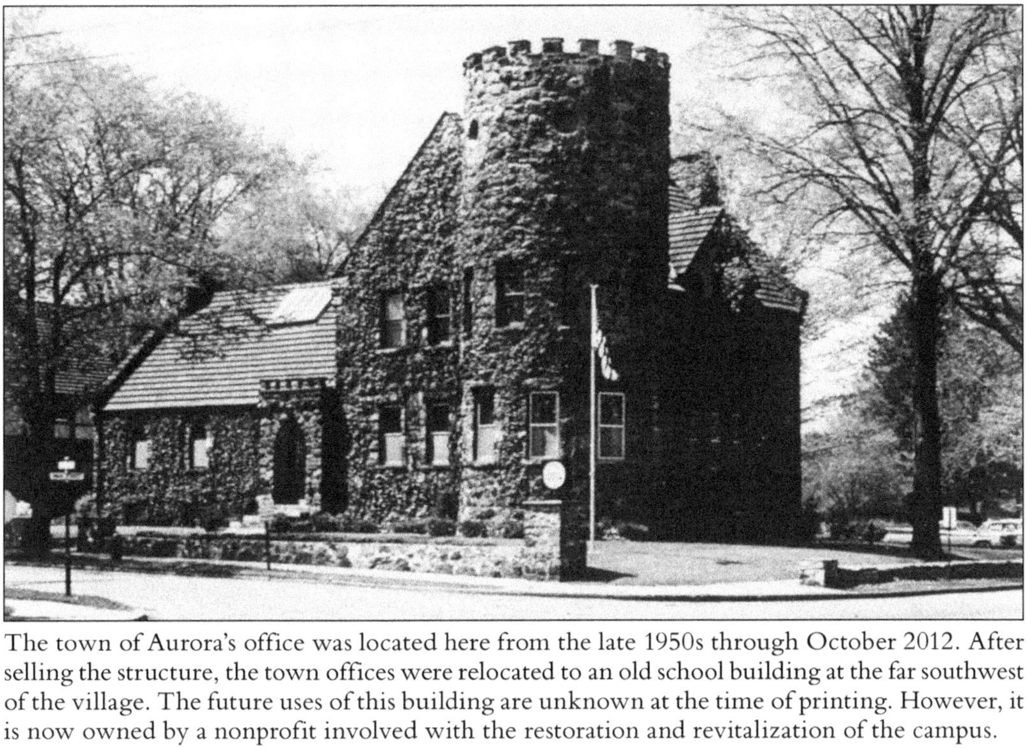

The town of Aurora's office was located here from the late 1950s through October 2012. After selling the structure, the town offices were relocated to an old school building at the far southwest of the village. The future uses of this building are unknown at the time of printing. However, it is now owned by a nonprofit involved with the restoration and revitalization of the campus.

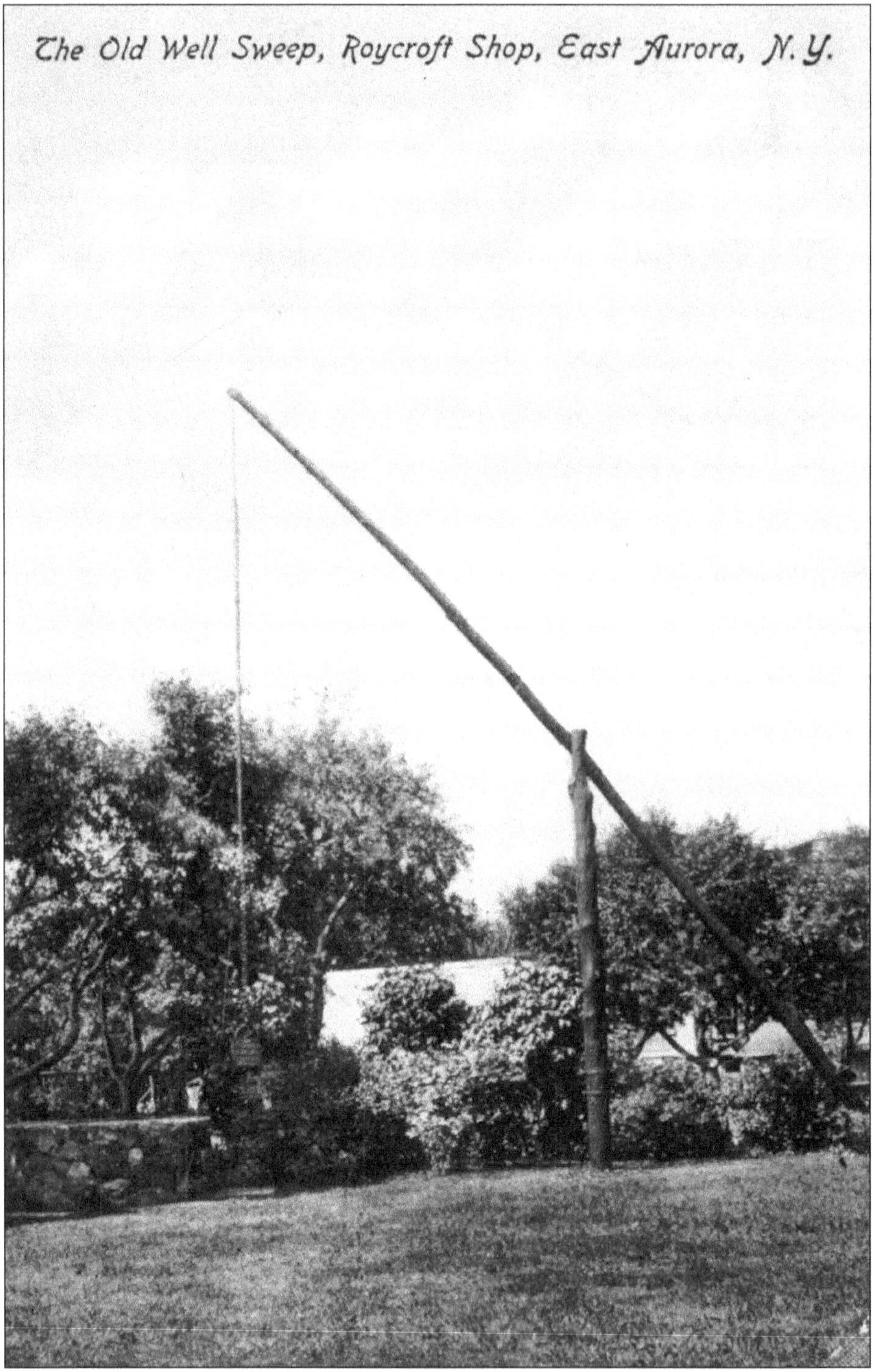


Giving the appearance of an old English village, the well sweep was used for fighting fires in the neighborhood but was really just a great photograph location. It is presently capped and under the asphalt of the parking lots south of the Print Shop. There are discussions ongoing as to the importance to its restoration and the dangers involved in an open well in a public area.

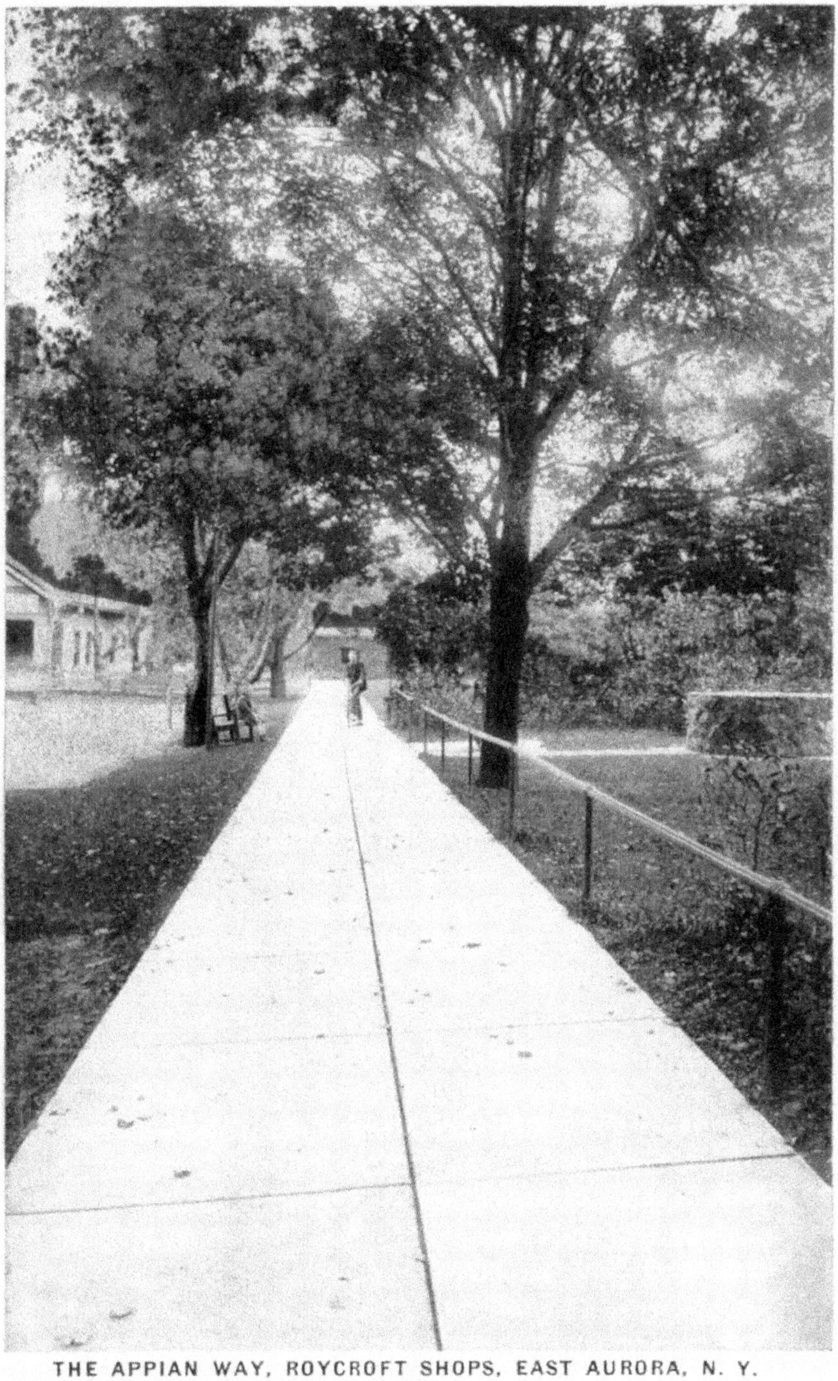

THE APPIAN WAY, ROYCROFT SHOPS, EAST AURORA, N. Y.

Hubbard's use of Roman nomenclature was just one of his eccentricities. The Appian Way, really just a long sidewalk that lead from the inn across to the Blacksmith, Copper, and Furniture Shops, was given this fancy name to entice customers across to the workshops. Today, it is a memorial walkway paved with bricks that can be purchased to help fund the restoration of the campus. This activity is organized by the Roycrofters-at-Large Association, which was founded in 1976.

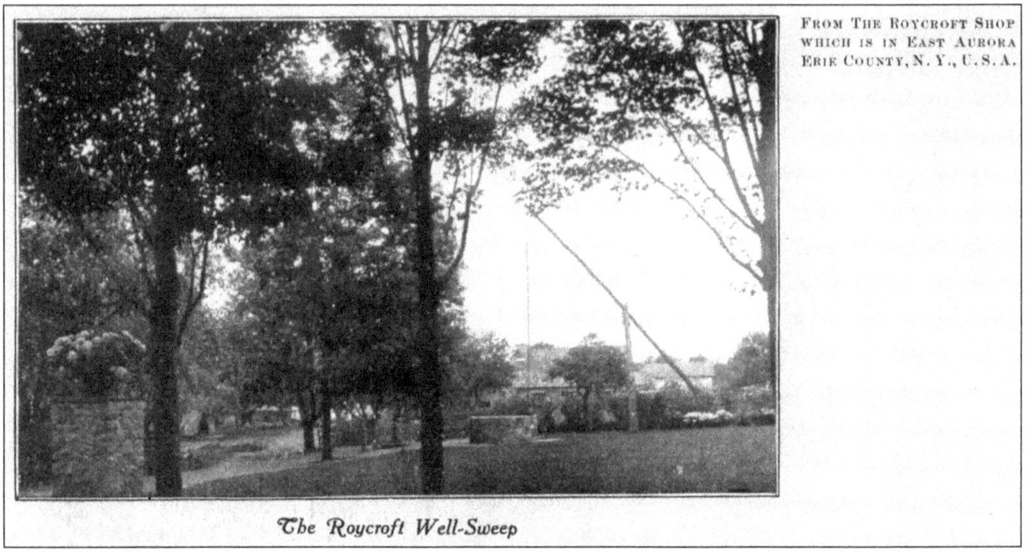


The view seen here around 1905 shows what some hope will be the future of the campus, a verdant treed garden across from the inn. There were many horticultural specimens and flowering trees and shrubs during Elbert's lifetime. Most of these trees were removed by his early demise in 1915. Many were taken to make space for the powerhouse in 1910.

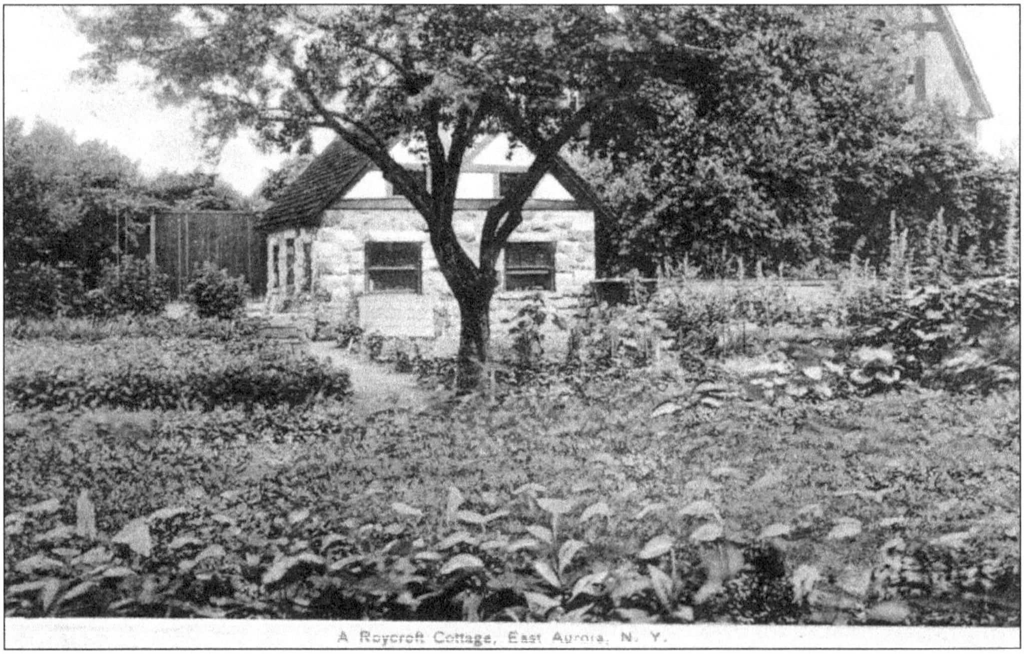


Again, a fanciful name for a straightforward view of the second Blacksmith Shop, built in 1899 and 1900. Yet the photographer makes this appear as a worker's cottage in some quaint English village of 100 years before. Gardens of both flowers and vegetables were found throughout the campus. The new three-story wooden Bindery and Furniture Shop building appears in the background at right. It was built in 1904.

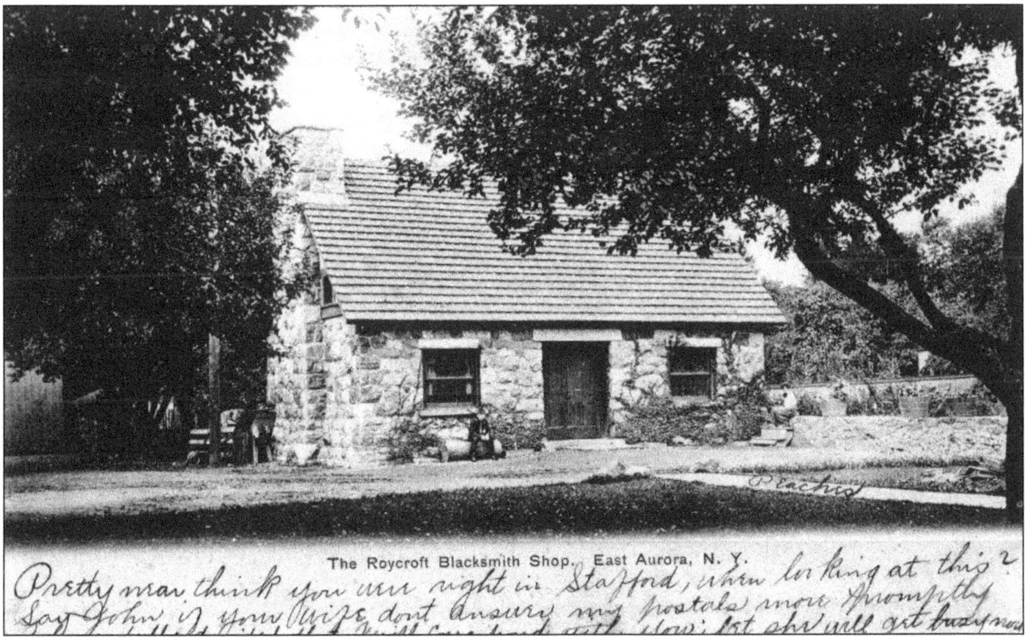


A view of the east facade of the second Blacksmith Shop is seen here. It became the campus's third permanent structure in 1899. When it was first built it had a dirt floor, hearth, and bellows in the exposed timber structure of one large room. This was soon to change as the Arts and Crafts Movement spread its philosophy nationwide.

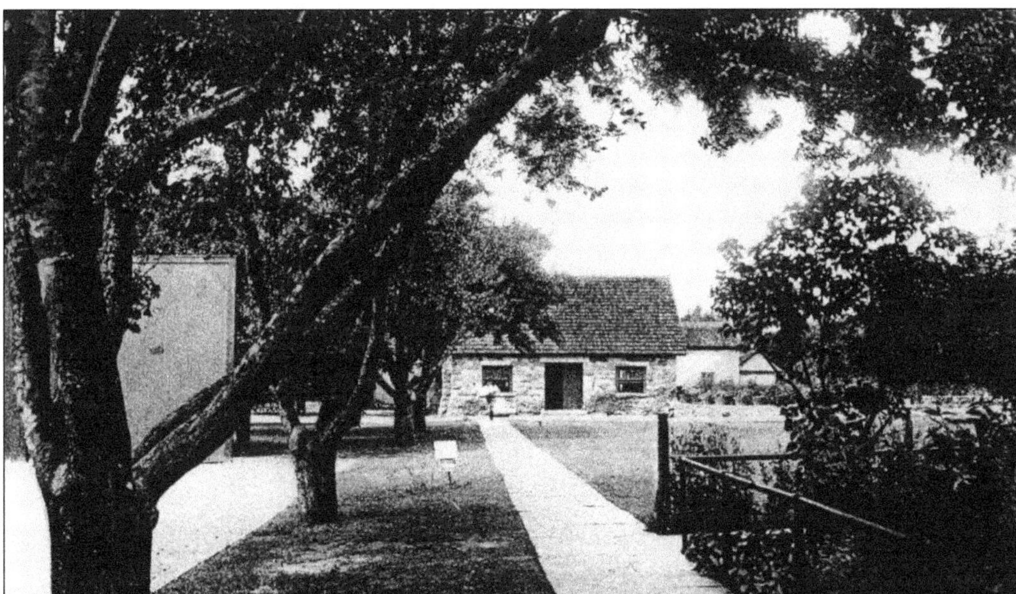


This rare card, maybe because of its typo, shows the cement handball court at left, which was used every summer as a screen for the projection of free movies for the community. In 1911, this space was used to build the Roycrofter's powerhouse.

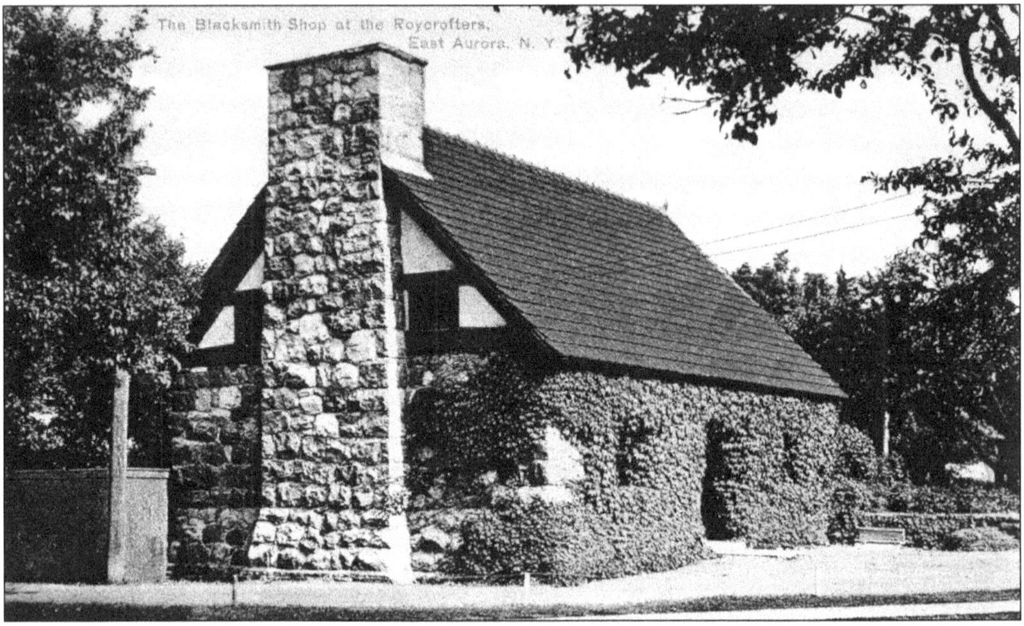


As the years passed, English ivy was allowed to grow up the stone walls to further beautify the building. Karl Kipp was the foreman of the new Copper Shop and art metal department, which was headquartered here. Blacksmithing with wrought iron was replaced by the Arts and Crafts material of hand-hammered copper. This craft is what the Roycroft is most known for today among collectors, and some items made here have commanded more than $100,000 at auctions.

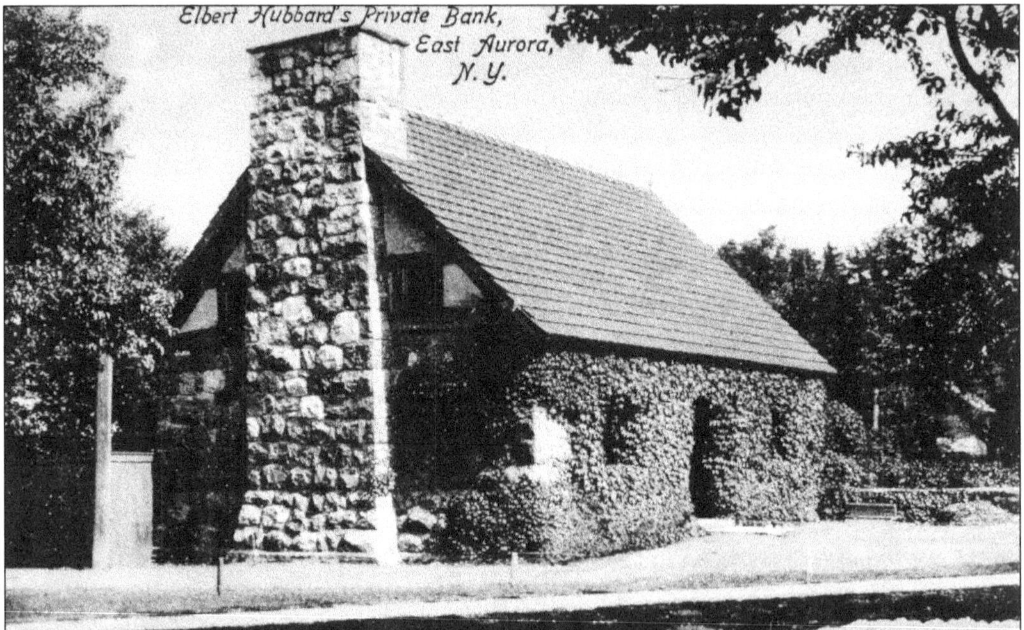


To emphasize his belief in personal savings, Elbert Hubbard set up a savings account for each of his employees. He also opened up an account in his newly chartered bank for each child named Elbert or Elberta. He deposited a gold piece into each of these accounts. The bank did not survive the Depression of the 1930s, however.

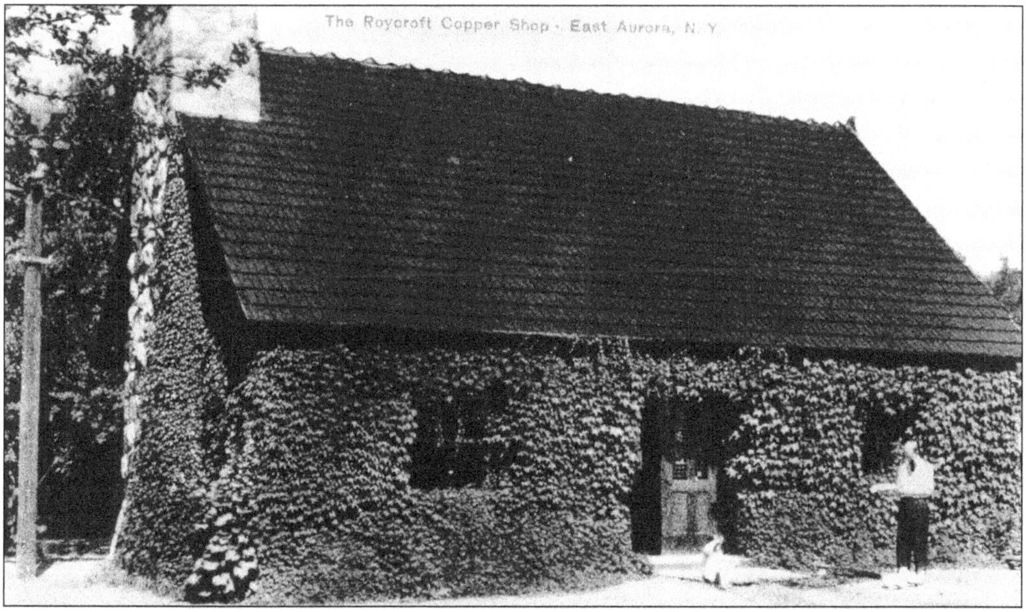


The master craftsman Karl Kipp stands outside his workshop with white doves at his feet around 1923. The small boy on the walk is Elbert Hubbard III (1921–2003), the only son of Bert Hubbard. He became a medical doctor just like his grandfather Silas. John, as he was known, lived and had his medical office on Oakwood Avenue, just a block away from where he sits here at age three.

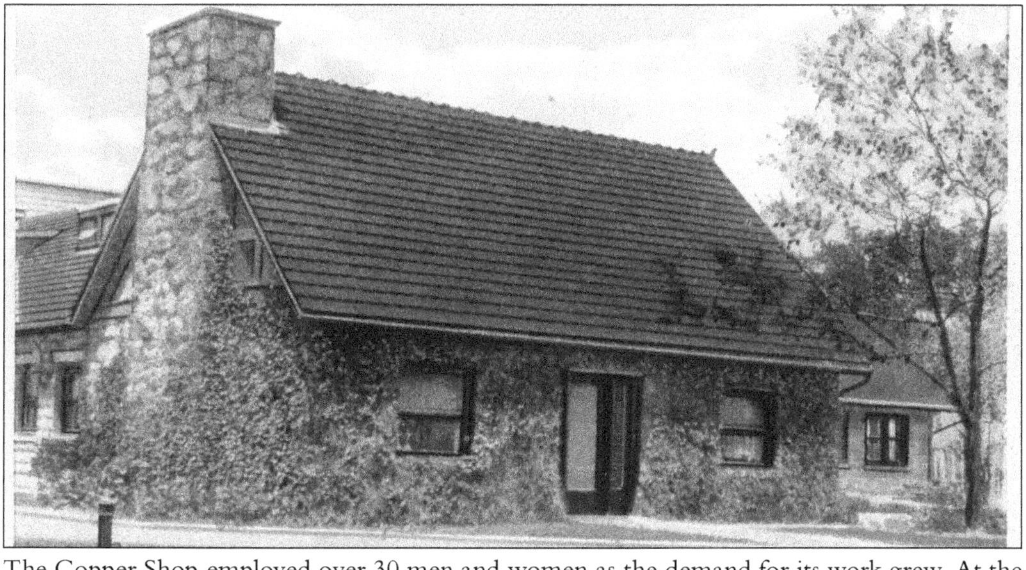

The Copper Shop employed over 30 men and women as the demand for its work grew. At the far right, the last addition to the building can be seen on the north side. It held the plating room, where the patinas and silver plating were added to the copper crafts. The Cooper Shop was the last of crafts shop of the Roycrofters to survive. Copper items made here were sold by catalog and in department stores throughout America until 1938, and they are highly collectible today. The Roycroft Gift Shop, as it became in 1938, continued to feature the original coppersmiths work well into the 1960s. Today, as the Copper Shop Gallery, the work of modern-day craftsmen and women of the Roycroft Renaissance is available.

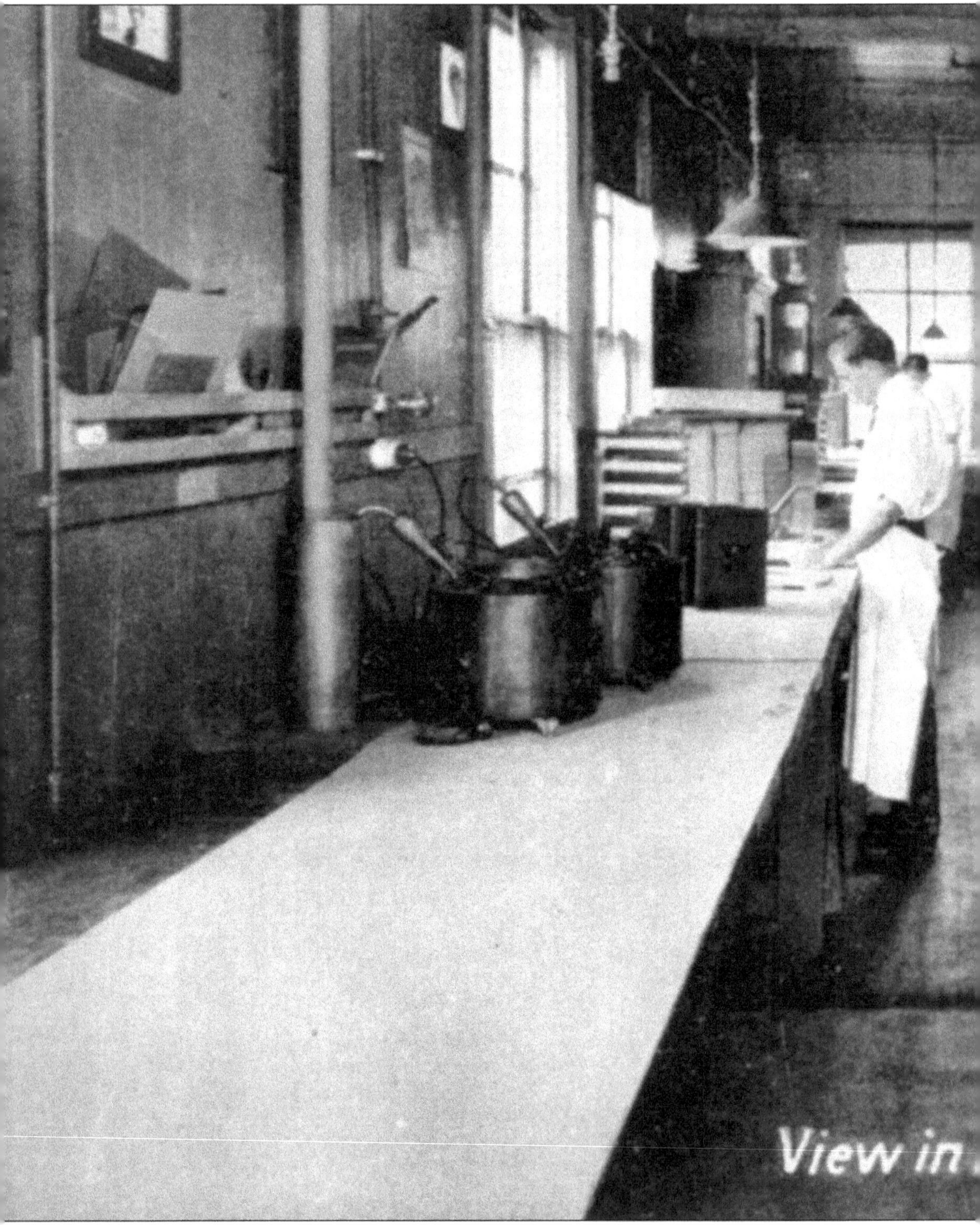

The first floor of the three-story Bindery and Furniture Shop housed the bookbindery where Louis Herman Kinder was foreman. The Roycroft Press was well known for the fine hand-

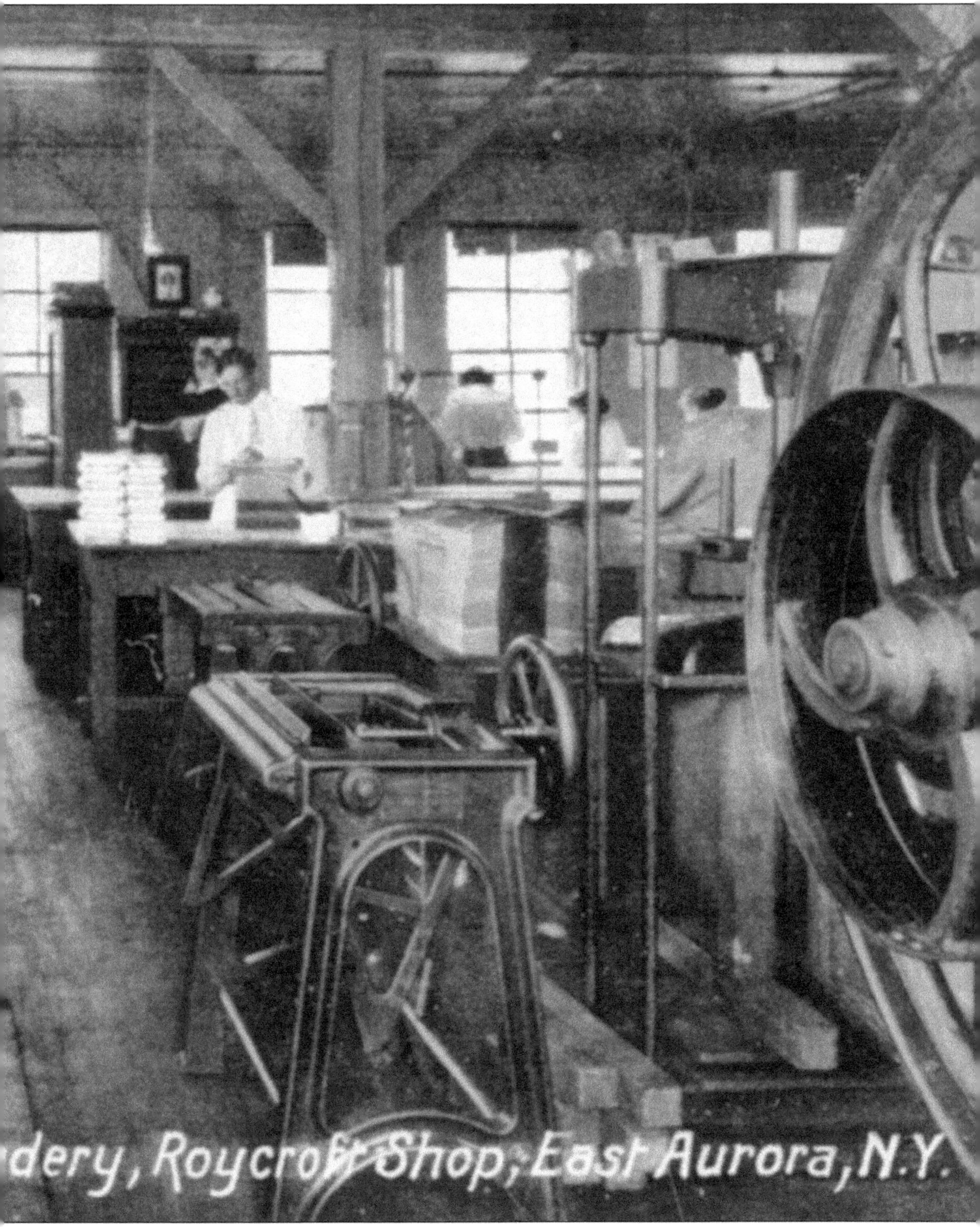


tooled, leather-bound books produced in limited editions. Some of the books that were made here sold for over $200 in 1905, an equivalent of $10,000 today.

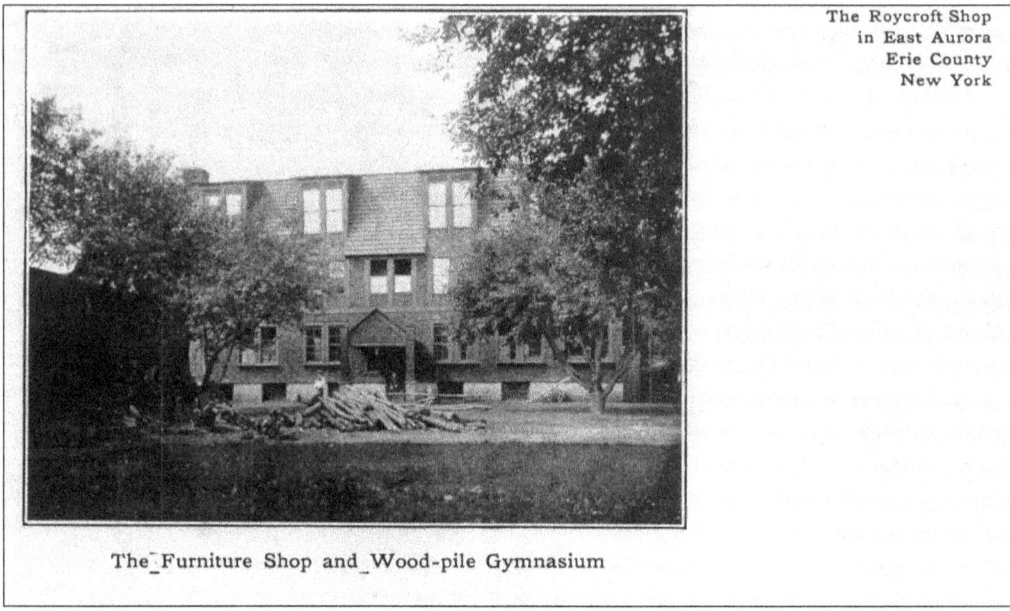


This first card to feature the new Furniture Shop, where the shop's Mission oak-style chairs and tables were made, employed about 20 to 25 craftsman regularly on two of the three floors. Local carpenters were hired, and no one designer is credited for what Elbert advertised as Aurora colonial furniture starting in 1901. Hubbard also thought that chopping wood was an exercise that could be enjoyed by workers and visitors alike, hence the gymnasium.

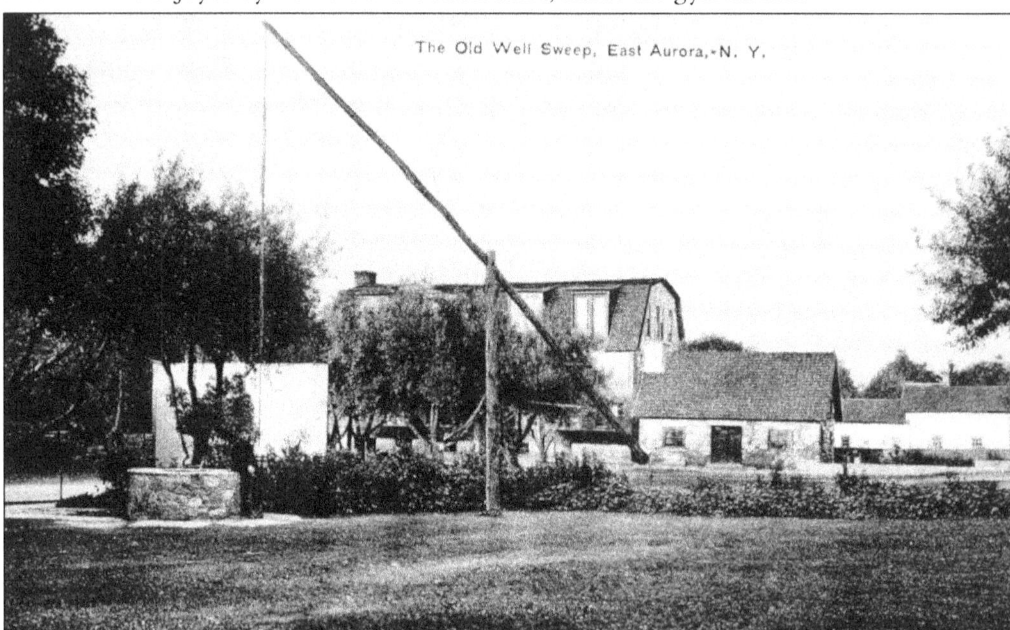


The handball court located behind the well sweep at left only existed for a short time. In the summers, this was used as an outdoor motion picture theater for the community. In 1910, a new building, one of the campus's last, was to be constructed here. The few remaining apple trees from the orchards that existed when the Hubbard's moved to the village were removed in this project.

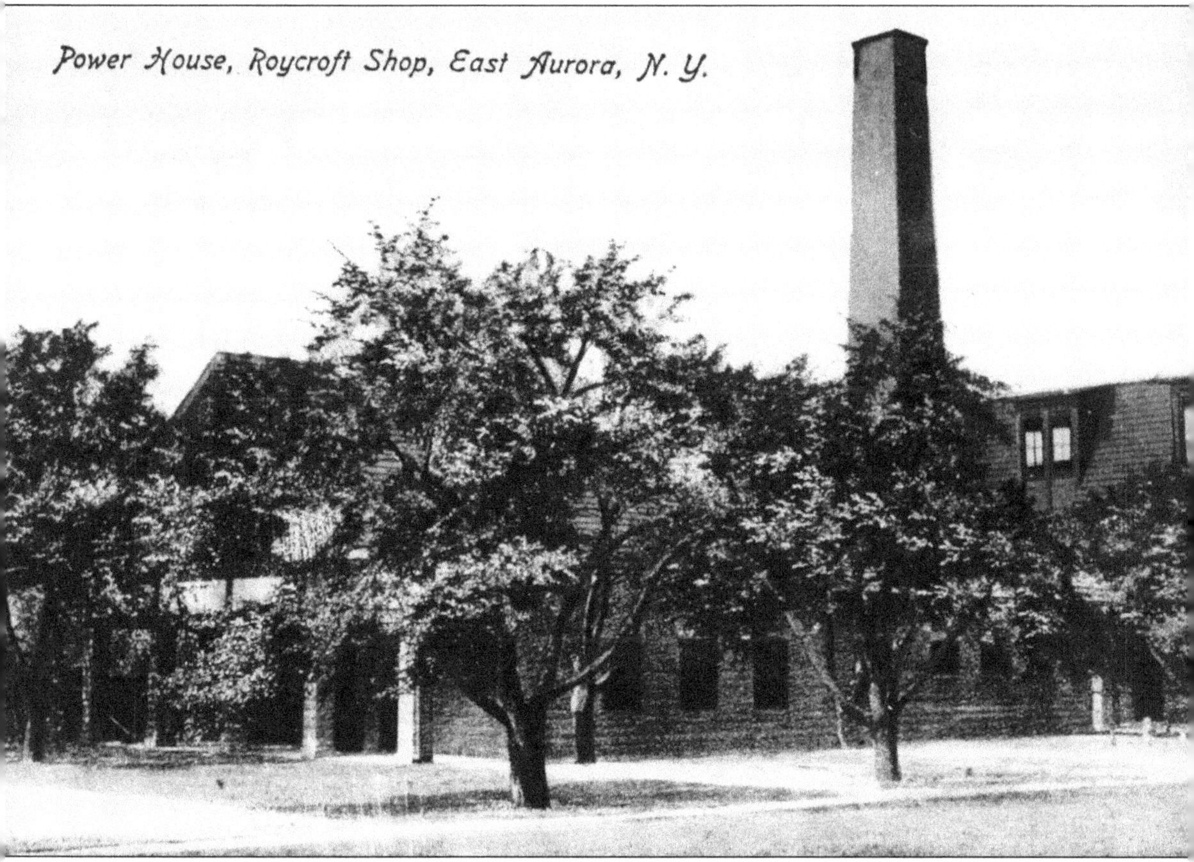


The powerhouse is a building with a story equal to the phoenix. Built to heat and power the campus and the inn with underground pipes, it was completed in 1910. Fired by coal boilers, it made the campus self-sufficient. However, when the Roycrofters, Inc., declared bankruptcy in 1938, all of the buildings were sold off individually after a failed attempt to remain as a publishing house for Samuel Guard's agricultural periodicals. When separated, the boilers were sold off for scrap metal for the World War II efforts. The building first became a church, and in the 1960s, it was turned into a multiuse edifice with medical and legal offices on the first floor and apartments above. In 1997, a fire broke out in the attic space of the wood-framed structure and destroyed the building. The remaining concrete walls were knocked down in a windstorm in 2005, and all seemed lost. But, its National Historic Landmark status proved its savior. The Roycroft Revitalization Corporation obtained grants and loans to rebuild the powerhouse as the new educational center for the campus. It now contains offices, classrooms, meeting rooms, and historic displays for the visitors and reopened in 2012. Enlarged photographs of the original boilers and the workers grace the walls.

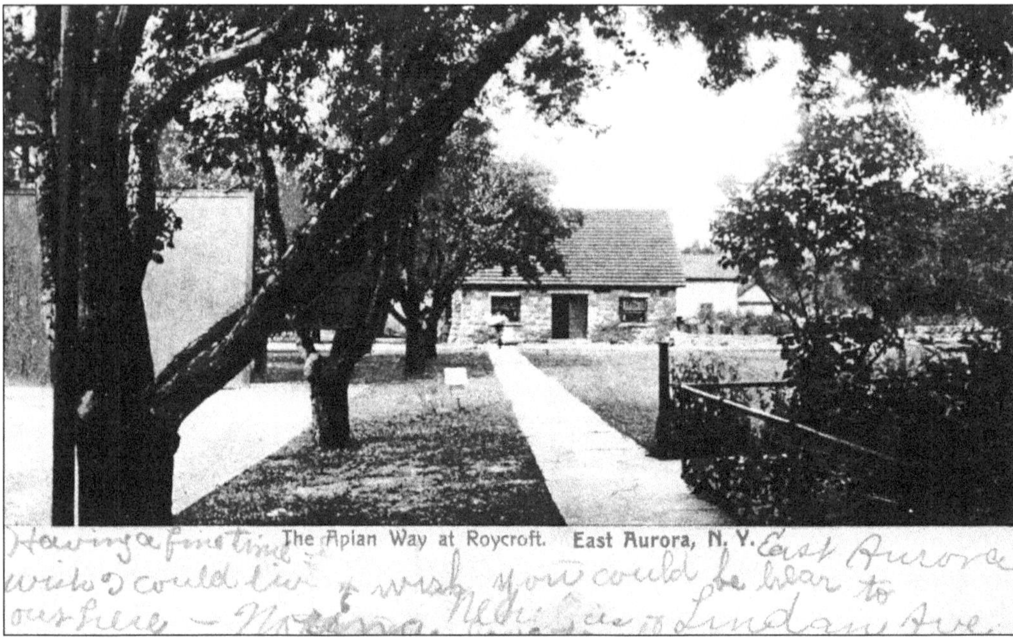


This is a rare card because of the typo in the spelling of "Apian." This is a card for the collectors and was printed around 1905. It even shows a please keep of the grass sign . . . or maybe another one of Elbert Hubbard's sayings regarding the need for exercise and fresh air and the location of handballs for the guests' use?

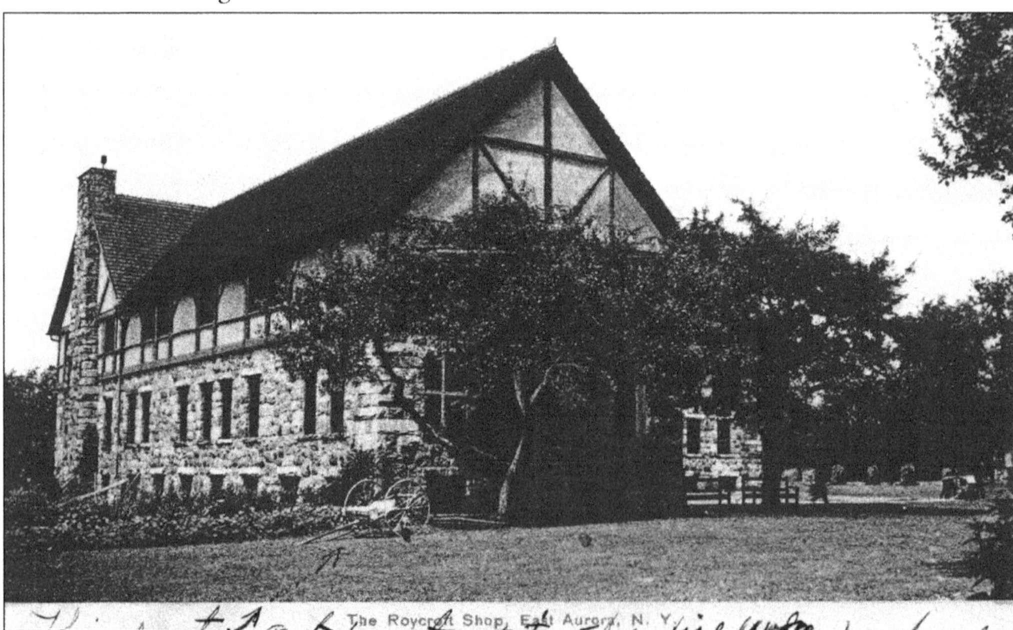


Another version of this card is shown earlier but is important for its owners statement, "This cart got burnt up in the fire we had." Actually a hose cart for fire protection, little is known about this fire, but fire has always been a hazard for the wooden buildings on campus. Fires in the 1920s, 1940s, 1960s, 1970s, and 1990s have scared the face of the campus, especially the Bindery and Furniture Shop, which lost its third floor in a massive blaze in the 1980s.

# *Five*

# Roycrofters at Play
## Fun and Games in the Village

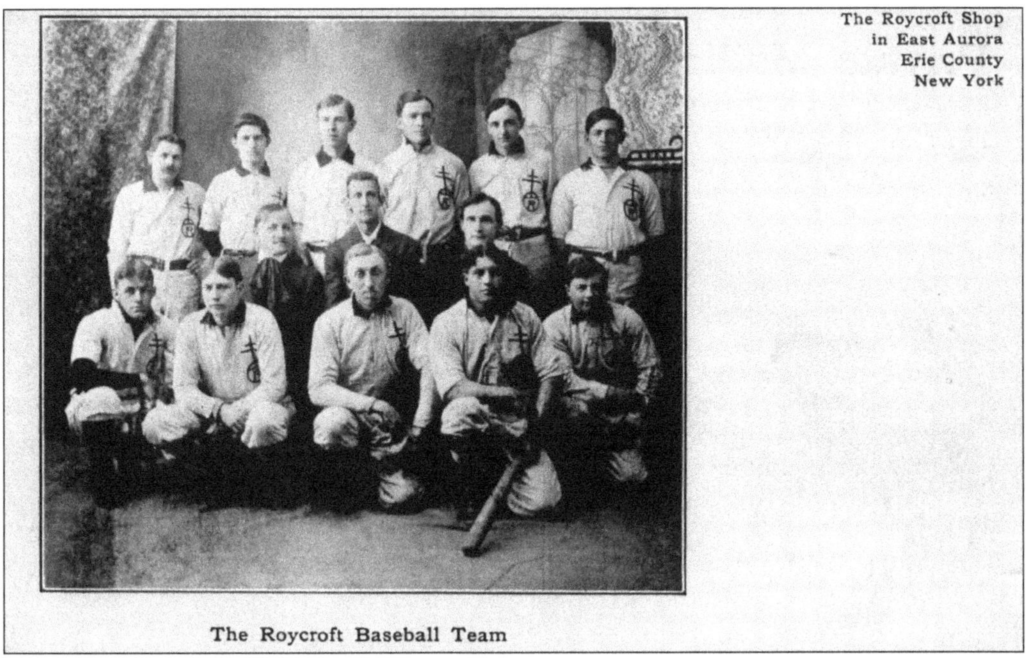


Yes, Roycroft had a baseball team! It is pictured here around 1903 to 1905. Two of its members became professionals. Wally Shang (1889–1965), born in South Wales, was the catcher in 32 World Series games before 1920. The team played many famous semipro teams, including the House of David from the commune in western Michigan, only a day's drive away across Canada. One of the rarest collectibles of Roycroftiana, if one were ever found, would be a Roycrofters team baseball uniform from this period. The shops made and sold many leather sport items, including baseballs, softballs, and medicine balls. Fun and games were a part of the Roycroft lifestyle. Elbert called exercise breaks for all the employees when he was in town and would throw the medicine ball around among the workers, men and women, alike. Visitors and inn guests were always invited to tag along on walks afield, some ending up at one of the Roycroft's three farms at the edge of the village. (Courtesy of the library of Jack Walsdorf.)

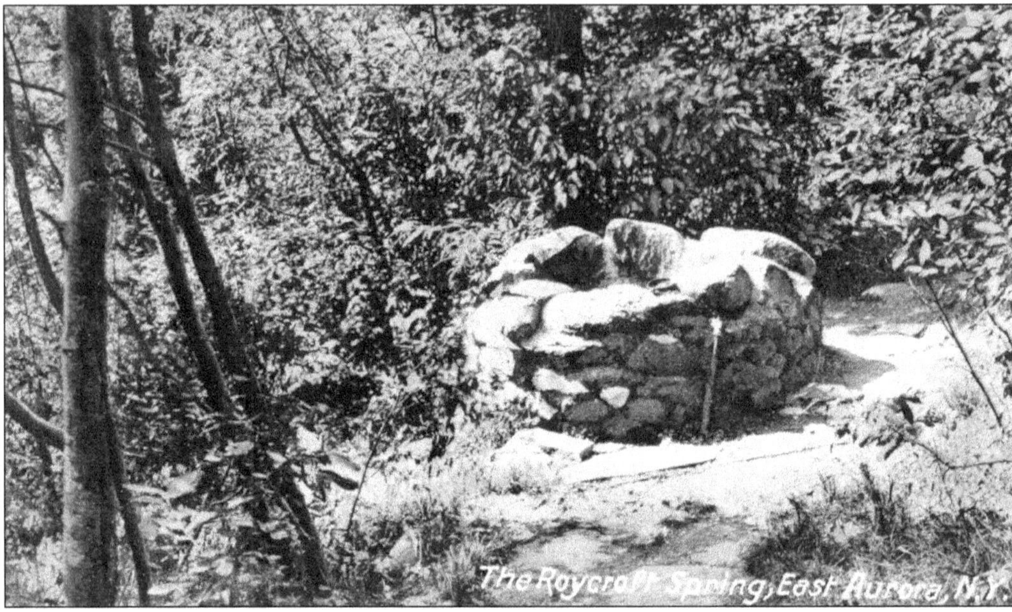


This natural spring found at the south end of the village was another short hike for Hubbard and company. The southern edge of the village rises up into the beginnings of the Allegheny Mountains. Just 10 miles south of the village is the highest point in Erie County, not mountains really by western standards. Fresh water and artesian wells and springs pop up throughout this glacial terrain.

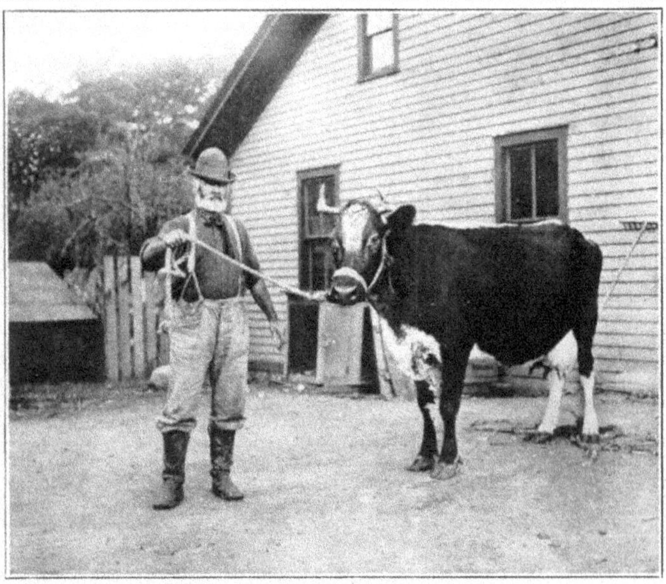

The Roycroft Shop
in East Aurora
Erie County
New York

*Ali Baba and June*

Always looking for humor in everyday life, Ali Baba and June became celebrities around early Roycroft. Ali Baba, also known as Anson Blackman, was a farmhand and horse trainer for many years before being hired by Hubbard. He was in charge of all the stock initially, though was promoted to traveling companion and valet by the late 1890s when this photograph was taken. He lived many years longer than Elbert and became a source of many stories for visitors.

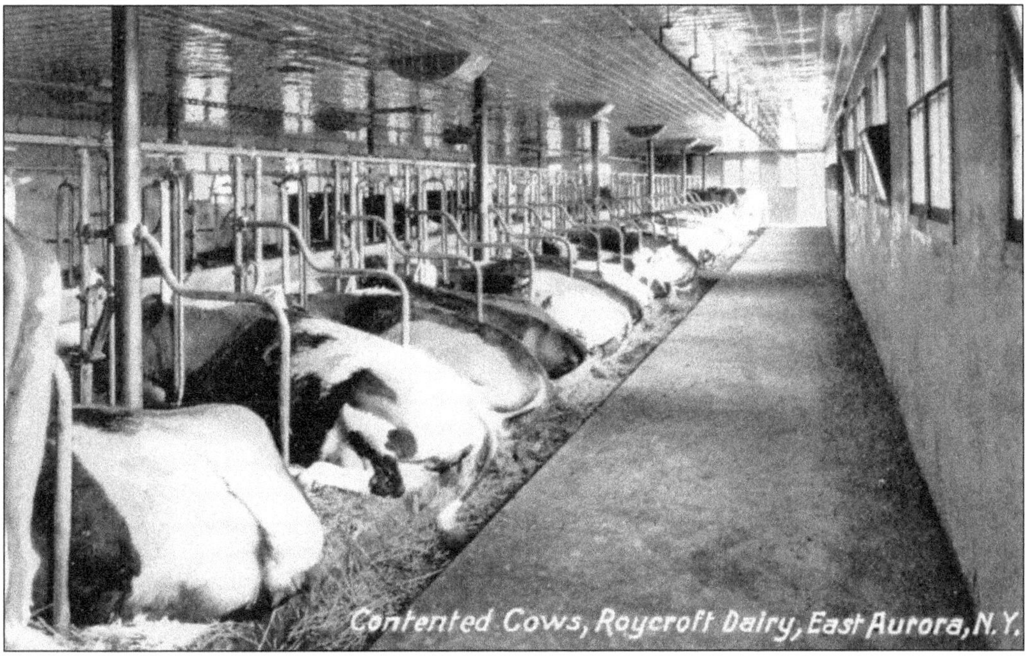


Western New York State is well known for its dairy farms. With the Roycroft Inn and dining rooms to feed the workers, many cows were needed to supply their needs. This barn, located on what is now called Hubbard Road, is also famous for being the place where Elbert Hubbard had painted the suffragette motto "Votes For Women" in 10-foot-tall letters. This image was published as a full page in *The Fra* magazine.

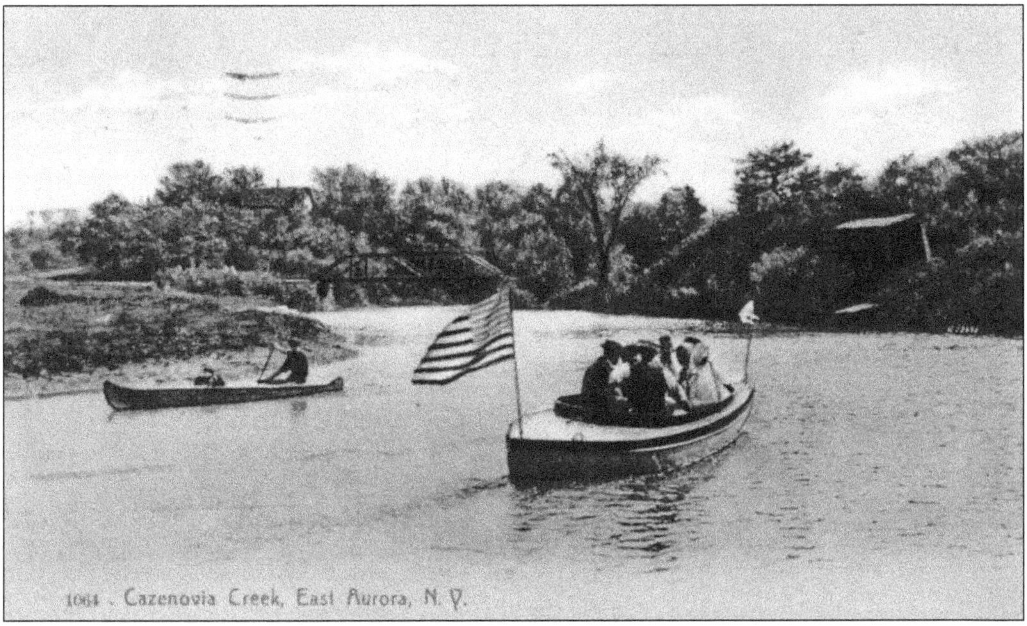


By the turn of the 20th century, East Aurora and the Roycroft became a tourist destination. Steam-powered small boats, rowboats, and canoes could be rented from the Donnor family, who owned the land at the creek side. Donnor's Park was located straight down South Grove Street, only a 10-minute walk from the campus.

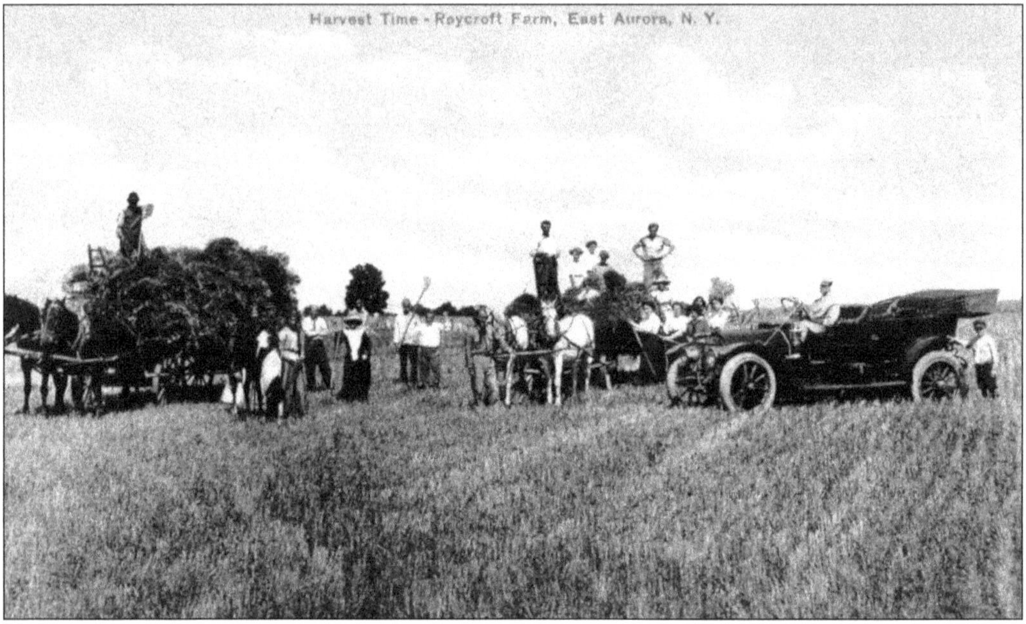


Always looking for a photo opportunity, Elbert poses with his many happy workers on one of his three farms. Note the eight-passenger limousine with chauffeur in the fields that brought Elbert Hubbard just in time for the shot. This image was used as an advertisement for the "Roycroft School of Life," a summer-long school program teaching all the aspects of "head, heart, and hand," leading to a graduation from the "University of Hard Knocks," Elbert's alma mater.

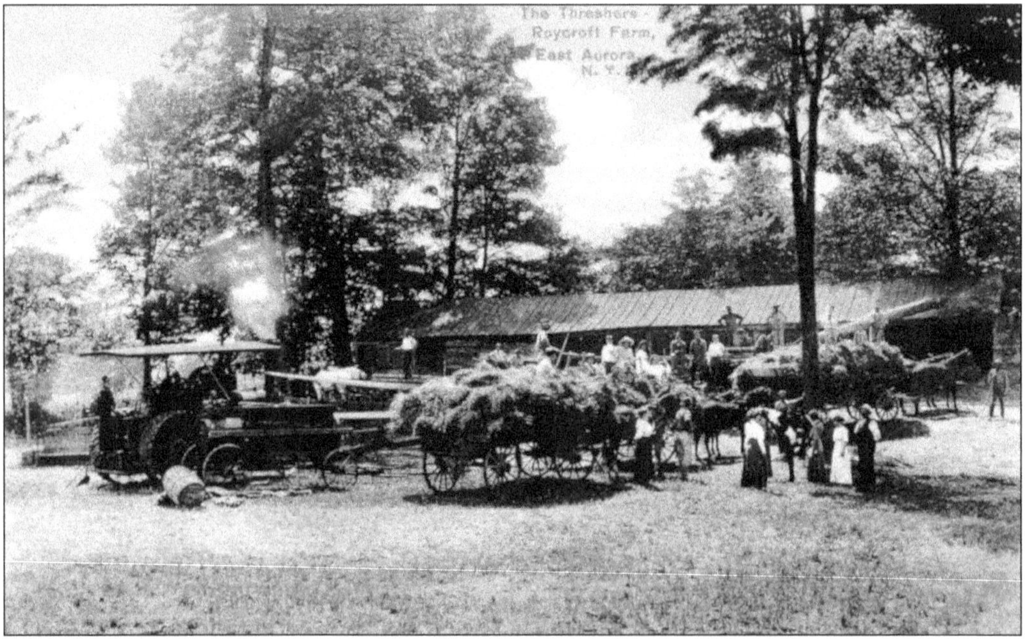


When the summer ended and the fields needed cutting and thrashing, Elbert would take employees from all of the departments to help bring in the harvest. Some important visitors and guests were also recruited to help with these chores.

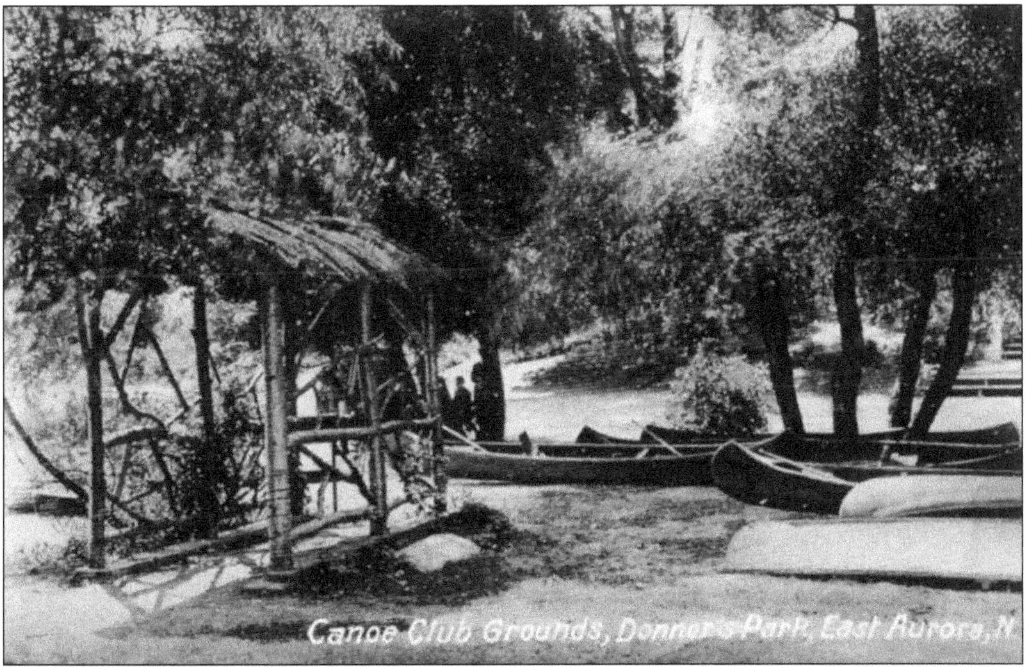


The Canoe Club was a popular activity for villagers and Roycroft guests. Run by the Donnor family for more than 30 years, Donnor's Park was at the end of South Grove Street. Abandoned in the 1950s, today there is no trace of its existence except for photographs.

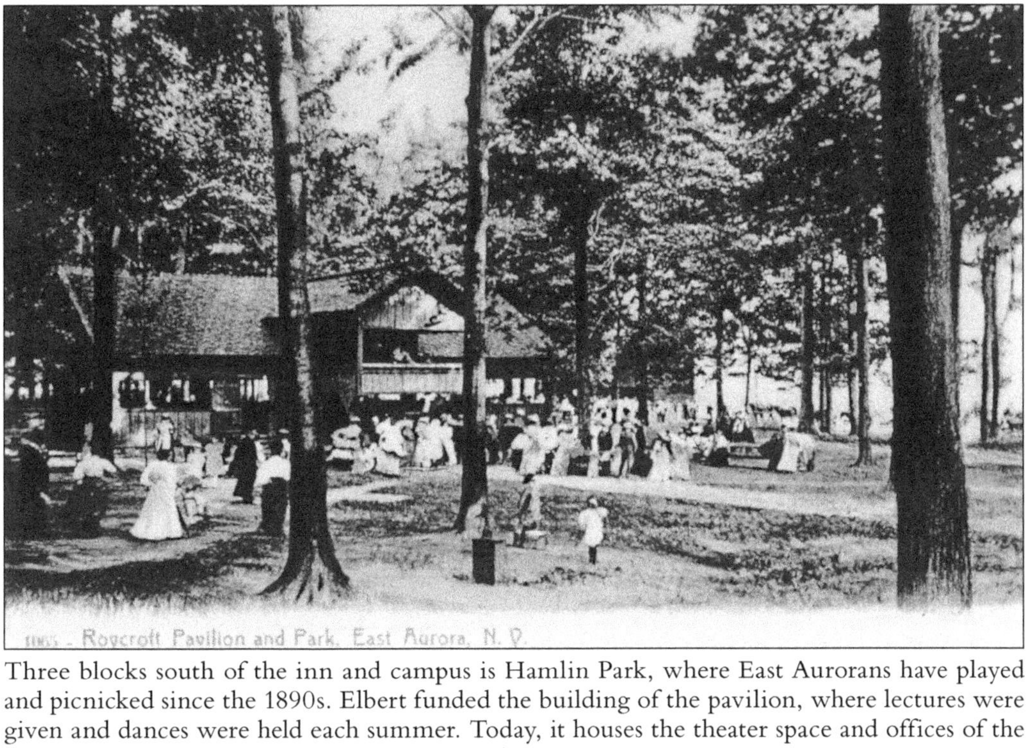


Three blocks south of the inn and campus is Hamlin Park, where East Aurorans have played and picnicked since the 1890s. Elbert funded the building of the pavilion, where lectures were given and dances were held each summer. Today, it houses the theater space and offices of the Aurora Players, a local troupe of actors since the 1950s.

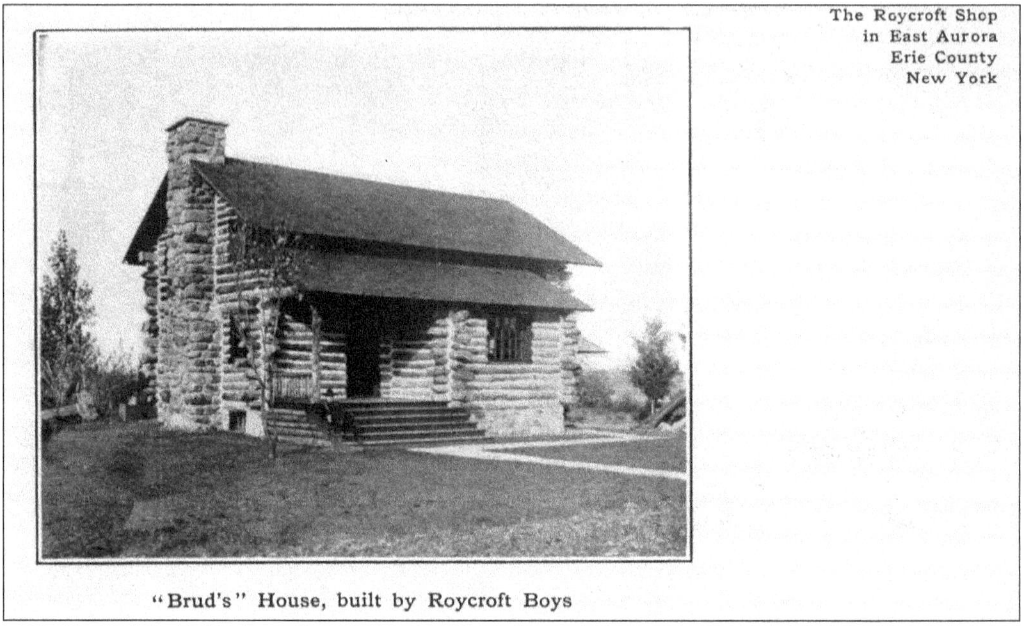


A log cabin is one of America's quintessential forms of architecture. Elbert "Bert" Hubbard II built his log cabin one block north of the campus. He was also nicknamed "Brud" by the Roycrofters, who had many names for each person among the community. Bert and his wife, Alta Fattey Hubbard, raised their family in this home until he built Hubbard Hill above the village in 1929; the family moved in the fall of 1929 just after the crash. Hubbard Hill, where Bert lived until his death in 1970, was a Tudor Revival–style manse with over 20 rooms.

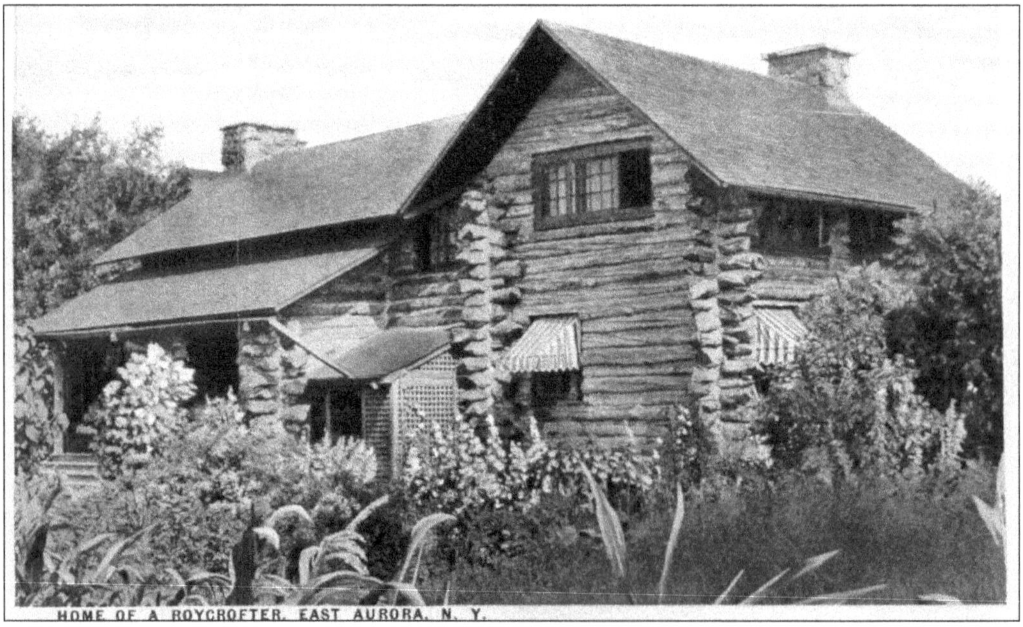


This photograph, taken around 1920, shows the additions to Bert's log home, now more than a cabin. With three children and a successful publishing empire, he was to begin building a large estate and home in 1928 on Maple Road at the edge of the village. This house still exists today with a tennis court and large trees hiding it from the casual observer.

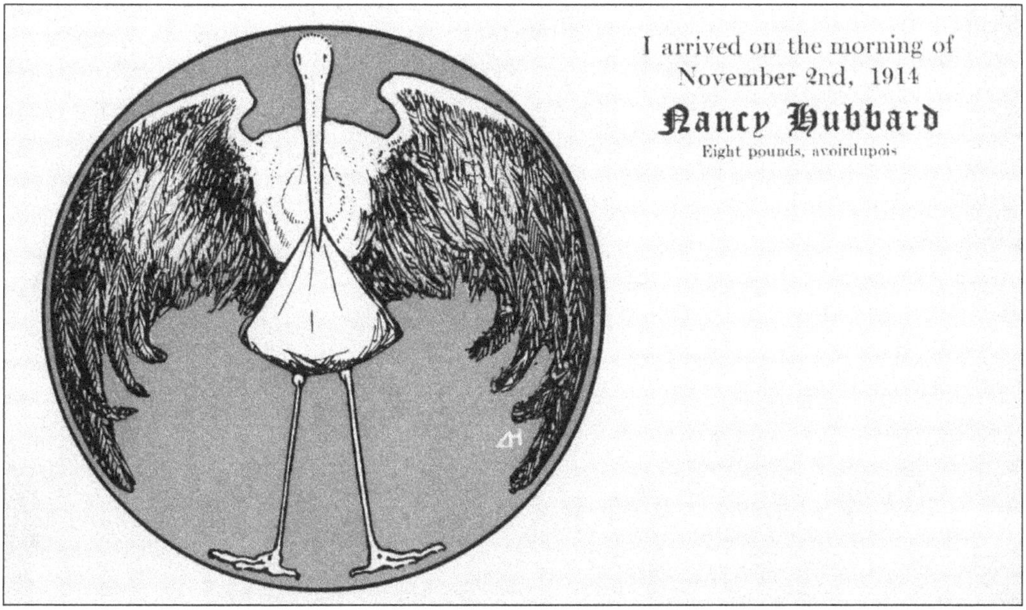


This rare card designed by Dard Hunter and issued by Bert and Alta Hubbard, announced their second daughter Nancy's arrival. She became one of the founders of the Roycroft Renaissance in the 1970s. Nancy taught school for many years before joining her father in his House of Hubbard book business, buying and selling the collectible Roycroft Press books. That business still exists today.

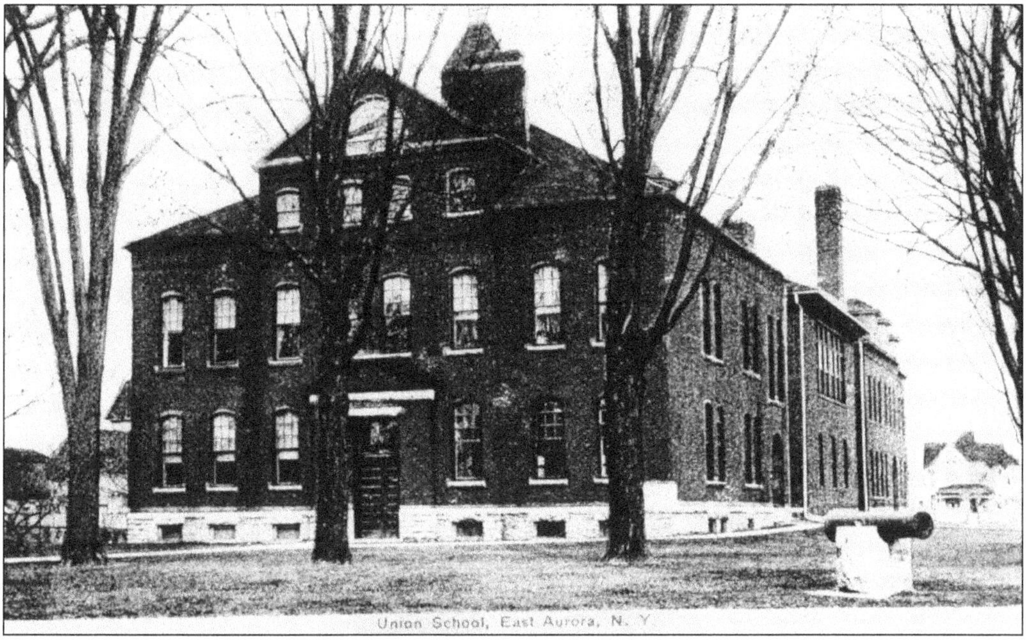


The school attended by the children of Elbert Hubbard and all his employees has existed since the 1880s. It has grown exponentially with the Roycroft's expansion. Today, this building, though much has changed, is the middle school of the East Aurora School District. Alice Moore was a teacher in this building when she boarded with the Hubbards in 1888, later to become the second Mrs. Hubbard.

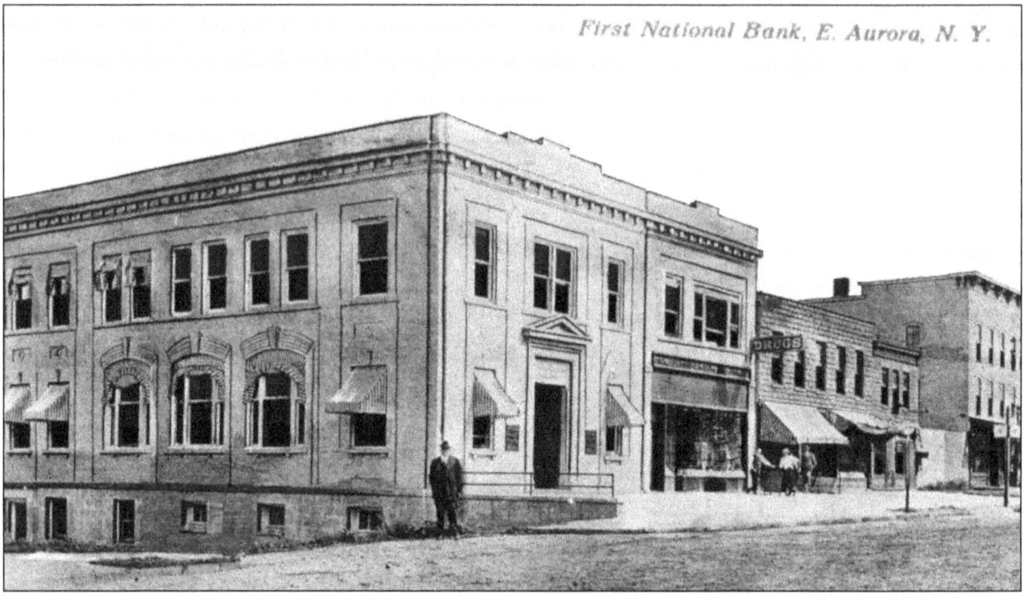


There were three banks in East Aurora in 1910, including Hubbard's Private Bank. The First National, pictured here, is still a bank today, and this block is virtually unchanged. A record price of $24,000 was paid at an auction for a national currency note issued in 1902 by this bank in the $20 denomination.

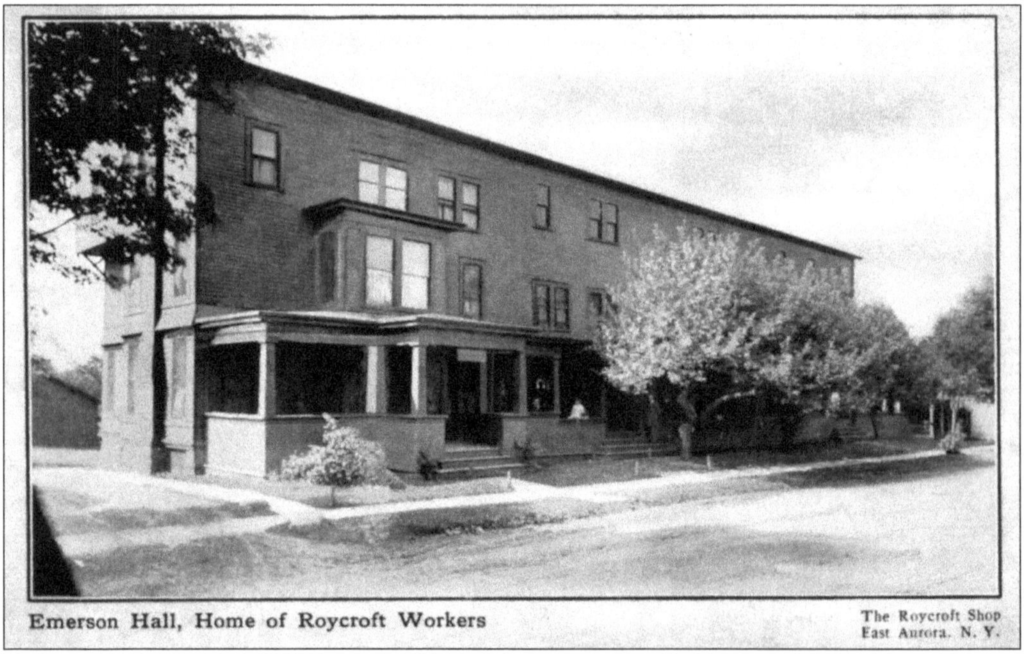


Housing was at a premium for the many workers coming to Roycroft. Elbert took the opportunity to build a second residential hotel two blocks away on Prospect Street. Named after one of his literary heroes, Emerson Hall housed workers and overflow for the inn. During the summers, it housed the School of Life and later became a women's dormitory. After the bankruptcy it became a home for unwed mothers run by the County of Erie. Today, it houses apartments. The Roycroft Stables were located behind this building.

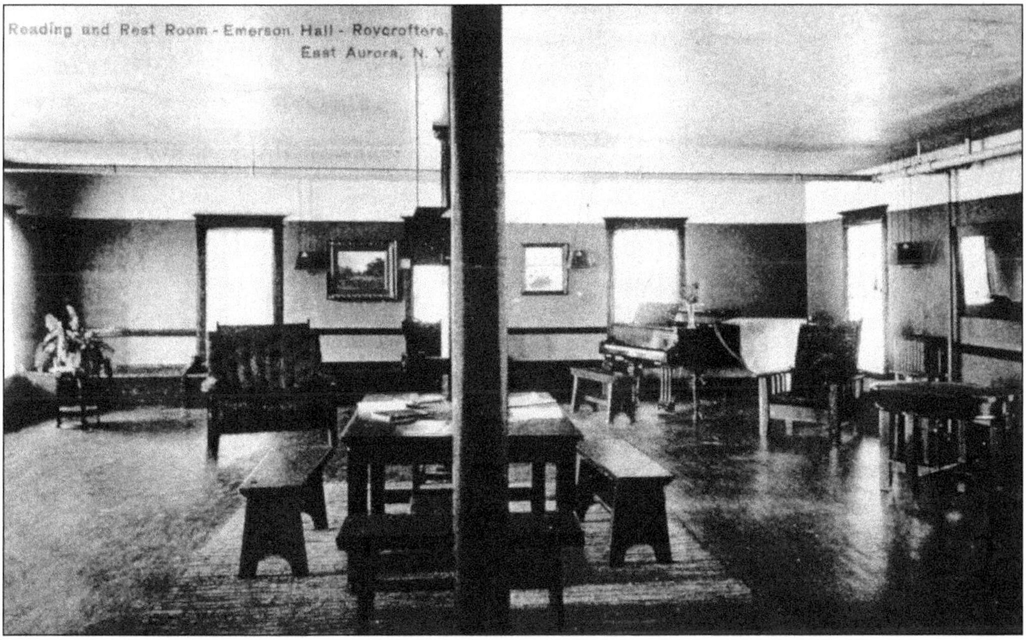


Inside Emerson Hall were some of the prime examples of Roycroft's furniture designs. Ali Baba benches, single and double morris chairs, fine paintings by Alexis Fournier, and hanging lanterns designed by Dard Hunter grace this common room on the first floor.

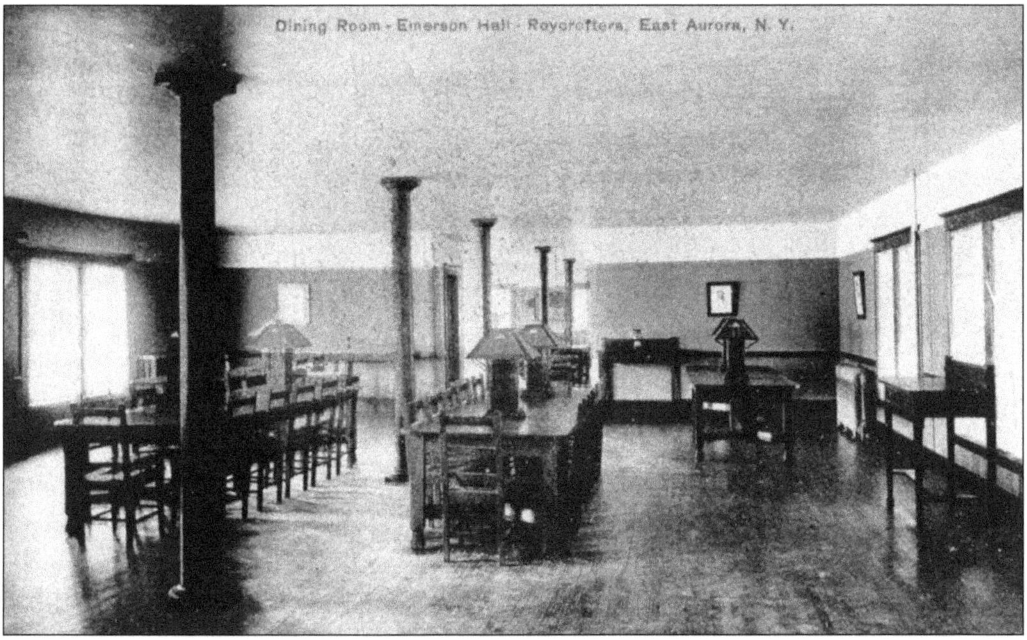


Also on the first floor was the hall's dining room, complete with the largest of the tables produced in the shops. Over 10 feet long, these eight tables, now known as Emerson Hall tables, held lamps of stained glass and oak, originally lit with natural gas before electricity came to the village.

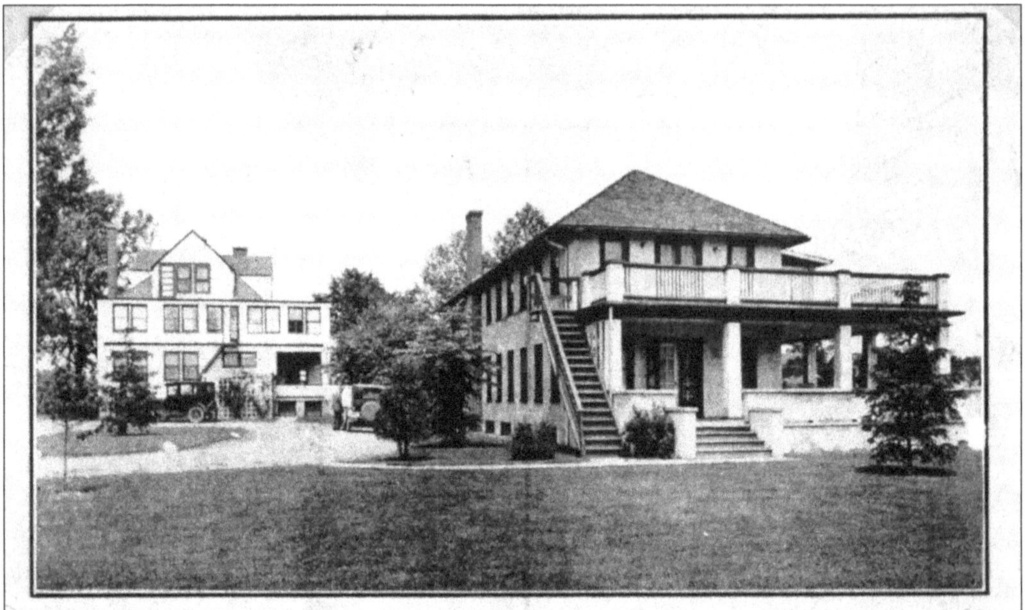

Rear View Children's Building EAST AURORA SUN AND DIET SANATORIUM, EAST AURORA, N. Y.

Only five blocks west of the campus was the Sun and Diet Sanatorium, famous for its "Green Juice Diet." It opened in the late 1910s and was popular into the 1930s. Elbert was a proponent of the natural foods movement. The Roycroft Press published the Sun-Diet's cookbooks and other ephemera. The sanatorium was founded by Dr. William Hays (1886–1940), who invented "food combining" to treat Bright's Disease and was a popular lecturer in the United States and Canada.

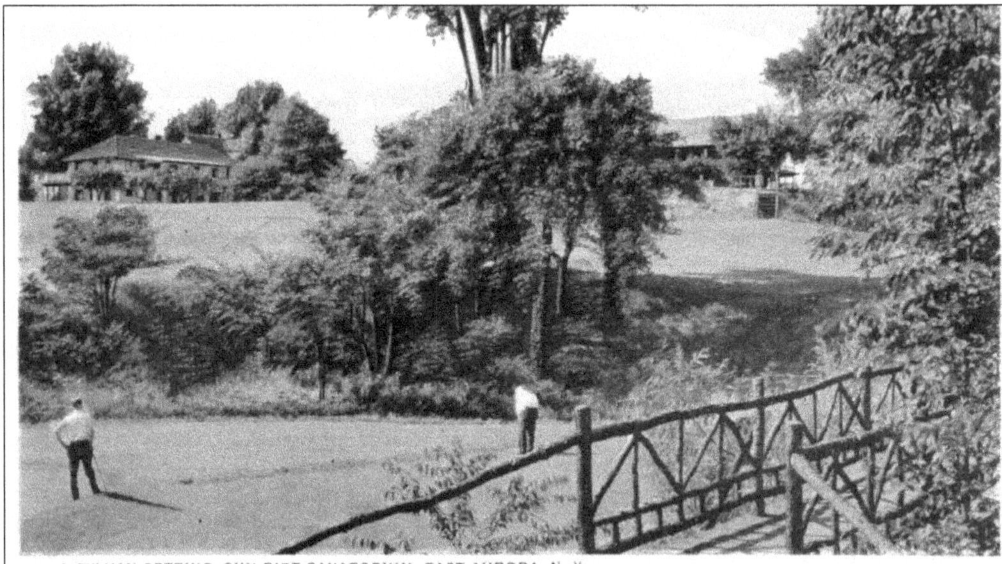

A SYLVAN SETTING. SUN-DIET SANATORIUM, EAST AURORA, N. Y.

Sun-Diet, as the sanatorium was also known, featured a small golf course, croquet lawns, and tennis courts along with water sports on the creek running through its grounds. Most of these buildings on Oakwood Avenue are still extant and have become apartments. East Aurora had more than a half-dozen "health homes" by 1920. Many of the health homes were for the stressed businessman to dry out away from the city life of Buffalo.

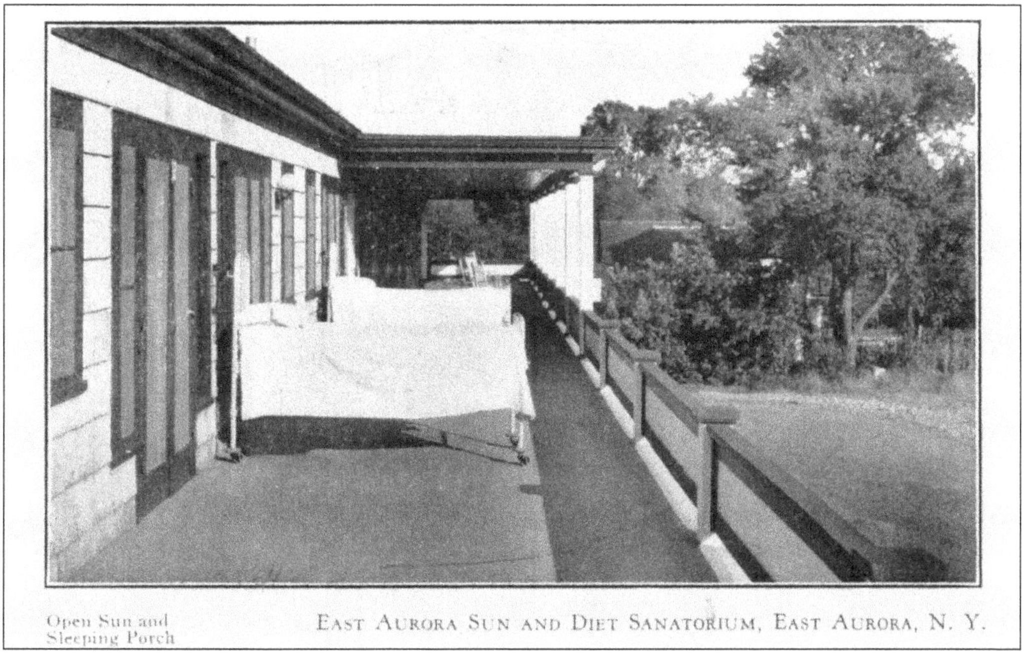


One of the popular treatments in the early 20th century was sleeping outdoors in all seasons, and the fresh air in East Aurora has always been plentiful. Sleeping porches were popular in bungalows and also a feature of the rooms at the Roycroft Inn. The craze became unfashionable by the 1930s, and rooms at the inn had radiators added.

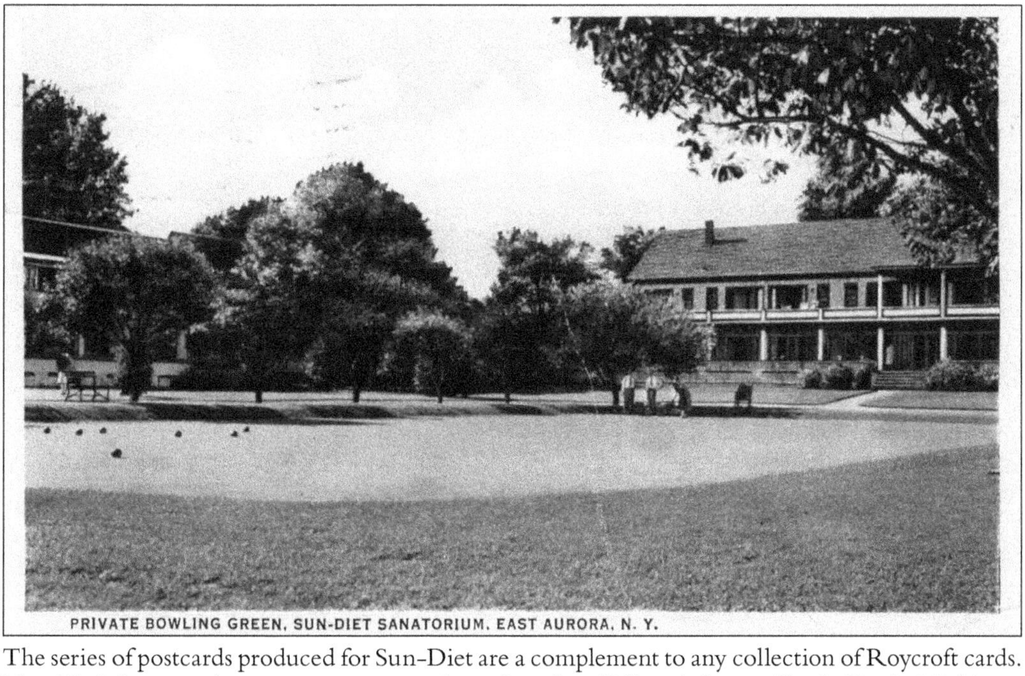


The series of postcards produced for Sun-Diet are a complement to any collection of Roycroft cards. New York State was home to many sanatoriums, based on Kellogg's famous Battle Creek, Michigan, location. About 70 miles southeast of the village was the large Bernarr MacFadden (1868–1955) Healthatorium, a five-floor building for his physical culture movement followers.

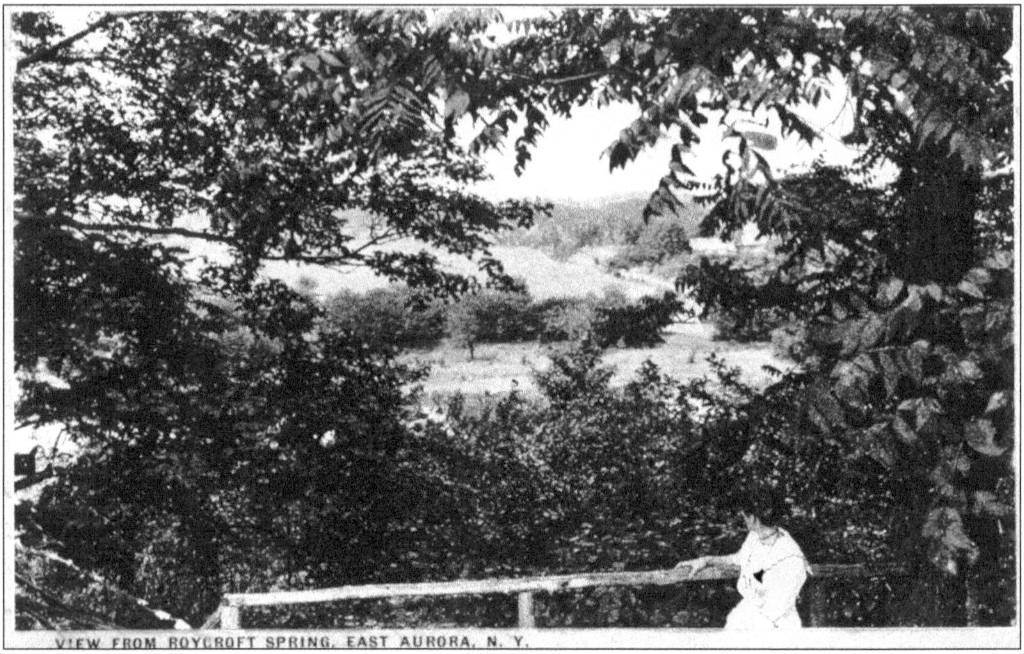


This woman is sitting overlooking Cazenovia Creek next to the Roycroft Spring, so named as it was in Roycroft Park at the south end of Grove Street. Elbert held impromptu talks here during the summers for the visitors and workers.

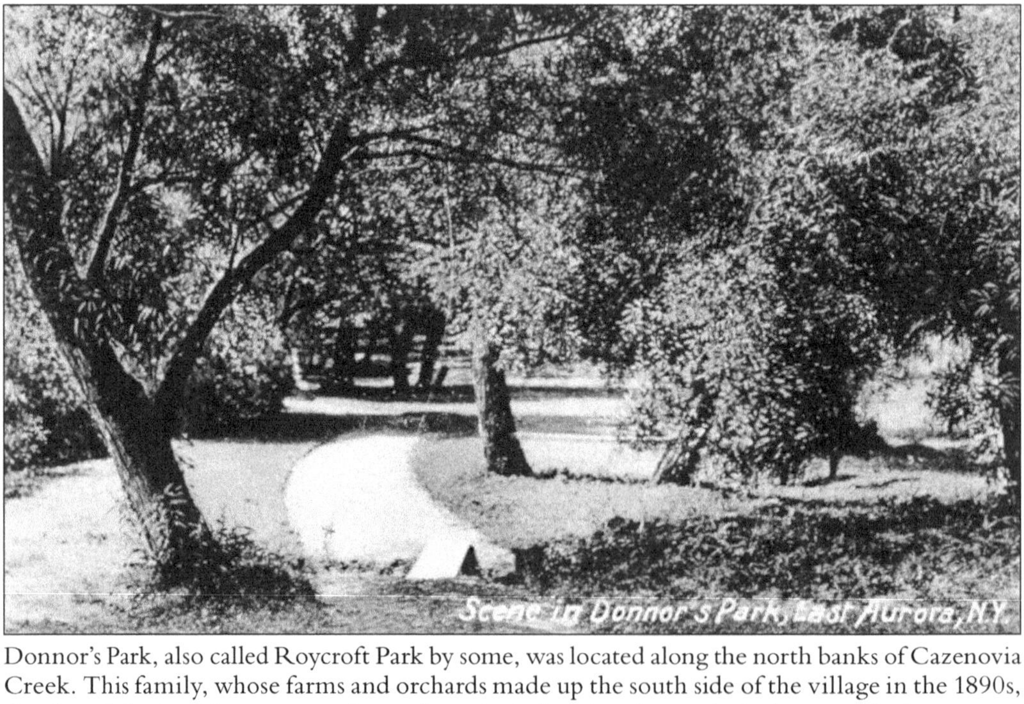


Donnor's Park, also called Roycroft Park by some, was located along the north banks of Cazenovia Creek. This family, whose farms and orchards made up the south side of the village in the 1890s, developed the land into an area for outings, including boating and picnic grounds. It was very popular area into the 1940s.

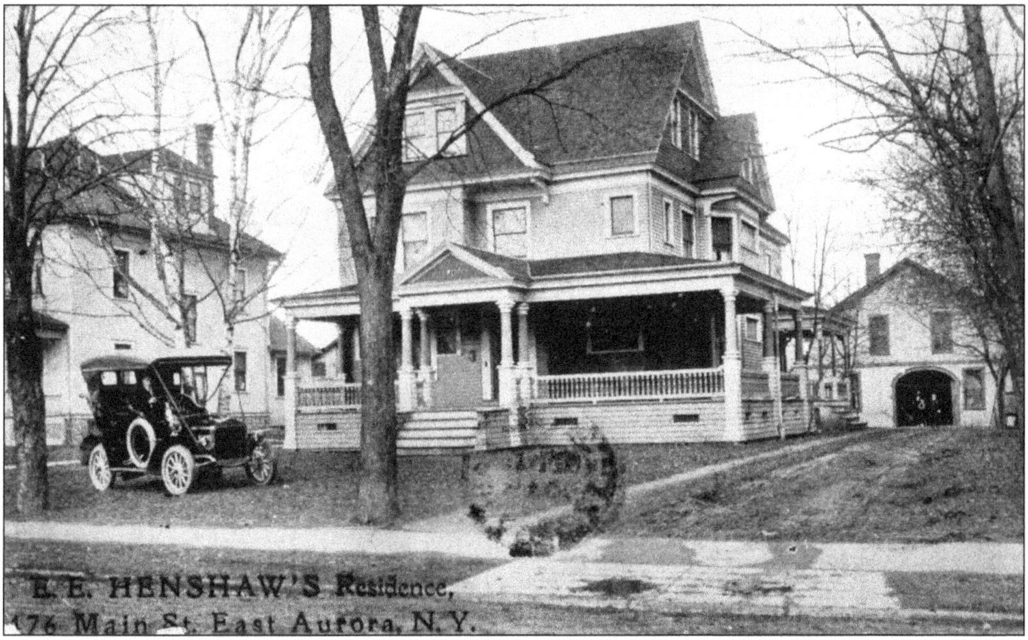

An example of one of the Victorian-era homes surrounding the campus is shown here. Many of these single family homes still stand, though some now serve commercial purposes. Henshaw was the owner of the local hardware store on Main Street, just east of his home. It operated through three generations of the family until the late 1980s.

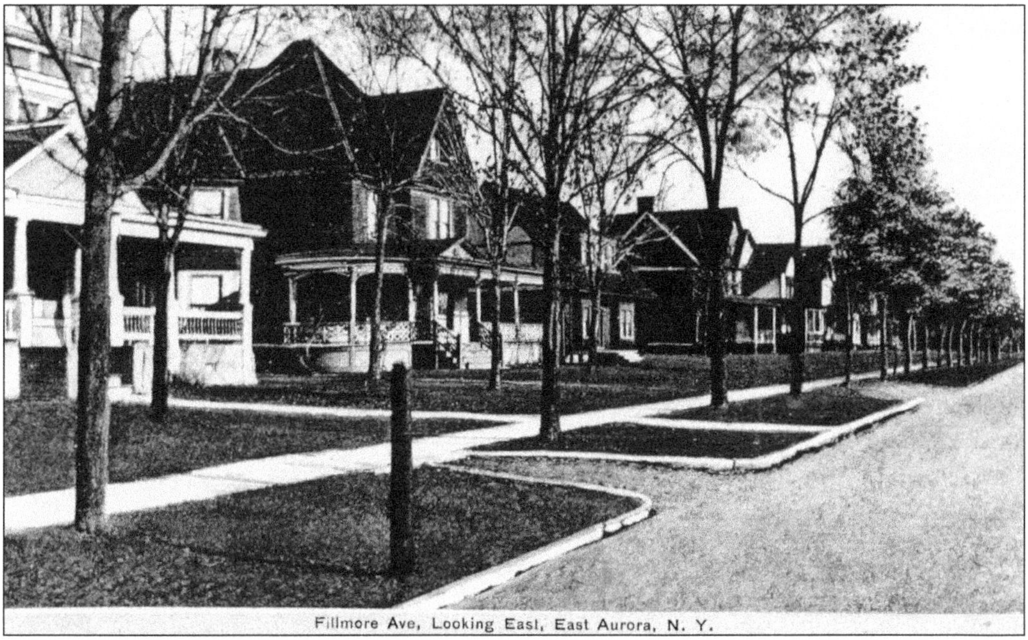

Fillmore Avenue, named after the other of Aurora's most famous residents, runs parallel to Main Street and looks much like this image taken around 1910. Many of these homes were owned or rented by craftsmen and other employees working on the campus two to three blocks away.

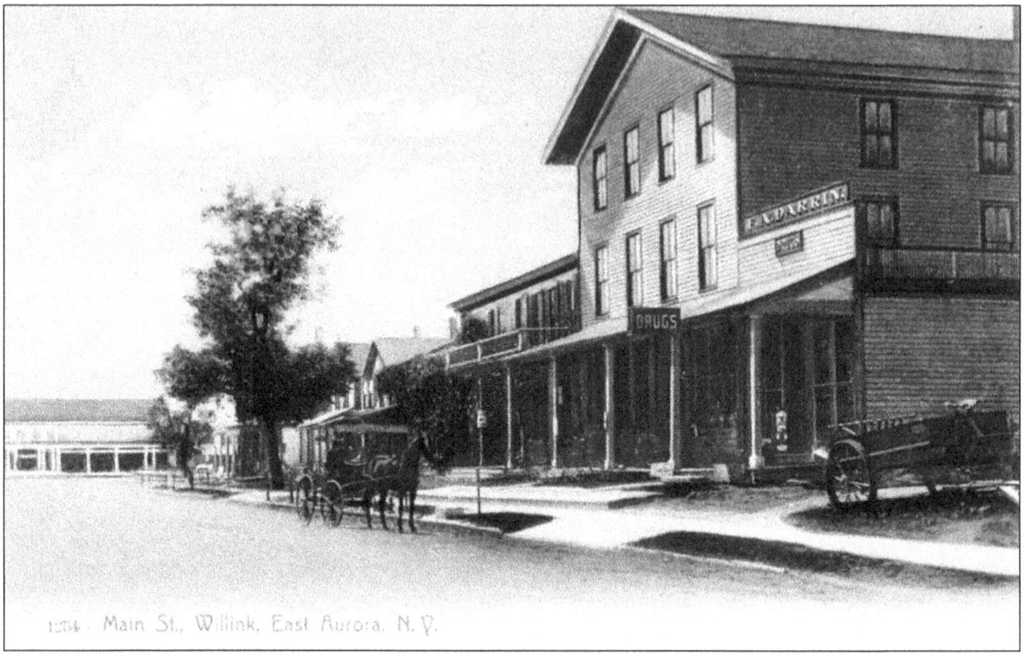


It was said that there were more saloons than churches in East Aurora in Hubbard's day. Today that is not true as six churches are along the thoroughfare and there are more restaurants than bars or saloons. Hubbard was a teetotaler and perhaps had an influence on this change.

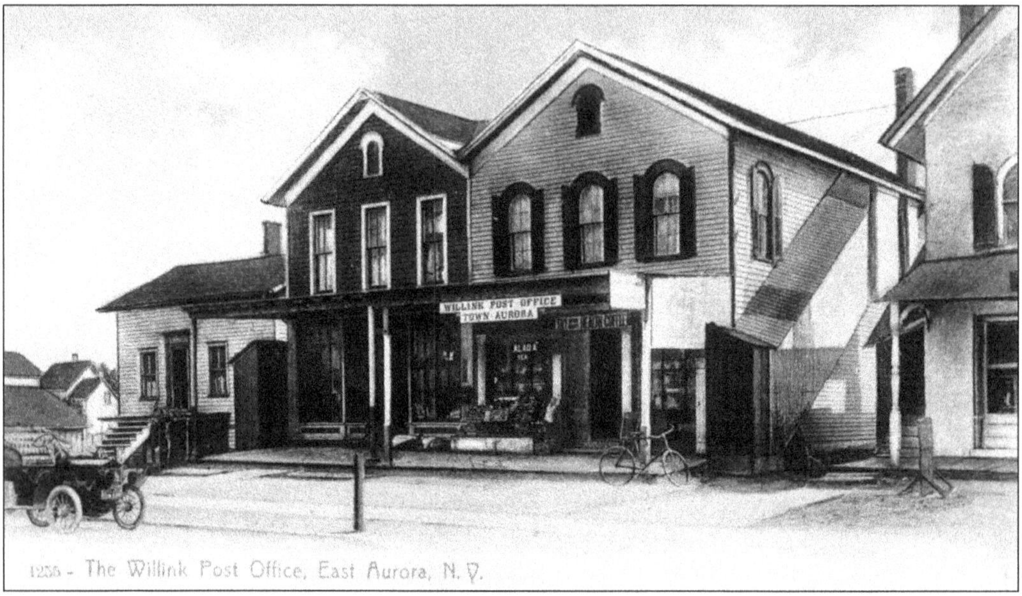


The village of Willink was named after Willem Willink, one of the Dutch investors in Western New York in 1804. Today, it is located at the east side of the village after being annexed during Elbert's day in 1874. Some of these Civil War–era buildings still stand along Hamburg Street and Buffalo Road, at the present traffic circle or roundabout. Willink was home to a one-room schoolhouse that became the artist studio of Canadian Eleanor Douglass (1872–1914), who was loosely affiliated with the Roycrofters. She was the cousin of Carl Ahrens (1862–1936), onetime art director and potter at the campus. Today, the building houses an art gallery.

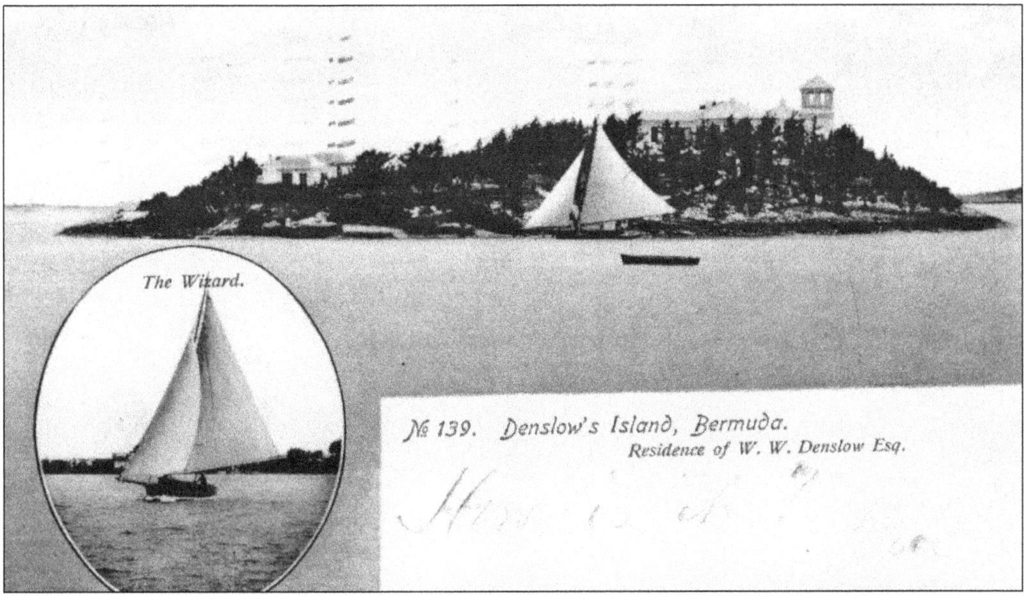


Although this card is not of the Roycroft proper, it has many connections to East Aurora. Sent to artist Alex Fournier from the Bermuda home of W.W. Denslow (1886–1915), it shows his yacht *The Wizard*. Denslow, after leaving the Roycroft as a staff artist in 1900, became world famous as the illustrator of L. Frank Baum's *The Wizard of Oz*. With the money he made from the various books, plays, and movies based on the series, he bought this island, set himself up as emperor, and demanded royal treatment wherever he sailed, especially New York.

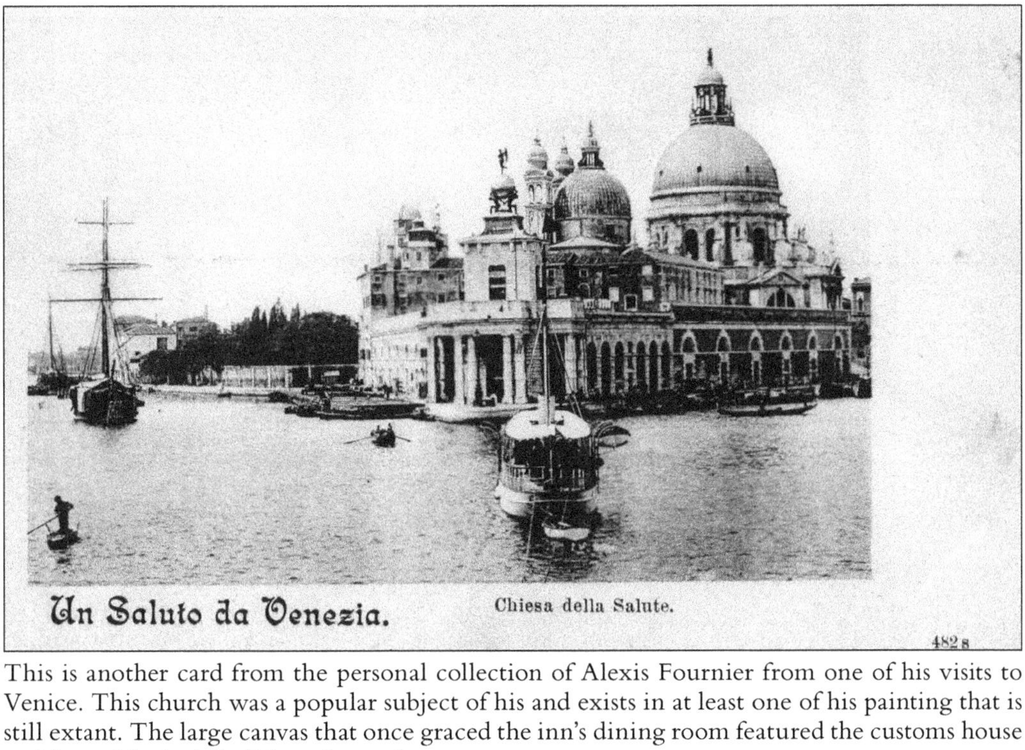


This is another card from the personal collection of Alexis Fournier from one of his visits to Venice. This church was a popular subject of his and exists in at least one of his painting that is still extant. The large canvas that once graced the inn's dining room featured the customs house and Santa Maria della Salute shown here.

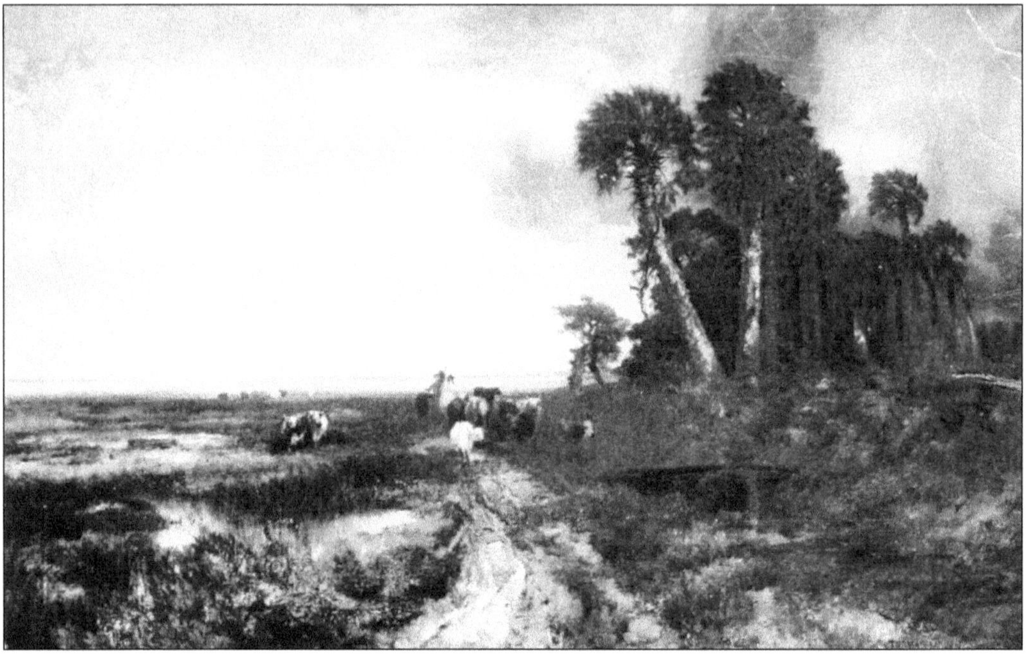

Fournier was known as the last of the American Barbizons, and this card is of a painting he paid tribute to in his famous series The Homes and Haunts of the Barbizons. He collected hundreds of postcards during his many trips to Europe. The author was very fortunate to find this collection still complete in the 1980s.

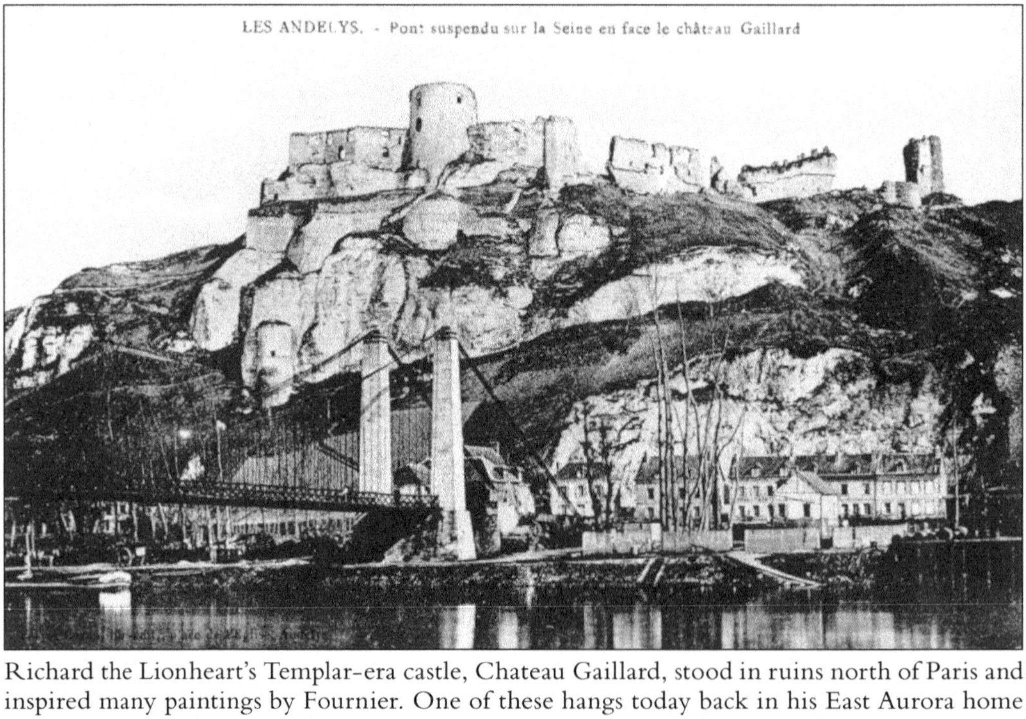


Richard the Lionheart's Templar-era castle, Chateau Gaillard, stood in ruins north of Paris and inspired many paintings by Fournier. One of these hangs today back in his East Aurora home and at least two other examples are known in the United States. Fournier was known to pay his bills to his tailor with artwork, so there may be many more in France as well.

*Six*

# The 1001 Epigrams
## Elbert Hubbard's Philosophy

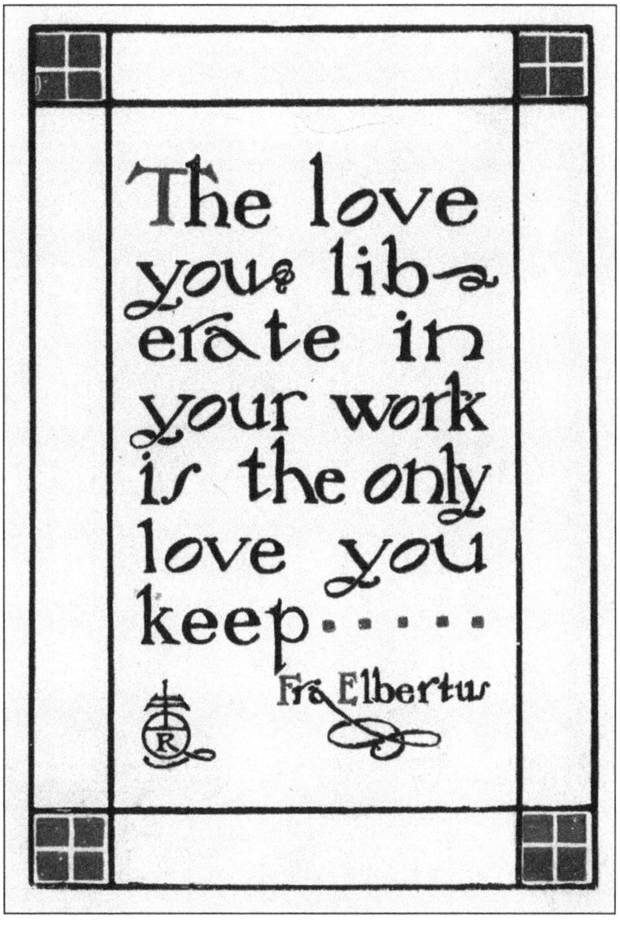


Carved into one of the large oak doors of the Roycroft Inn, this may be Hubbard's most famous motto. The typeface used on this card was designed by Dard Hunter in 1905, the same year the inn opened to guests. Many versions of this card exist and are a must for the postcard collector. (Courtesy of the library of Jack Walsdorf.)

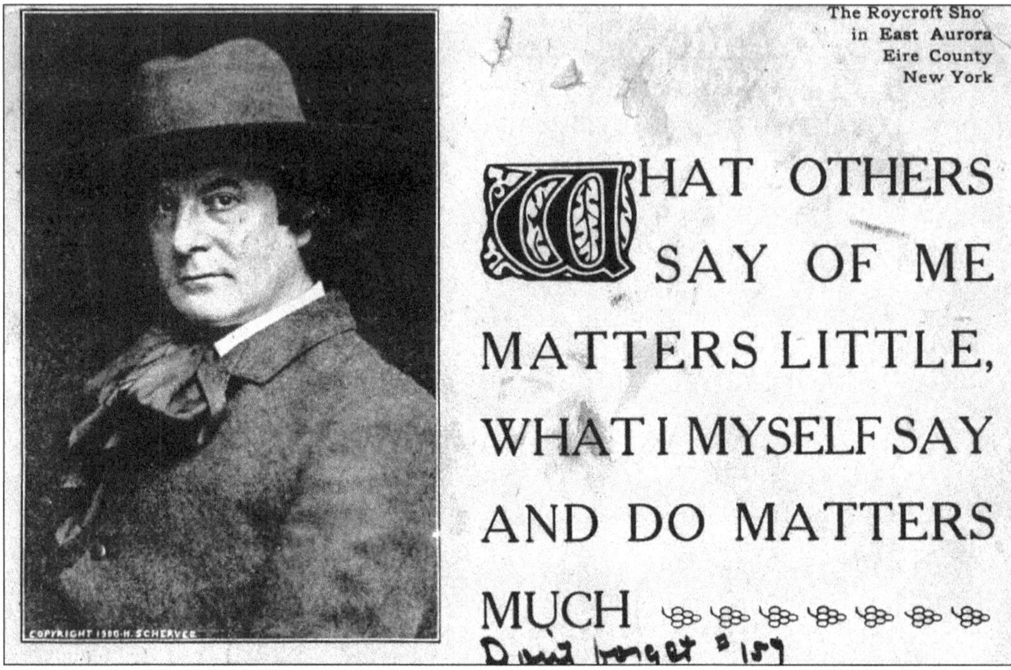


After the scandal broke in 1901 of Hubbard's affair with Alice Moore, he adopted an attitude of being above all the hoopla. But ever the one to capitalize on publicity, he created a number of motto cards reflecting his attitude. This card is one of the earliest printed around 1902 to 1903.

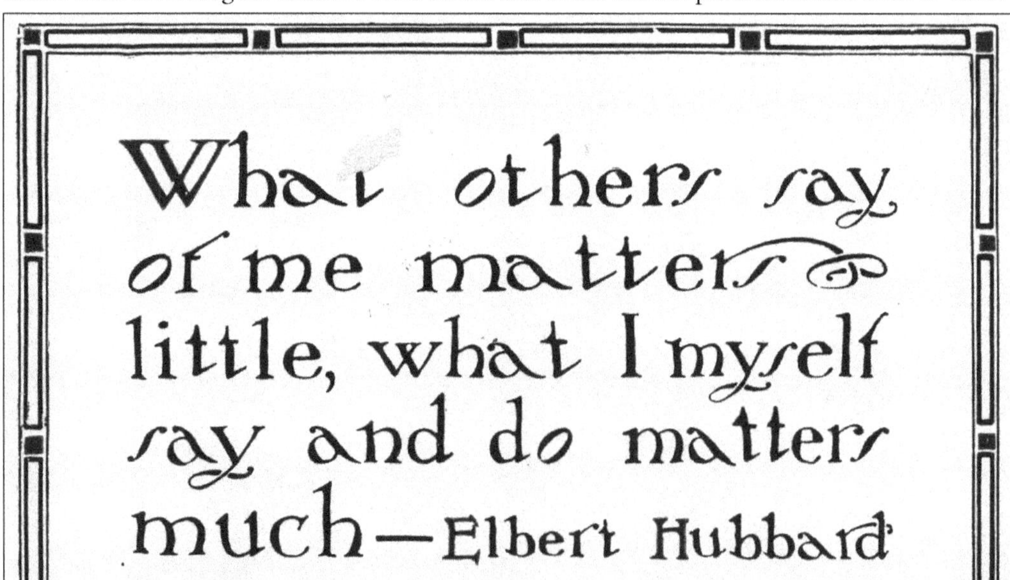


Utilizing the same sentiment but from 1905 after his divorce from Bertha and subsequent marriage to Alice Moore, this card shows that he still needed to keep his name before the public. His flamboyant lifestyle, especially with his newly recognized daughter Miriam, age 10, who was born during the first marriage, took some getting used to by many of his flock.

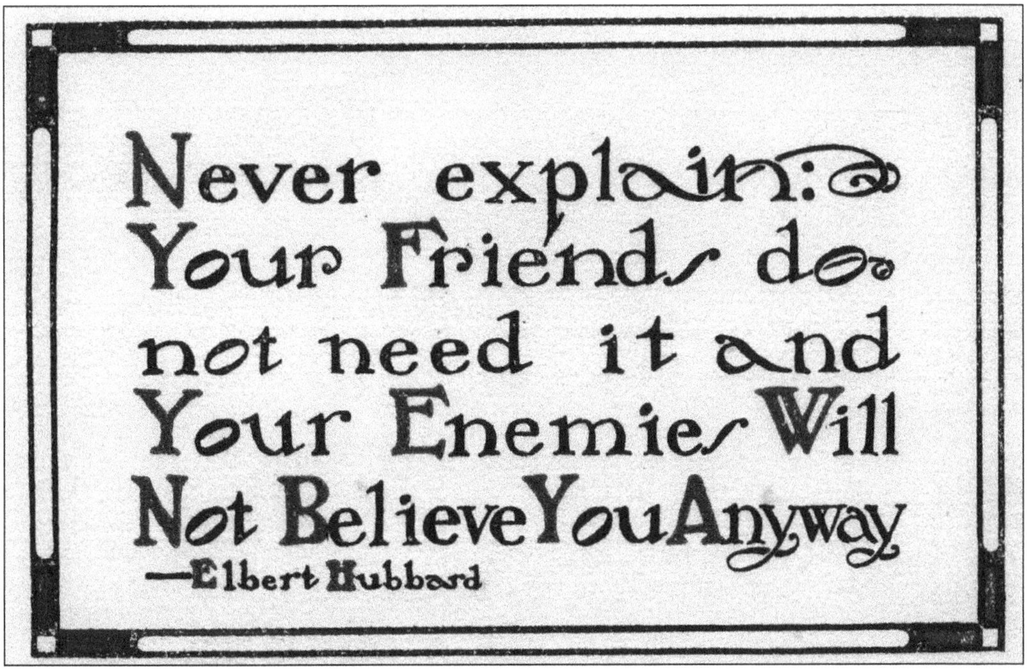


Continuing in the same vein, Hubbard gave inspiration to many to go out and do what they thought right and proper without explanation. He wanted the masses to get on with the work at hand and make the world a better place. A humanist philosophy many would say.

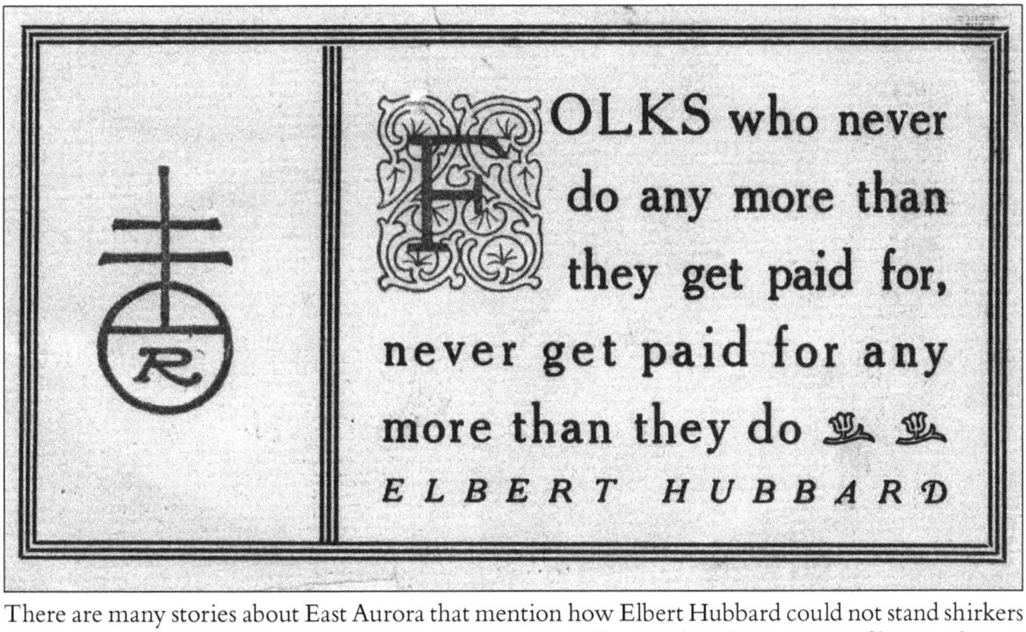


There are many stories about East Aurora that mention how Elbert Hubbard could not stand shirkers or people who were too sure of themselves. He paid well enough to keep many of his employees 20 years or more, as long as they did their work and got along with the community.

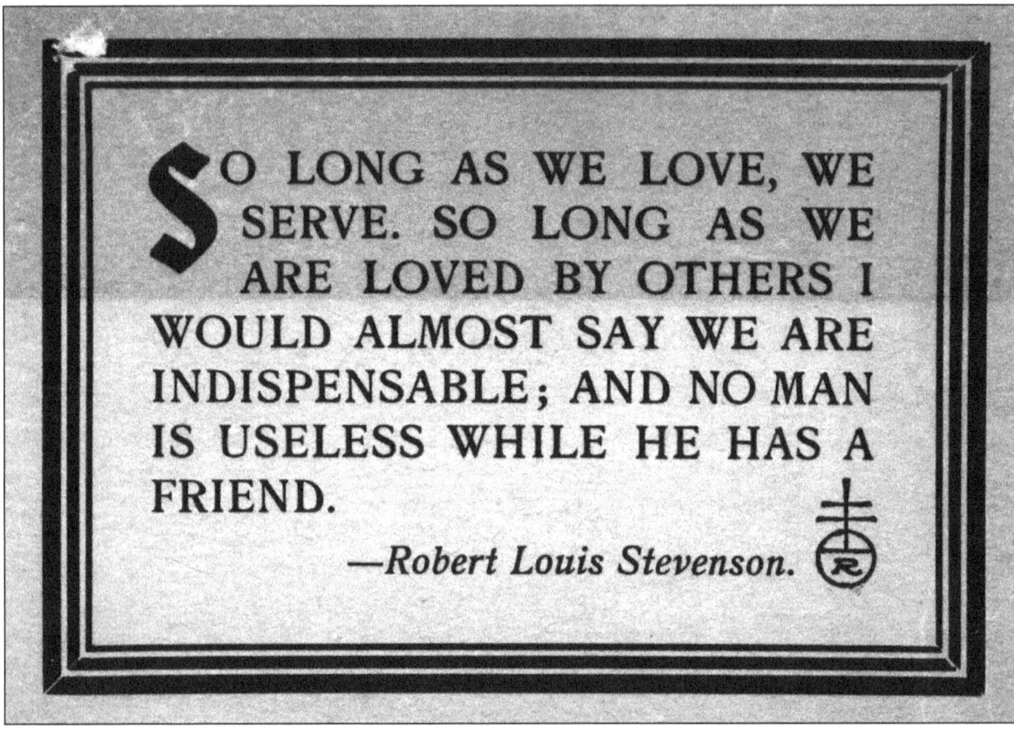

SO LONG AS WE LOVE, WE SERVE. SO LONG AS WE ARE LOVED BY OTHERS I WOULD ALMOST SAY WE ARE INDISPENSABLE; AND NO MAN IS USELESS WHILE HE HAS A FRIEND.

—*Robert Louis Stevenson.*

Hubbard published many mottos that were quotes from his favorite authors, such as R.L. Stevenson, and he had also written short biographical essays of them in his *Little Journeys to the Homes of the Great,* which ran monthly from 1894 through 1909. Published as a 14-volume set memorial edition in 1916, it is now available to all online on Project Gutenberg.

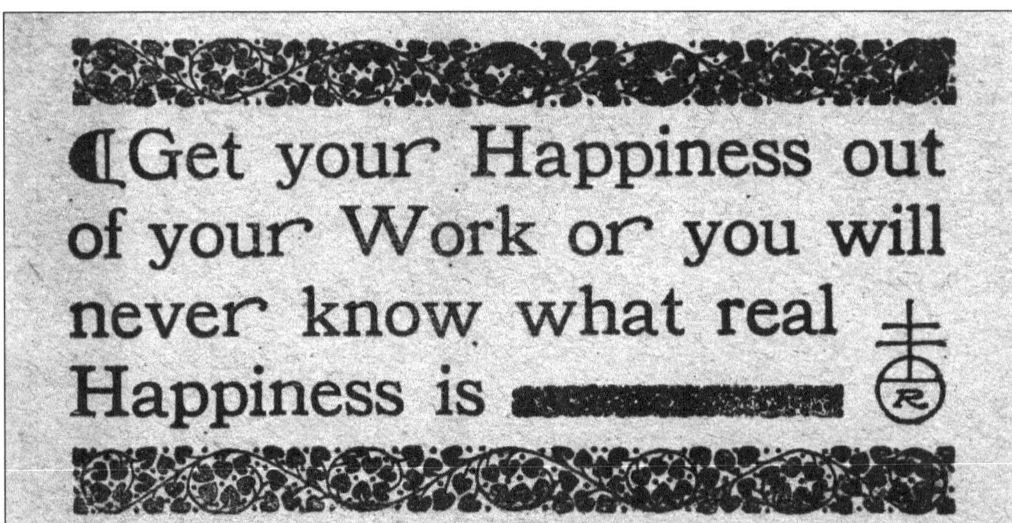

¶Get your Happiness out of your Work or you will never know what real Happiness is

The Arts and Crafts Movement in America as well as Britain believed that a man or women should find "joy in his work," and Ruskin and Morris were both quoted often by Hubbard. Here, he Americanizes the theme and adds the Roycroft logo as a seal of approval.

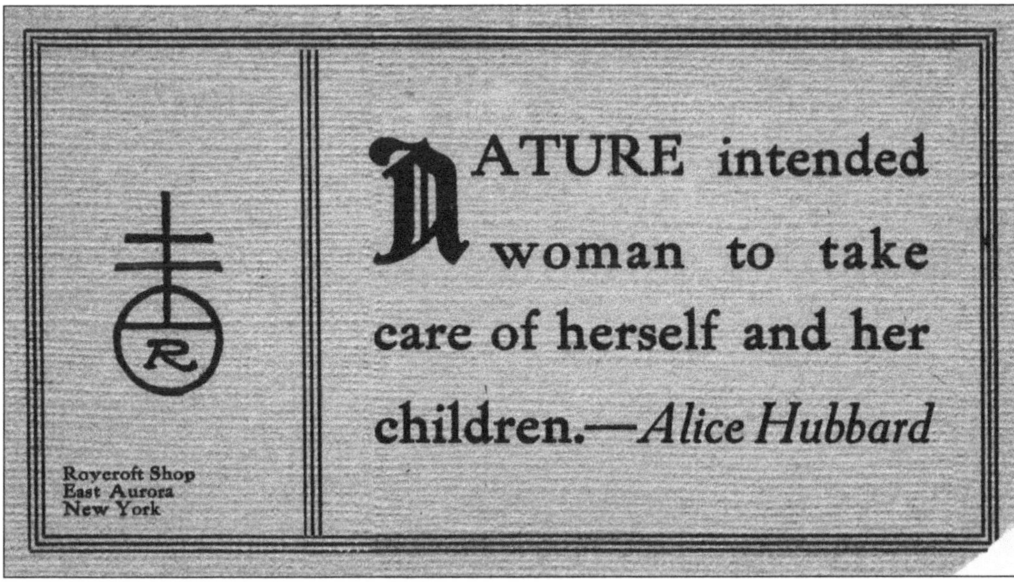


Hubbard is credited for many more epigrams than he actually minted. Here, his wife and muse, Alice, makes a statement about the power of womanhood and motherhood, one of her favorite causes.

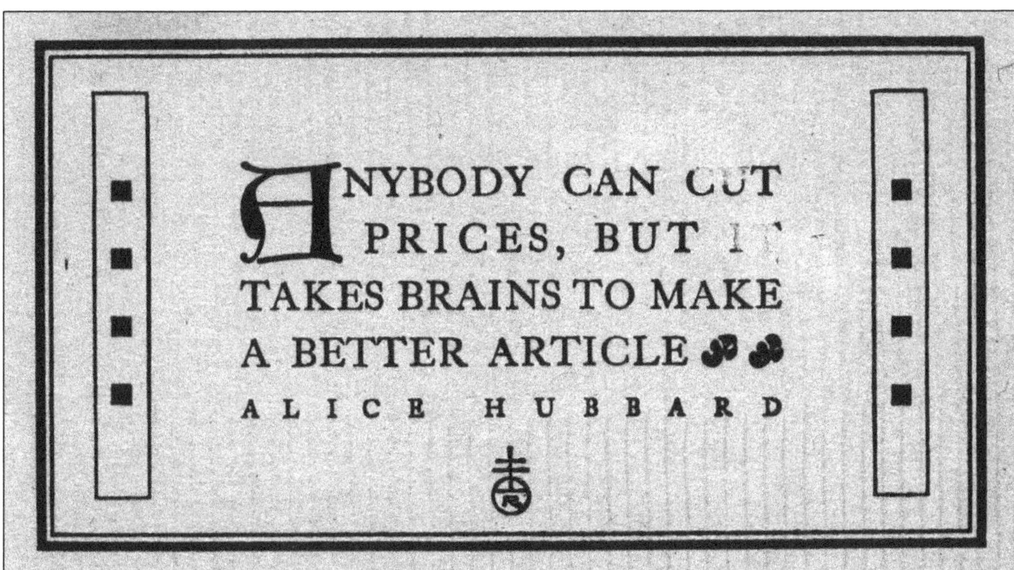


Most do not know that it was Alice who ran the shops after their marriage in 1904, not Elbert. Alice, with two master degrees and years of teaching, was very well qualified to run the business she inspired. However, there was much dissent at first from the male department heads, and some even left the corporation until after her death in 1915 aboard the RMS *Lusitania*.

IT is only by Labor that Thought can be made Healthy, and only by Thought that Labor can be made Happy.

R U S K I N

John Ruskin (1819–1900) was considered the father of the Arts and Crafts Movement in the United Kingdom in the mid-19th century. He believed and taught his students that a balanced person must labor and be educated to be a truly healthy individual. His students, like William Morris and Oscar Wilde, carried this message around the world by the turn of the 20th century.

Horse Sense

IF you work for a man, in heaven's name work for him. If he pays wages that supply you your bread and butter, work for him, speak well of him, think well of him, stand by him, and stand by the institution he represents. I think if I worked for a man, I would work for him. I would not work for him a part of his time, but all of his time. I would give an undivided service or none. If put to a pinch, an ounce of loyalty is worth a pound of cleverness. If you must vilify, condemn and eternally disparage, why, resign your position, and when you are outside, damn to your heart's content. But, I pray you, so long as you are a part of an institution, do not condemn it. Not that you will injure the institution—not that—but when you disparage the concern of which you are a part, you disparage yourself

—ELBERT HUBBARD

Hubbard was considered by many in his day a communist or socialist because of his community of Roycrofters in East Aurora. However, he became a friend of the capitalists with his many work-oriented lectures, published works, and mottos; the most famous, of course, was his *A Message to Garcia,* first published in *The Philistine* in March 1899. This epigram reduces that sentiment into one concise mailable postcard, even able to slip into a pay envelope.

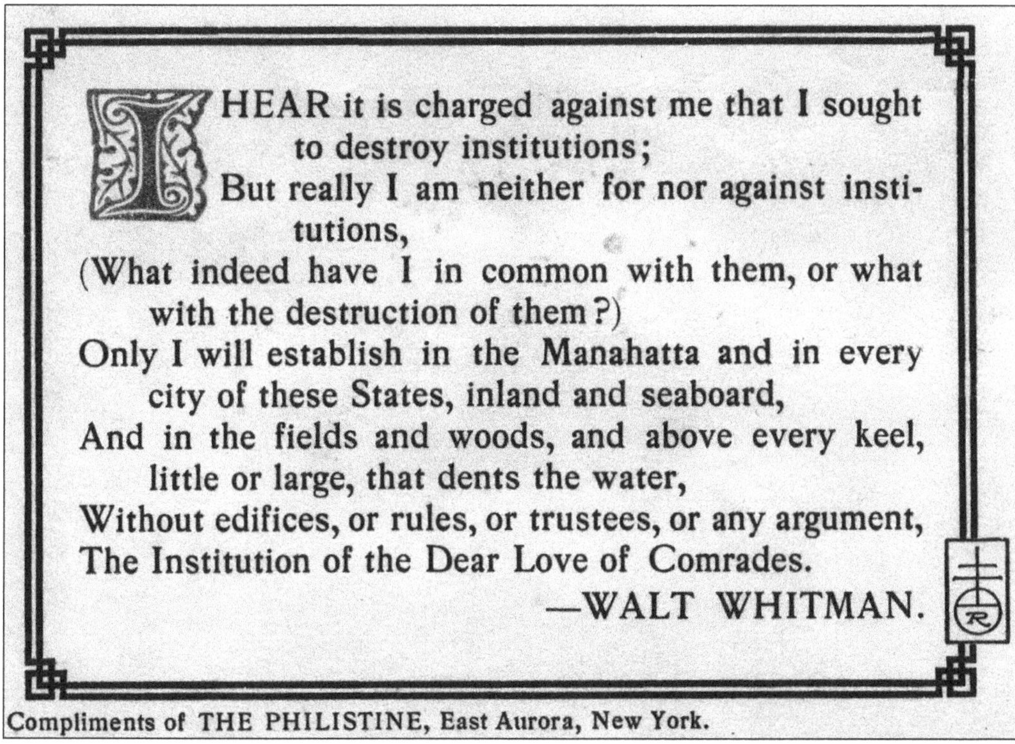
I HEAR it is charged against me that I sought
to destroy institutions;
But really I am neither for nor against institutions,
(What indeed have I in common with them, or what
with the destruction of them?)
Only I will establish in the Manahatta and in every
city of these States, inland and seaboard,
And in the fields and woods, and above every keel,
little or large, that dents the water,
Without edifices, or rules, or trustees, or any argument,
The Institution of the Dear Love of Comrades.
—WALT WHITMAN.

Compliments of THE PHILISTINE, East Aurora, New York.

Walt Whitman's (1819–1892) writings were published many times at the Roycroft Press. Elbert was a follower of Whitman's American transcendentalist philosophy that man could work with nature and create beauty on the earth, which Whitman wrote about in his "Leaves of Grass" and "Song of Myself," published by Hubbard in 1904. This card was a free motto sent out to buyers of his books and periodicals, as it also advertised *The Philistine*, where Whitman's shorter poems were published.

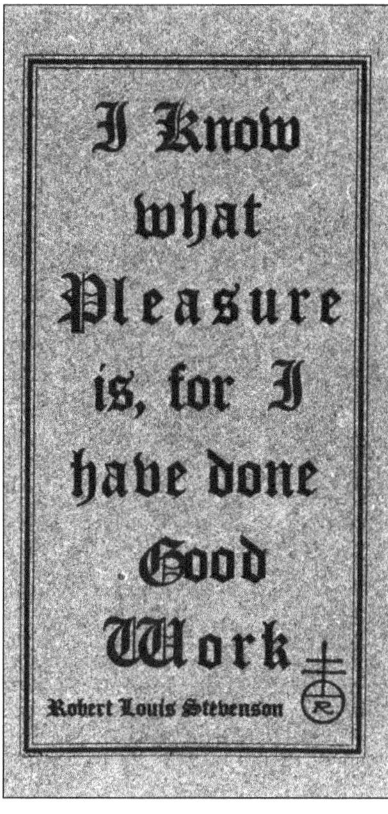
I Know what Pleasure is, for I have done Good Work
Robert Louis Stevenson

Much admired by Hubbard, Stevenson was a contemporary of his, but one he never got to meet as he died in Samoa the year that he was beginning his literary journey. He read aloud Stevenson's stories to his boys and reprinted some of the shorter ones at Roycroft Press in fine handmade paper and limited editions, including "Virginbus Puerisque," "Will O' the Mill," and "The Essay on Walt Whitman," all done in many editions and fine leather bindings.

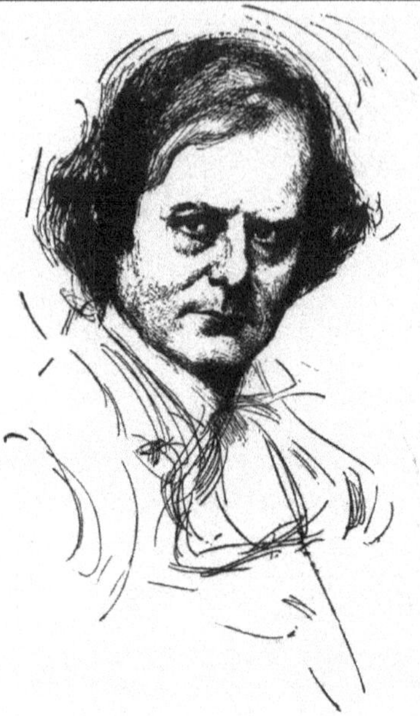

FROM THE ROYCROFT SHOP, EAST AURORA, ERIE COUNTY, NEW YORK

DEAR ROYCROFTER:—I send you our Catalog of Choice Things. If you will select your Christmas Wants soon, I will take a Personal Interest in filling your order. ¶ Do you realize what that means? Try it and see. With all kind wishes ever

Your Sincere

Elbert Hubbard

Hubbard utilized the postcard like no other marketer of his time to sell not just his philosophy, but also the many items made in his craft shops on the campus. The Print Shop kept busy not only printing the cards but also the catalogs offering Christmas gifts each year, starting in 1899 with one of the finer books available. The last catalog was issued in the summer of 1938.

# THE FRA PLATFORM

**Work**
**Health**
**Happiness**
**Brotherhood**
**Good Roads**
**Co-operation**
**Equal Suffrage**
**Human Service**
**Manual Training in Public Schools**
**Universal Peace through Arbitration**
**Tree-planting and Forest Preservation**

**Good cheer and courtesy, even under provocation**
**The keeping of promises, even to those who can not enforce them**
**The Kindergarten System, and its introduction into the higher grades**
**A Patriotism that will include other countries, with no lack of love for our own**
**No war of aggression, except on a popular vote of all the people, including women**

**Disarmament by means of mutual agreement; and a constant campaign of education until this is brought about**
**A Square Deal for cats, dogs, horses, cows, birds, guinea-hens, guinea-pigs, rabbits and all other animals, wild and domesticated**
**The taxation of church property and all educational or philanthropic institutions that are not supported through and by taxation**

**Are You With Us? THE FRA, East Aurora, N. Y.**

Handed out at his many talks and lectures, this card espoused what Elbert Hubbard believed was in the air in America at the turn of the 20th century: a platform of clean living, fresh air, a good job, votes for women, training children in the crafts, and replanting the forests. All of these were also taken up by the 4-H, the Boy and Girl Scouts, the creation of the national parks, and the evolution of manual training in the schools for all. Some things were not agreed on by many, but still on the agenda for *The Fra* were taxation of the churches, pacifism education to prevent further wars, and giving protection to all animals.

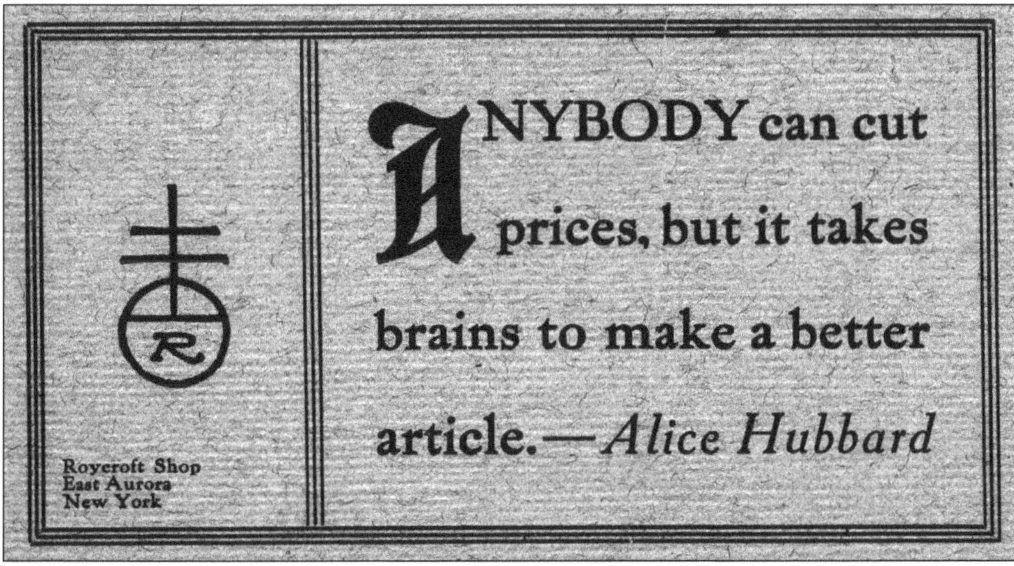


Alice was always looking to educate the public. Now as Elbert's wife, a well-known personage, she had the platform of his presses and periodicals as well as her own books. She was also a major supporter of the suffrage movement as a marcher, lecturer, and financial supporter. She hosted many famous people like Susan B. Anthony from nearby Rochester at events on the campus. She was not to live to vote herself, but her daughter Miriam continued her protests and voted for the first time in 1919.

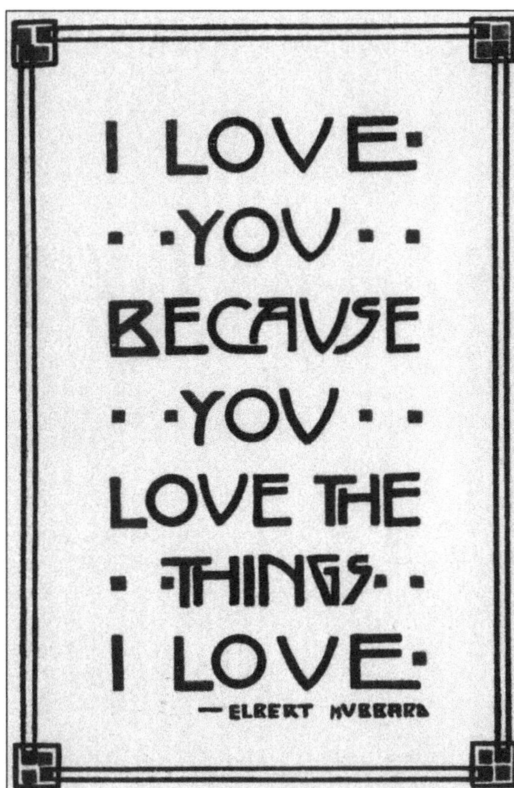


Hubbard had this motto printed in many typefaces and borders, a statement shared by many and written to his muse and second wife, Alice. This Dard Hunter design was popular well into the 1930s.

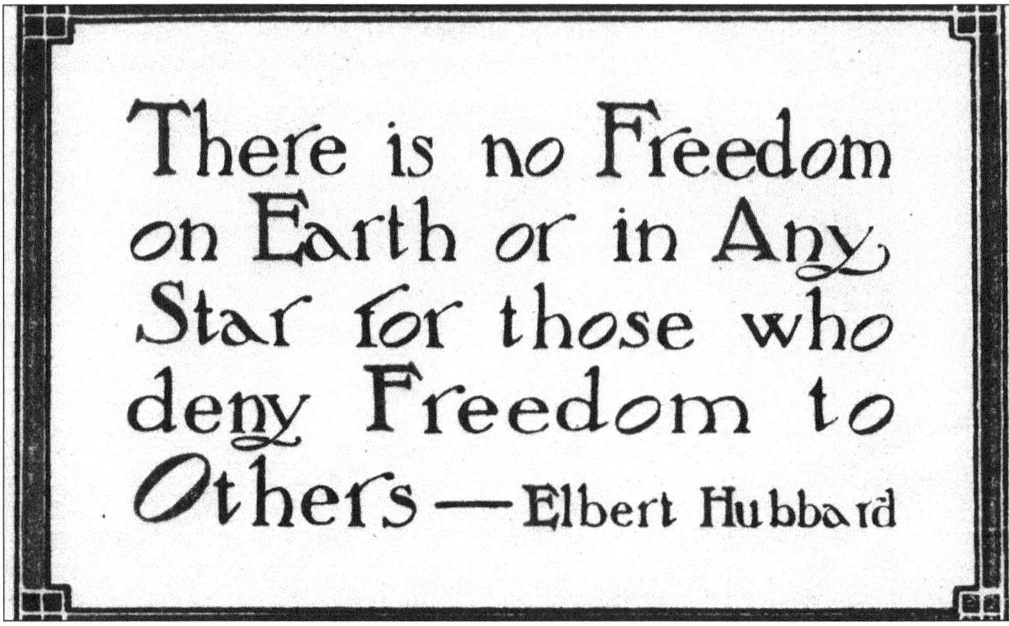


Hubbard meant this epigram not only about humans, but also as a plea for the rights of animals. He was an avowed pacifist and was not a hunter, even as a child, as far is known today. He was actively trying to keep the United States out of World War I when he booked passage on the RMS *Lusitania* in 1915. Hoping to meet with the Kaiser in Germany as well as heads of state in the Allied powers, he died in the Irish Sea as a victim of the same war.

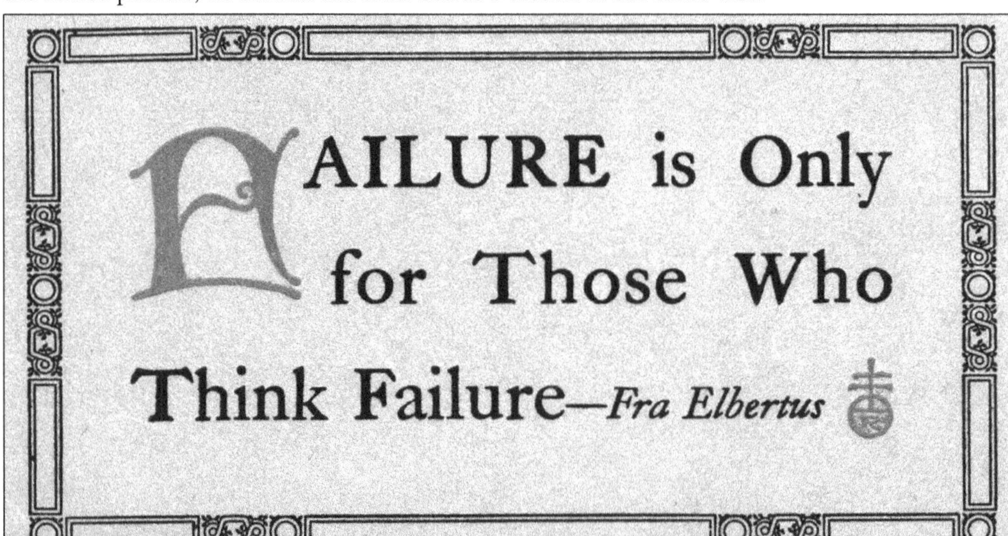


Hubbard almost never failed, starting with his salesmanship that led to becoming co-owner of one of the major mail-order houses in the United States by the age of 30. He had everything except formal education; his wives were both much better educated than he. Yet he never let that stand in his way, and he became an inspiration to tens of thousands of readers and followers throughout the world. A man who adopted his surname a generation later was to take this and create a religion, something Elbert Hubbard never wanted to do. They are not related, although this is confused by many.

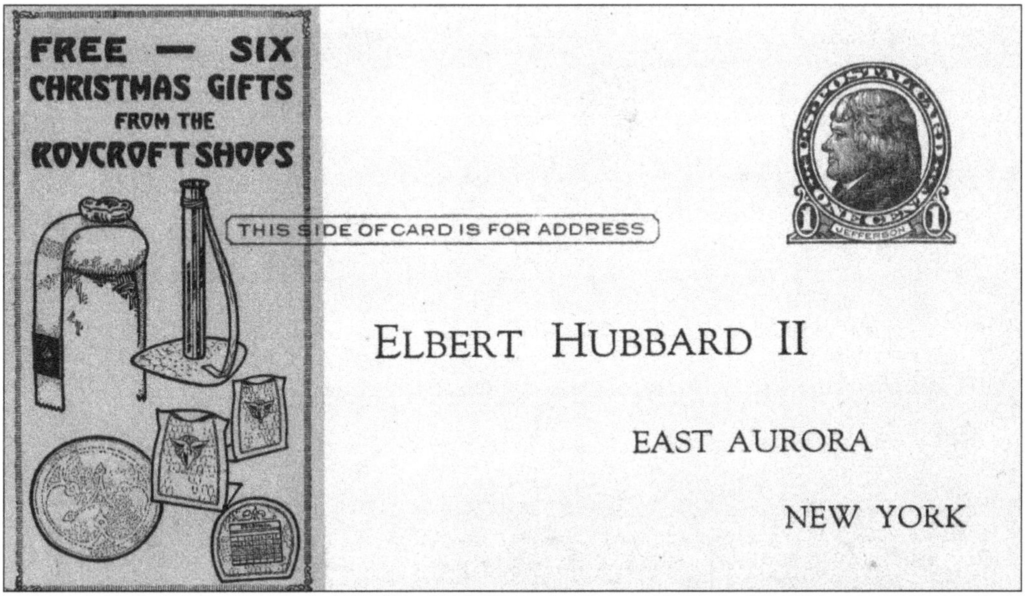


Bert Hubbard, Elbert Hubbard's son, was never known for being a philosopher or epigrammist but was happy to continue to print those of his father until the end. Advertising was something he had learned and learned well. The Roycroft continued to employ 500 people well into the 1930s, and Bert actually spent more years at the helm than his father. This order card was issued in the early 1920s, which was a very successful and profitable time for East Aurora.

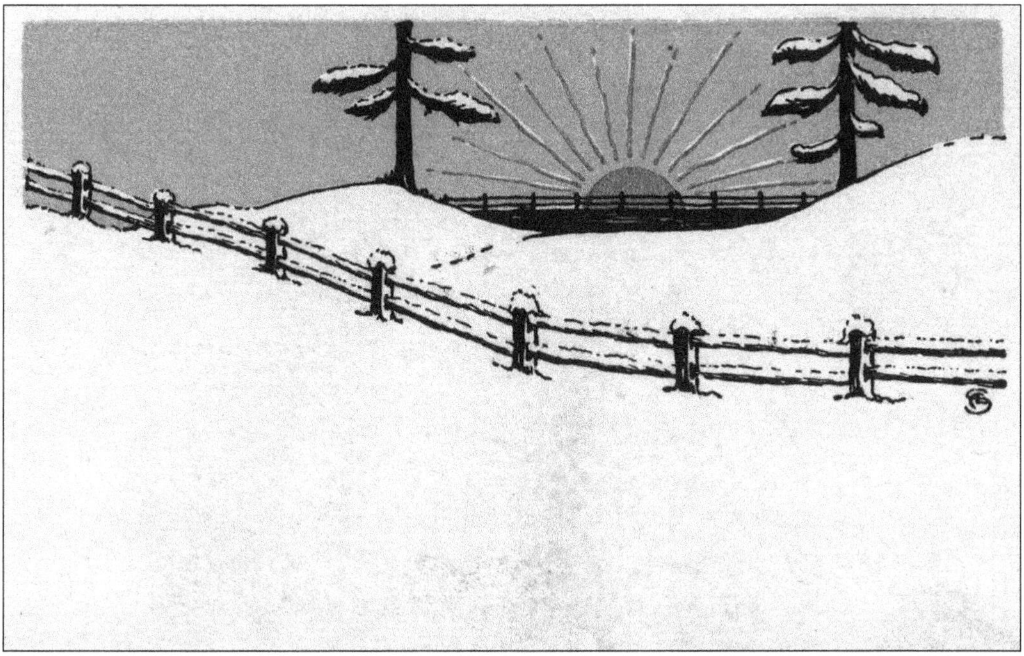

Bert was the innovator of the Christmas postcard, utilizing his staff artists like Merle James. James illustrated the two cards on this page and was on staff into the 1920s. He was the father of East Aurora native Betsy James, who became the wife of famous artist Andrew Wyeth and mother of another generation of artists. Today, their home Harmony Castle is a lovingly restored private bungalow home on the east side of the village.

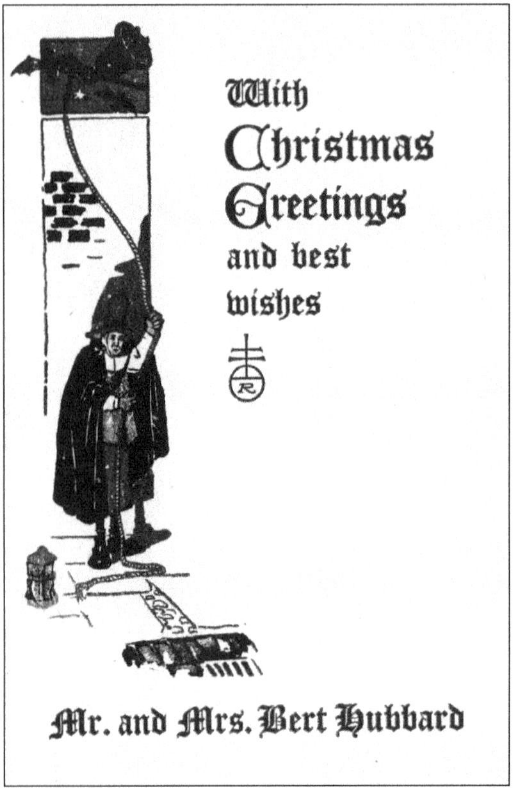


A favorite of ephemera collectors, Christmas cards and postcards from the Arts and Crafts era and especially those printed for the Hubbards are rare. The Roycroft Press issued a foldout brochure and sent sample books to stationery stores throughout the country for special imprinting. One of these sample books came up at a regional auction house about 15 years ago and sold for more than $1,000!

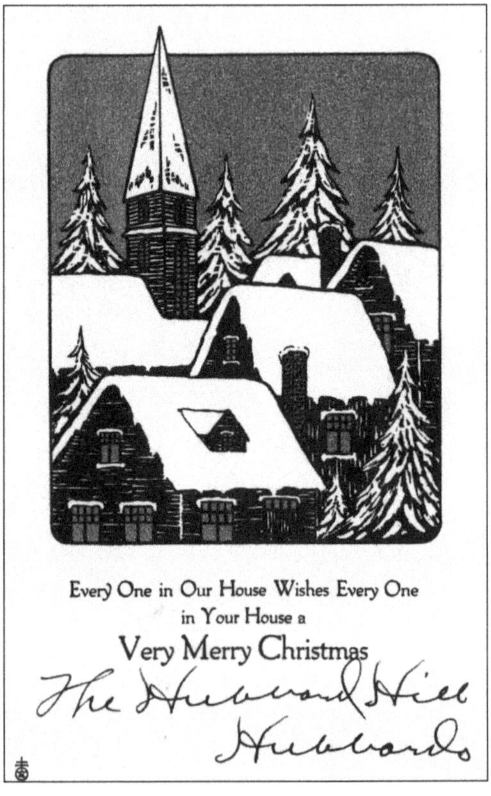


This very rare card, sent out just after the Hubbards arrived at their new home for their first Christmas there, was printed as the crash of 1929 happened. This was to be the beginning of the end for the handcrafted era, and nine years later the presses shut down. Bert and Alta were able to remain in their Hubbard Hill estate overlooking the village until their deaths; Alta in 1965 and Bert in 1970. The house was sold in 1970 outside the Hubbard family.

This rare advertising card displays Hubbard's merchandising invention of giving something free just for trying a product. This was the genius concept that was developed into the "premium" to sell Larkin soap, which he then continued at the Roycroft. He also gave away free publications and mottos, and to those likely to become long-term customers, he sent free copies of his limited edition books with a bill to follow a month later.

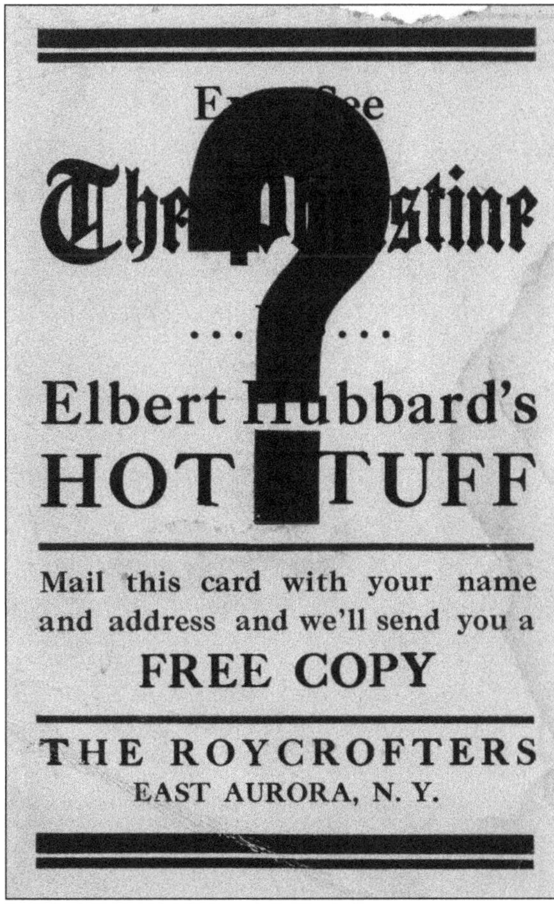


Hubbard's words and even his image were co-opted by others to sell their wares. Not a Roycroft card but Hubbard's image and one of his famous lines when being pilloried by the media, this user got one thing wrong. Elbert Hubbard never smoked or drank and even printed a famous essay, "The Cigarettist," in 1910. Reprinted many times and offered to all workers who had the evil habit, he did though produce ashtrays and cigar and cigarette boxes in fine hammered copper. (Courtesy of the library of Jack Walsdorf.)

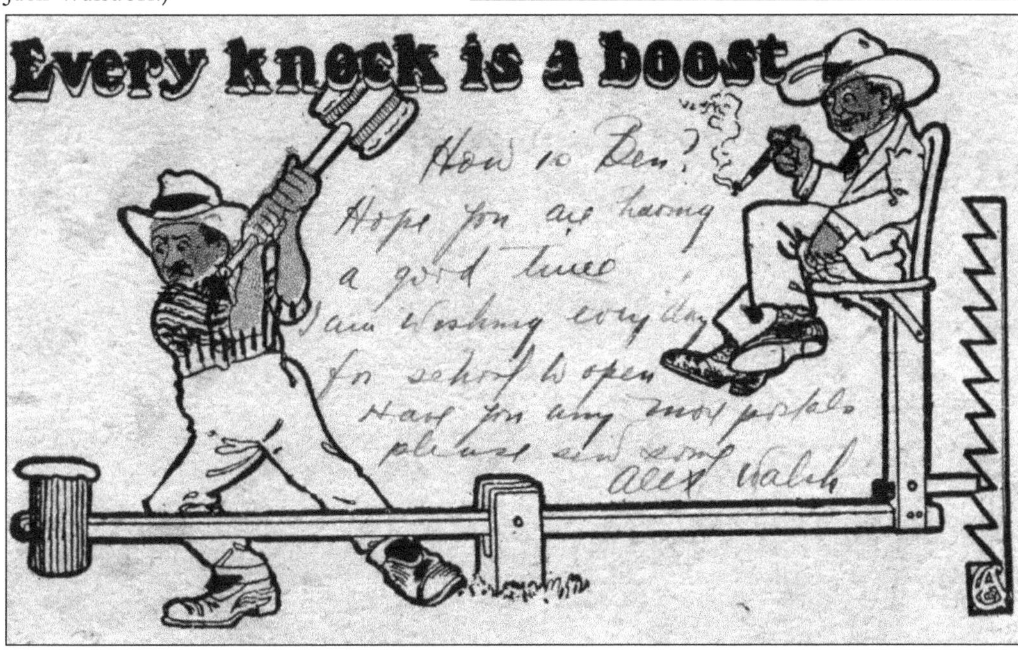

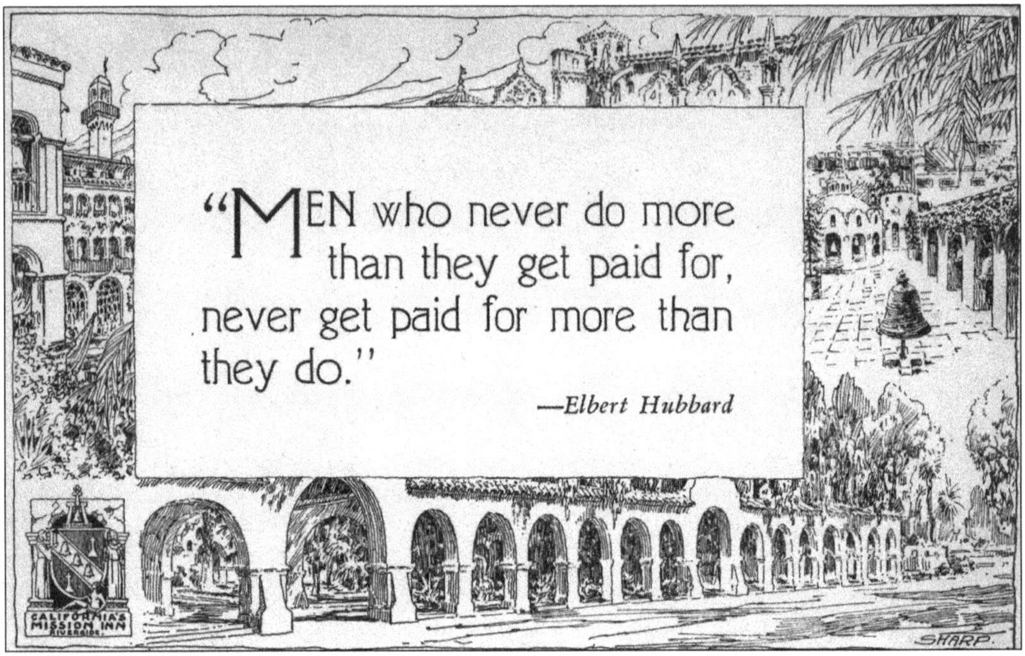


Frequently repeated and reprinted, though not always given credit, Elbert had many followers in California. The founder of the Mission Inn in Riverside, California, was a customer of the Roycrofters for cards, booklets for advertising, and also fine oak furniture, some which still remains on site in their museum. (Courtesy of the library of Jack Walsdorf.)

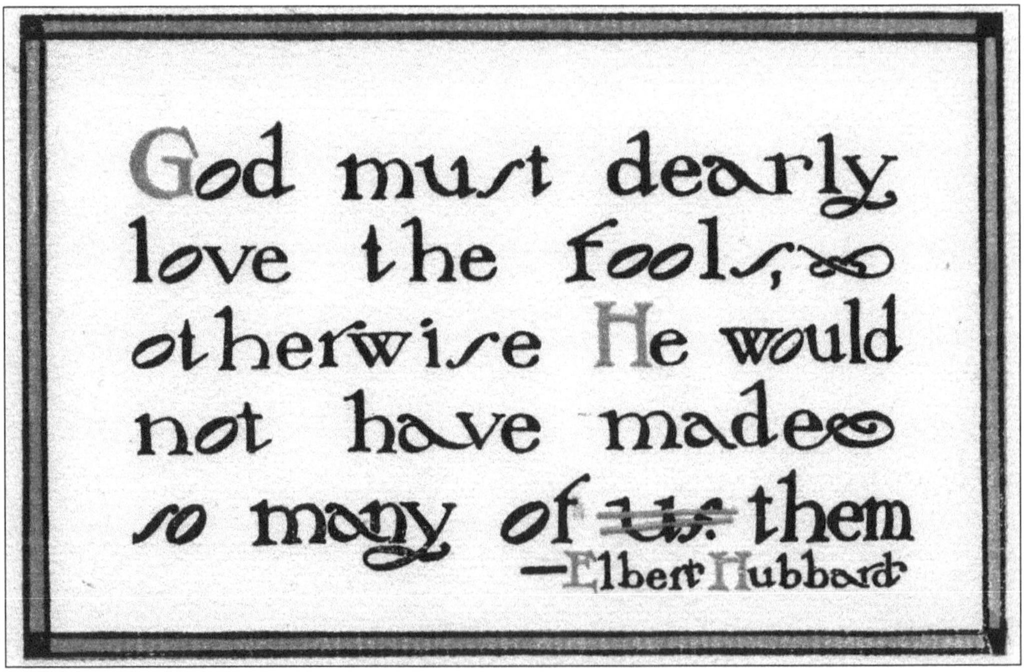


Hubbard always had a fine sense of humor and laughing at himself was always something that brought his crowds closer. This wonderfully designed card, also using Dard Hunter's famous script, is one of the author's favorites.

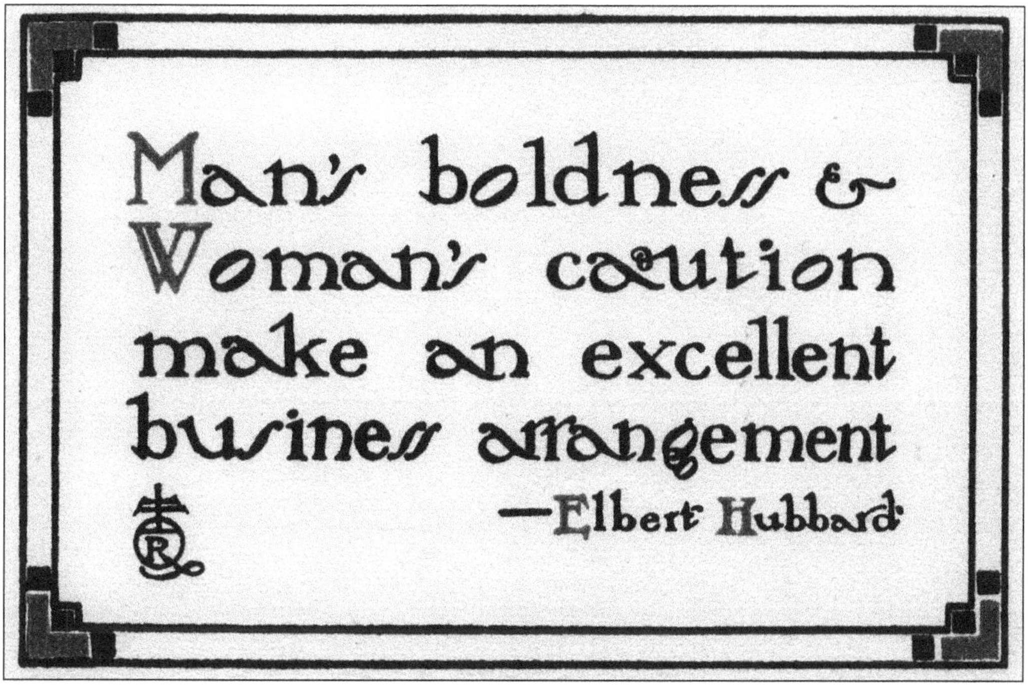


Utilizing a two-color design, he was always showing deference to his wife, Alice. This was somewhat uncommon in his first marriage. Bertha Crawford, his first wife, was a high school graduate and knew Latin and German. She edited his early writings, yet was not the muse that Alice was, his soul mate as he said many times.

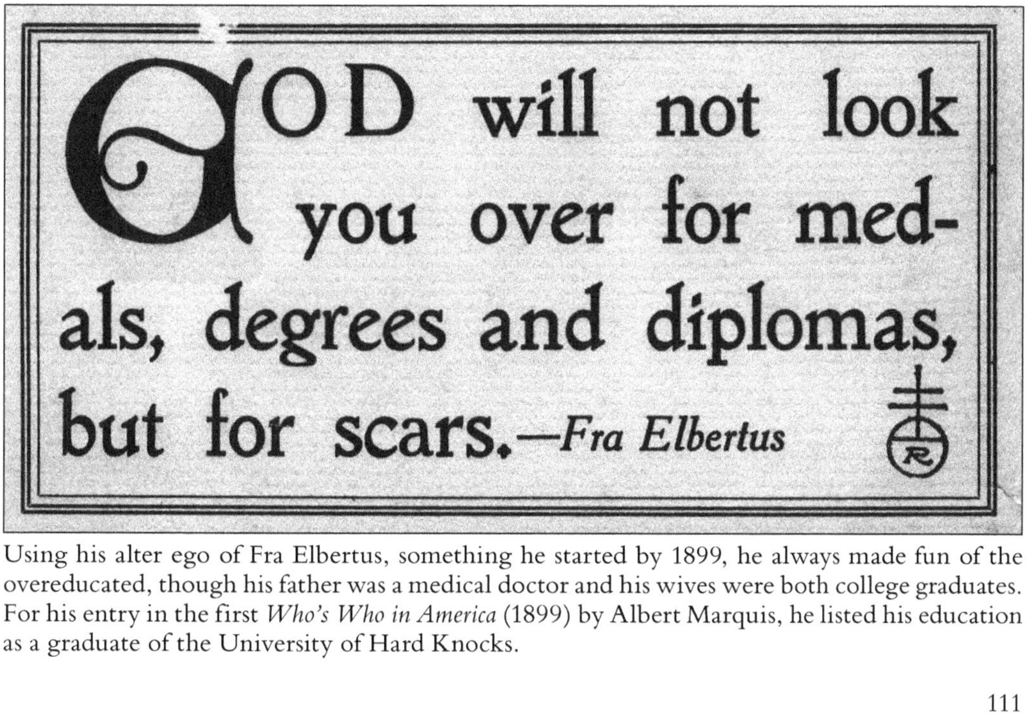


Using his alter ego of Fra Elbertus, something he started by 1899, he always made fun of the overeducated, though his father was a medical doctor and his wives were both college graduates. For his entry in the first *Who's Who in America* (1899) by Albert Marquis, he listed his education as a graduate of the University of Hard Knocks.

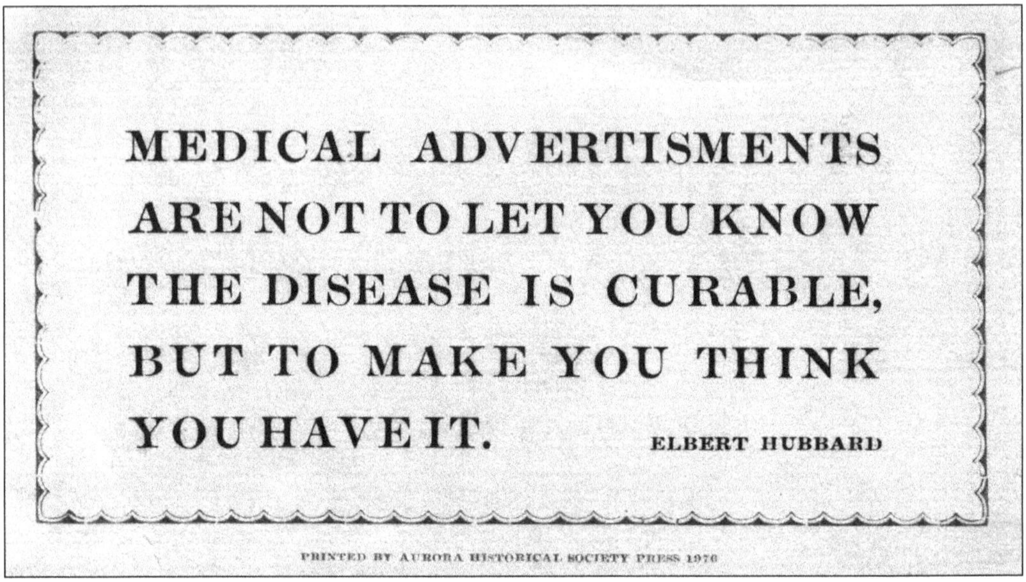


Elbert was always knocking the classical medical profession in his epigrams and lectures with arguments often arising from his own father in the audience in the inn's music salon at his Sunday lectures (sermons). This card was printed by the handpress that was set up by the Aurora Historical Society in the cellar of the chapel (town hall) in the 1960s. Curator Roger Kline operated it on weekends until his death in the 1980s. These were mementos given away to visitors.

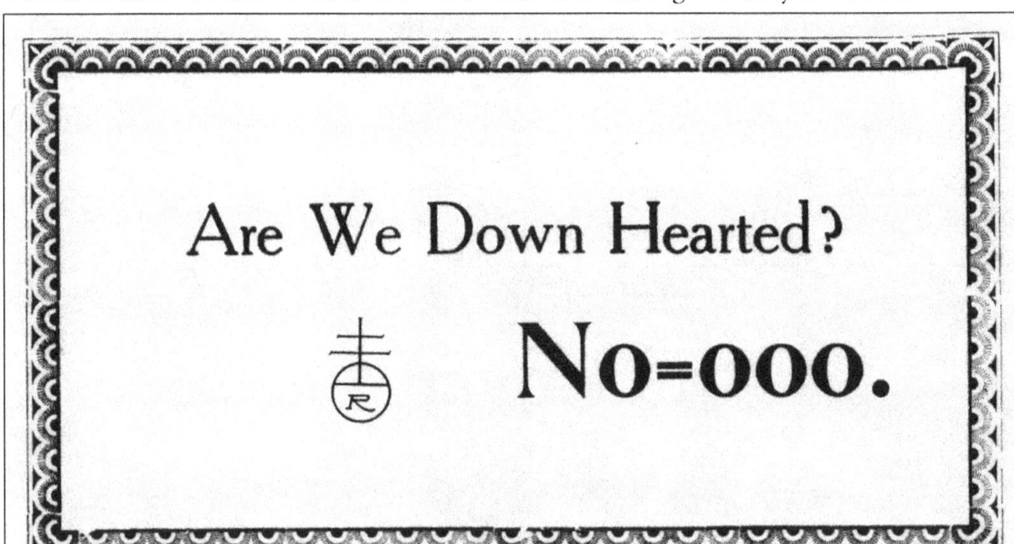


Also printed by Roger Kline, this card showed Elbert Hubbard's granddaughter Nancy Hubbard Brady's favorite epigram. An original hand-colored copy hung framed just inside her home's front door. It was also said to have always hung in her classroom when she taught school. She was one of the three founders of the Roycroft Renaissance movement in the early 1970s. It was inspired by the Princeton Exhibition of 1971, which asked to borrow some of her favorite Roycroft items, including a rare leaded lamp by Dard Hunter and a bust of her grandfather by Jerome Connor, among other things.

*Seven*

# The Years 1938–1995
## The Campus as a Phoenix Rising from the Ashes

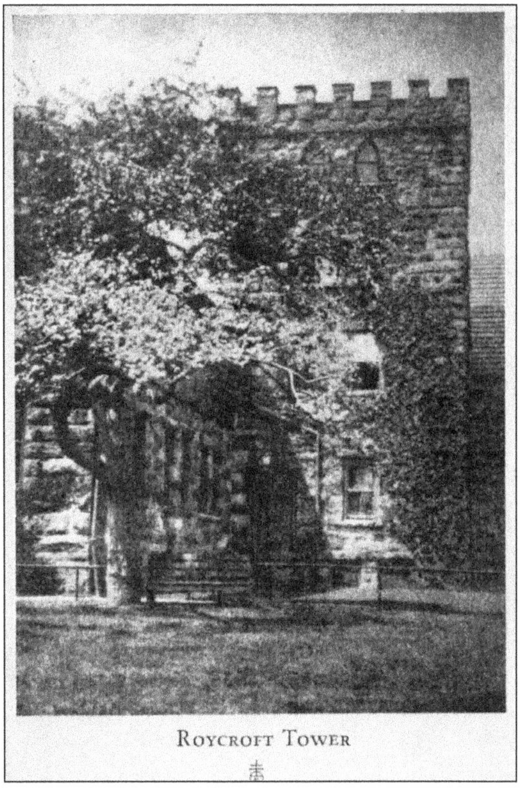


The Print Shops tower has always stood as a reminder of the Roycroft's past. From 1938 through the mid-1980s, the Roycroft Inn was all that came to mind to people who grew up and lived in the area. Few knew of its important contribution to history when they drove past this tower. (Courtesy of the library of Jack Walsdorf.)

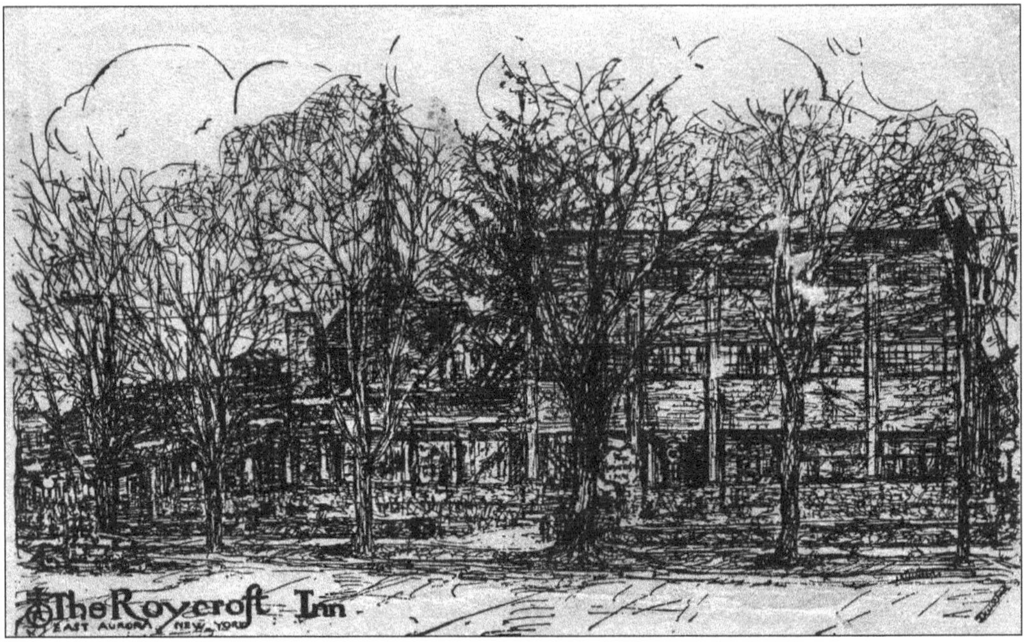


The Roycroft Inn's rooms were closed for a short time in the late 1930s and again during World War II; however, it remained a restaurant known for its food. This drawing by a local artist for a small series of cards was sold at the Roycroft Inn and the Gift Shop across the street in the 1950s. The cards are quite rare today and were needed for a complete time line of the campus's history.

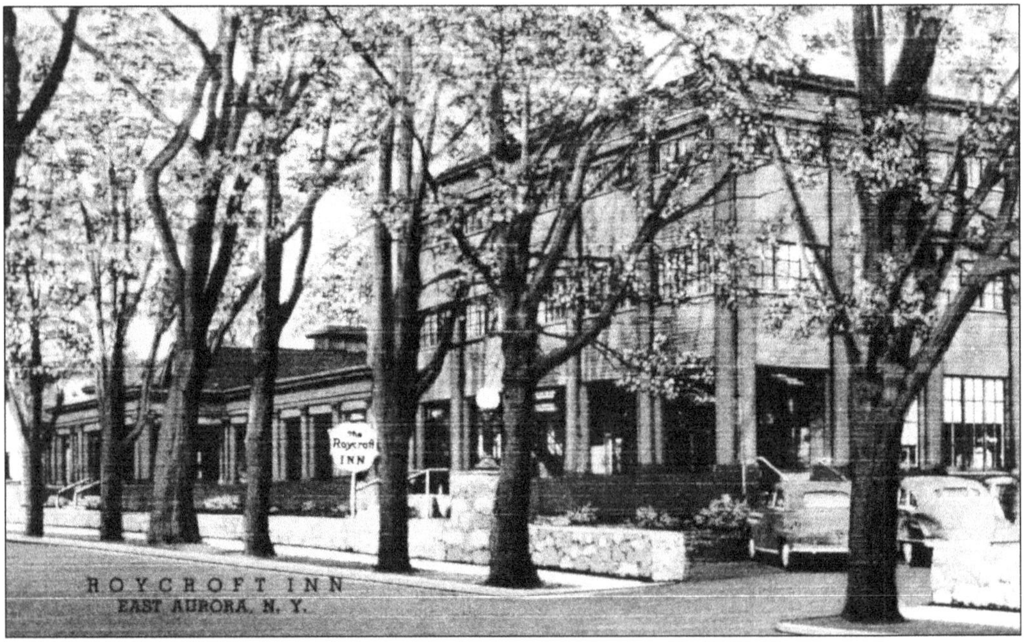


This is a more commercial card from the same time period where one will notice that the gardens are now a parking lot at the south end of the inn. The old signs have been replaced by neon and many vestiges of its Arts and Crafts era glory are gone. It is more noticeable on the inside than in this image.

By the same artist as the card on the previous page, this drawing shows the modernization that has taken place. The original and now very collectible Roycroft furniture has been sold off at auction and replaced for more "horsey" decor. The Tack Room decor remained until 1971.

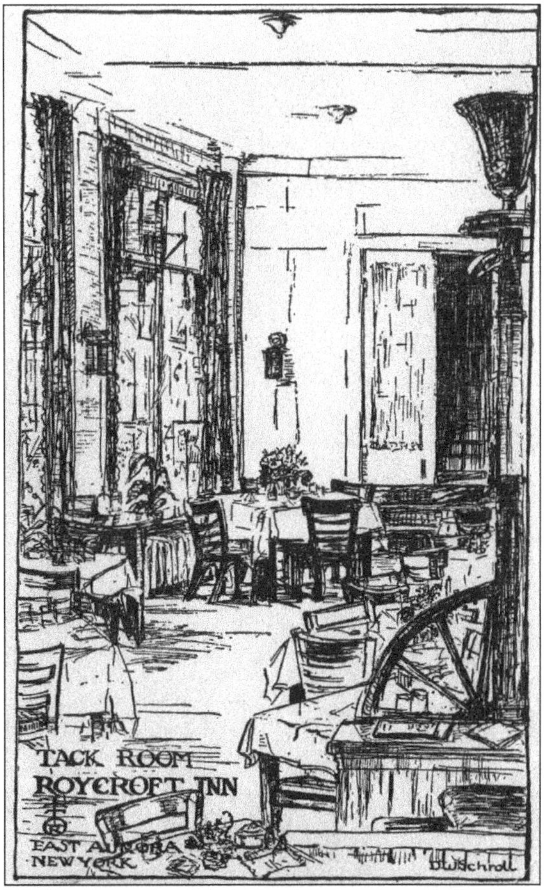


This card is from a short and yet famous time in the inn's history. This is the era of the ownership of restaurateur and stable owner Edwin Miller, from around 1960 to 1965. Eddie, as he liked to be called, stuck a deal with the new AFL football team, the Buffalo Bills, to host their summer training table and accommodations here. The most famous of those players, Jack French Kemp (1935–2009), served as the local congressman from 1971 to 1989 and vice presidential candidate in 1996. In the mid-1980s, he helped the author and his wife obtain National Landmark Status for the Roycroft Campus, to which the world of Arts and Crafts is forever in his honor.

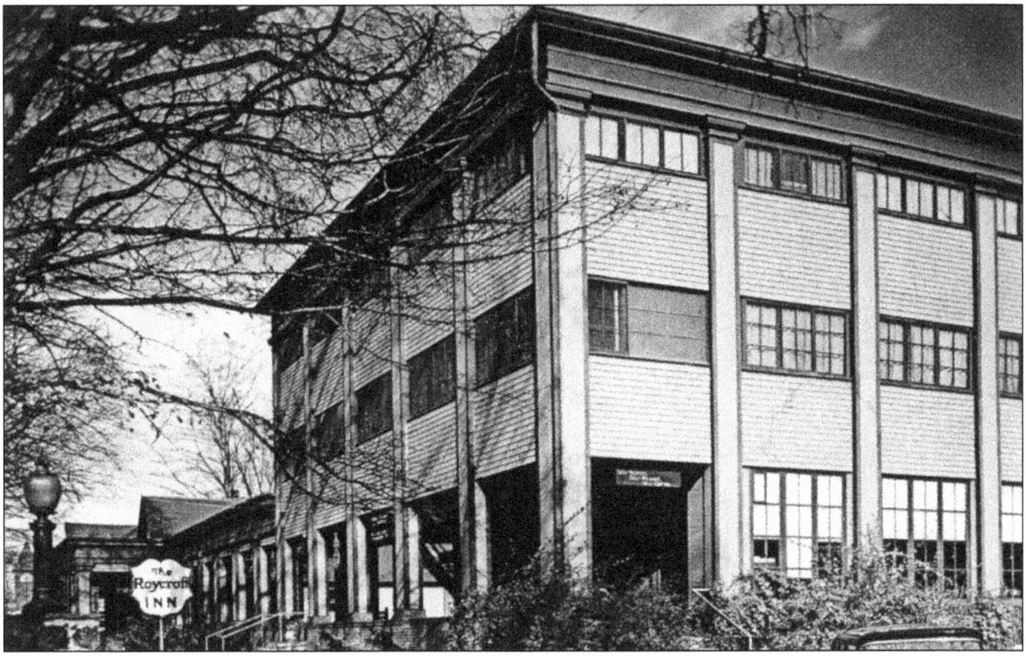

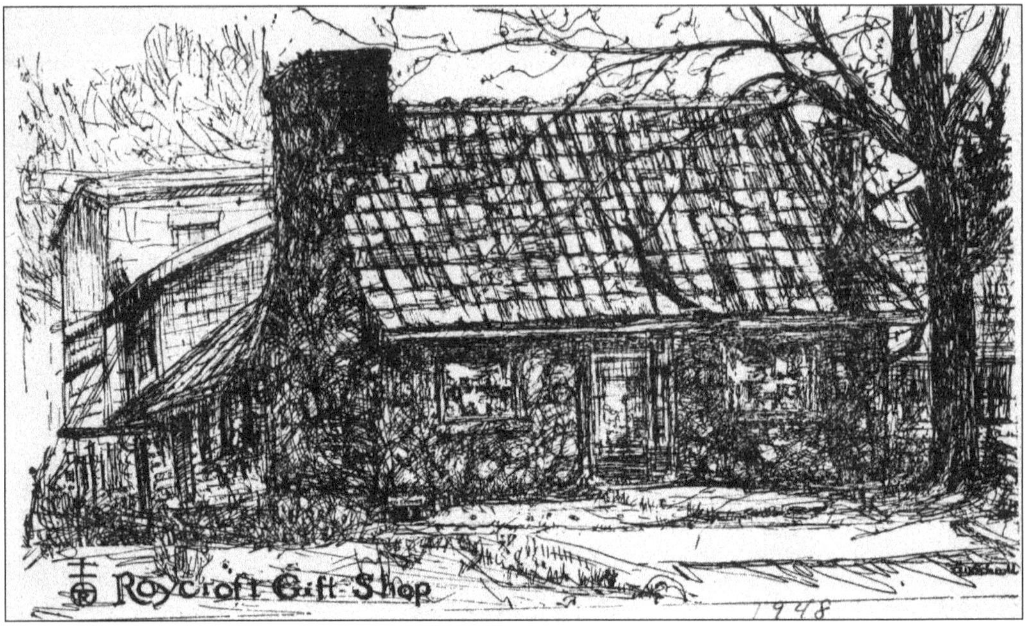


The Copper Shop was the only building to remain open in the winter and summer after the close of the other shops in 1938 until a short period in 1976 and then again after its sale during a major restoration in 2004. The Roycrofters, under Bert's directorship, had leased the building to tenant operators starting during the Depression era.

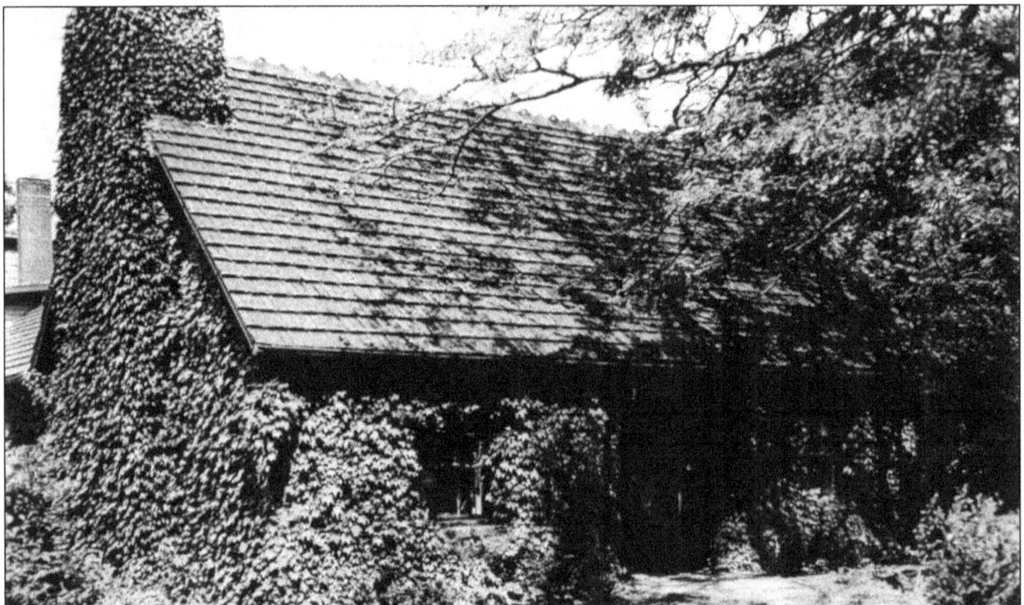

This photograph, taken around 1965, shows the Gift Shop when it had become known as one of the foremost fine shops for fine silver and china. A local bride registered her gift list here for her choices, something that continues up to this day. The exterior has remained unchanged in its footprint since the northern addition in the late 1910s. Items made by many of the former craftpersons continued to be produced into the 1970s. Later, the new work inspired by the old and made by Roycroft Renaissance juried craftpersons was sold here.

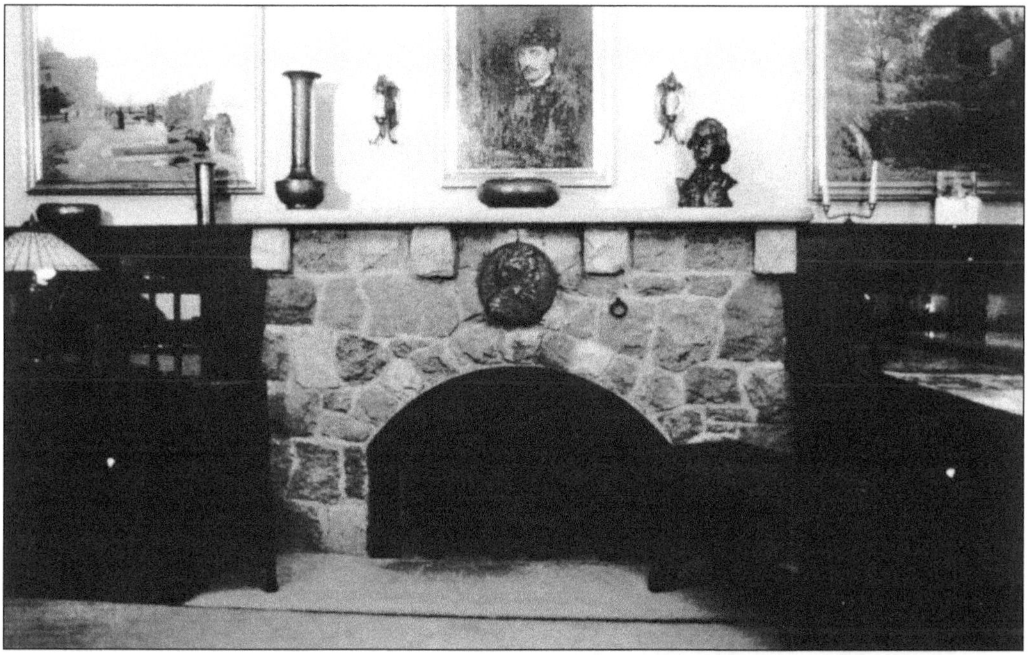

Around the corner from the campus at 363 Oakwood Avenue is a bungalow built by the Roycrofters in 1910 for master leather worker George ScheideMantel and his wife, Gladys, the daughter of Alice Grant (known as "Mother Grant"), the inn's chef. Unchanged on the exterior, today it is the Elbert Hubbard Library and Roycroft Museum. In 1985, Gladys gave her home to the Aurora Historical Society with all of its original furnishings. The society moved their museum from the Village Hall on Main Street to this beautiful house. The house came with the stipulation that it was a trade for Gladys to move into the local assisted living facility. At the time, she was 100 years young and her only concern was for her cat and her gardens. Both were well taken care of until her passing at age 106 in 1991. George's home workshop is located on the second floor. Rare examples of all Roycroftiana are found inside.

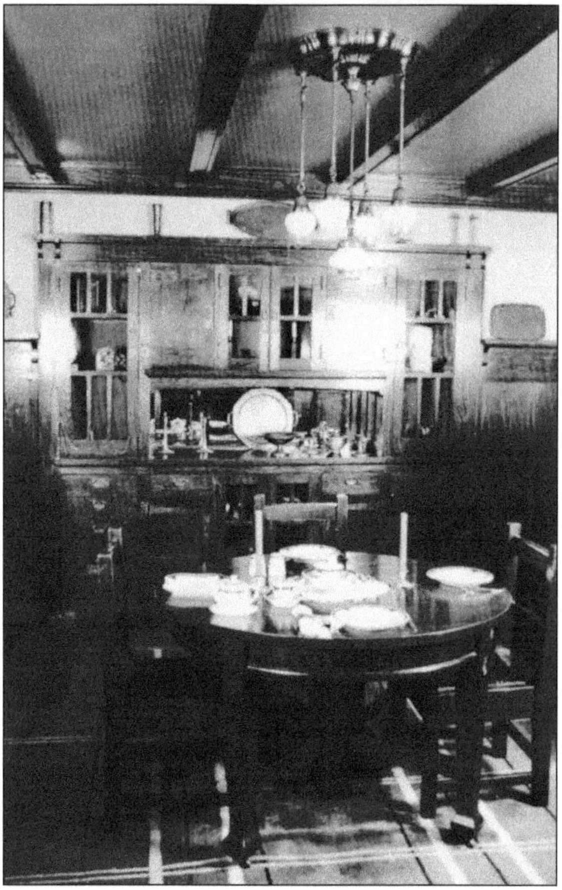

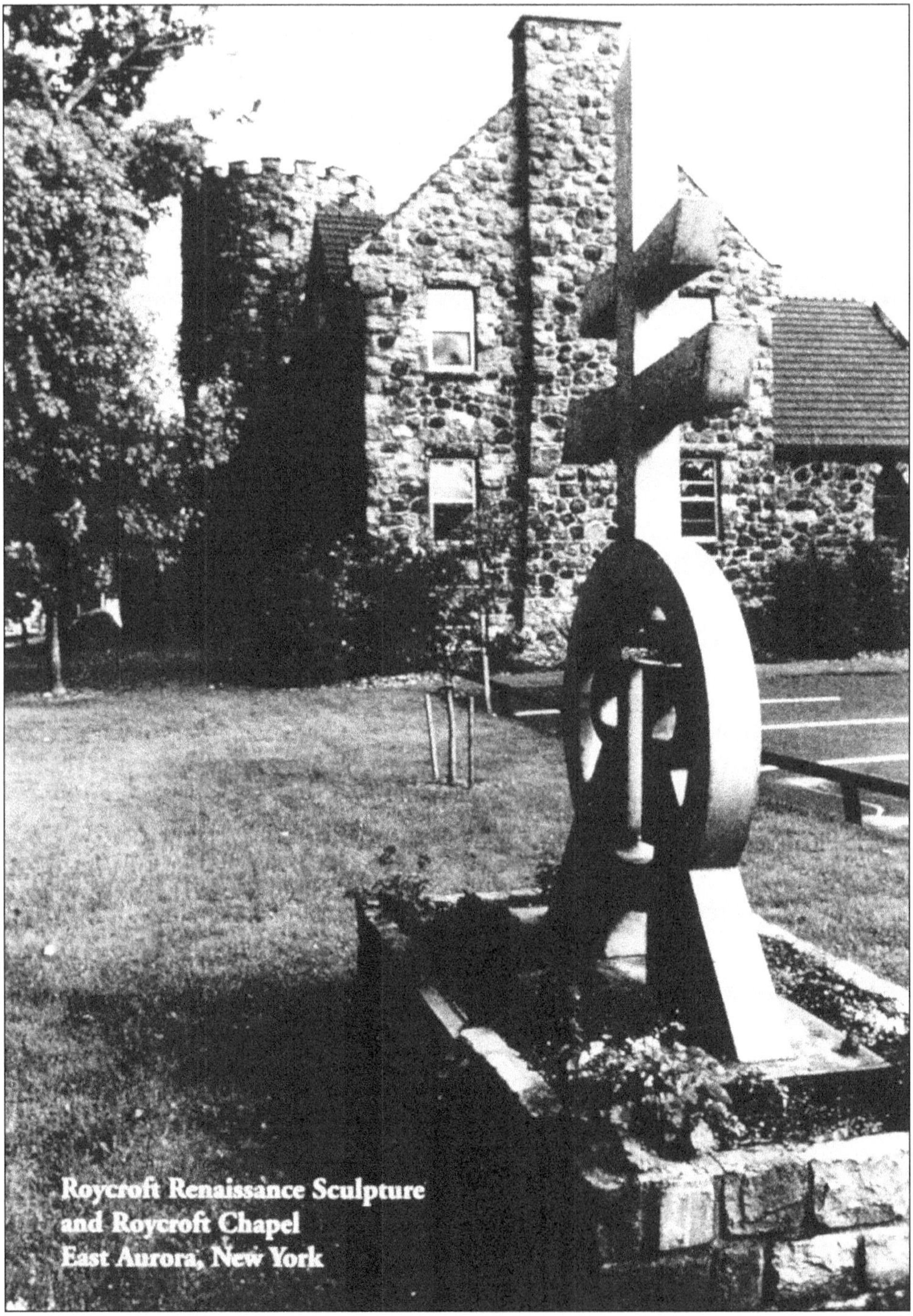


This sculpture, designed and crafted by blacksmith Paul Boccolucci in 1986, stands today facing Main Street as the mark of the new era, now into its fourth decade. The double "R" trademark is registered to the Roycrofters-at-Large-Association, which was founded in 1976 and was to be used by juried craftpersons throughout the United States. Miriam Hubbard Roelofs, Elbert and Alice's only child, unveiled this artwork with a smash of a champagne bottle in 1986, which was a very memorable event.

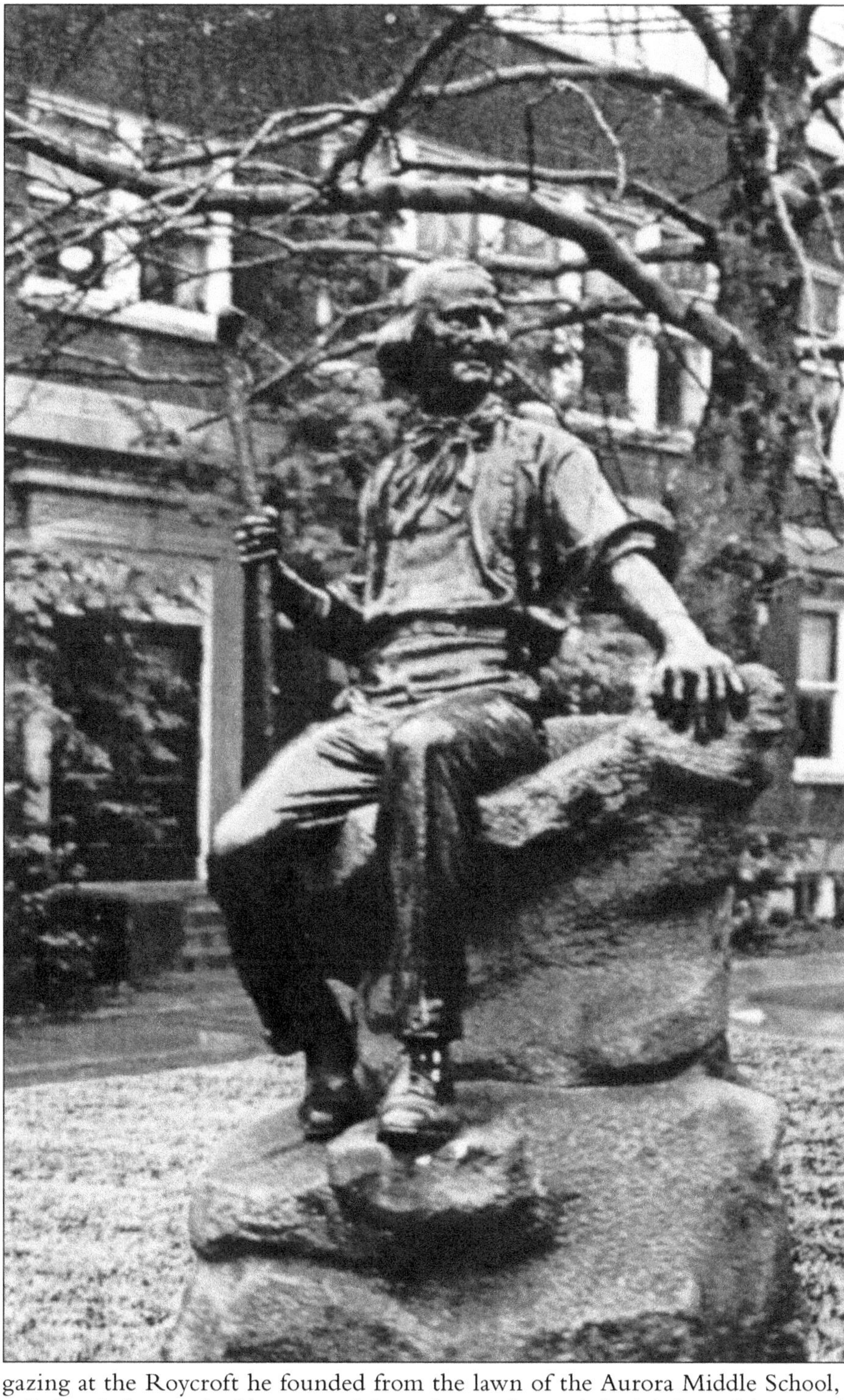

Now gazing at the Roycroft he founded from the lawn of the Aurora Middle School, Elbert Hubbard's heroic bronze had been saved from destruction and the joining of the war effort of World War II. Many in the community want to see it and its neighbor, Michelangelo, moved back across the street to celebrate the rebirth of the campus.

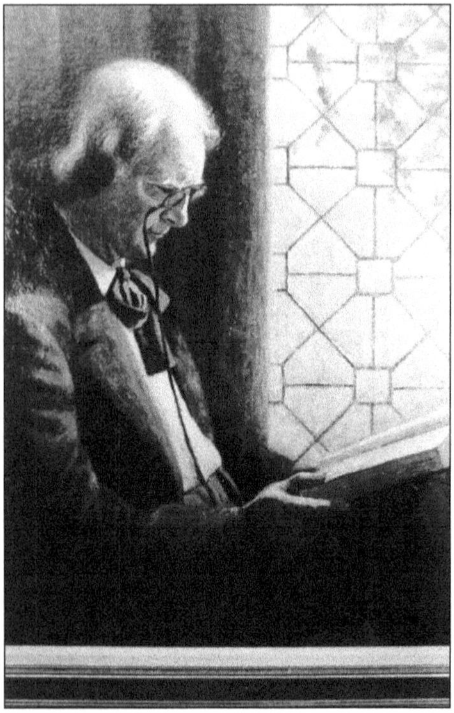

This oil painting of Elbert Hubbard, based on a popular photograph taken a year before his death, hangs in the Elbert Hubbard Roycroft Museum on Oakwood Avenue in the village. Only open for limited hours and arranged tours, it is a must for any visitor to the village, and the campus is only a short walk away. These cards are still available for the collector at the Gift Shop within the museum, which also has a fine book shop featuring Roycroft and Arts and Crafts history books.

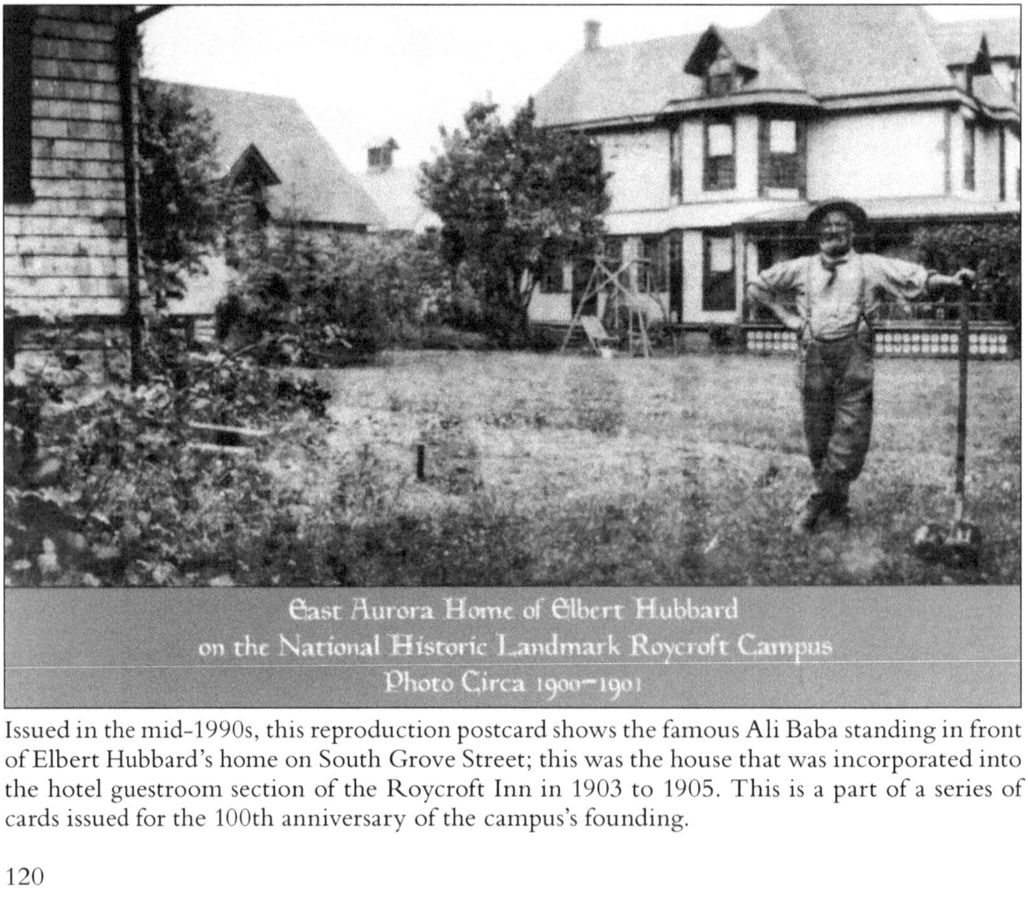


Issued in the mid-1990s, this reproduction postcard shows the famous Ali Baba standing in front of Elbert Hubbard's home on South Grove Street; this was the house that was incorporated into the hotel guestroom section of the Roycroft Inn in 1903 to 1905. This is a part of a series of cards issued for the 100th anniversary of the campus's founding.

Largely forgotten by most except as a restaurant and group of old buildings, the campus was marked as a historic site by the Erie County Sesquicentennial Commission, who placed this sign on the street in front of the chapel in 1971. Only a year later, rare Roycroft items traveled to major art museums in New Jersey, New York, Illinois, and California as a part of the famous Princeton Exhibition of the American Arts and Crafts Movement organized by Dr. Robert Judson Clark (1937–2011) of Princeton University.

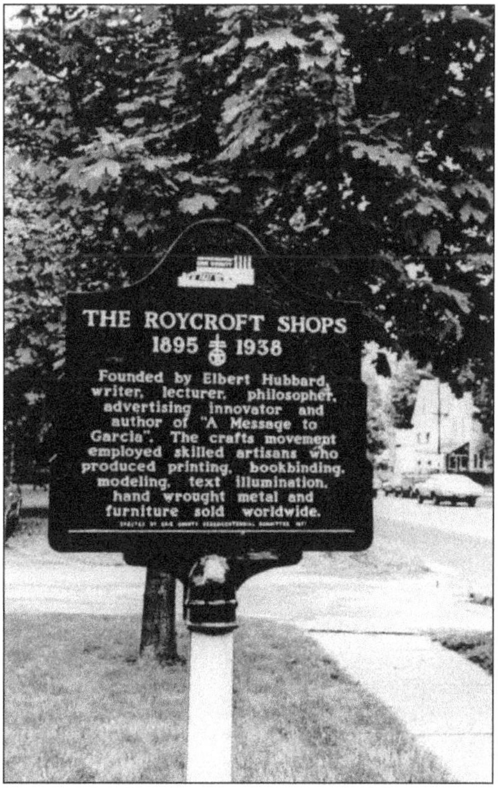


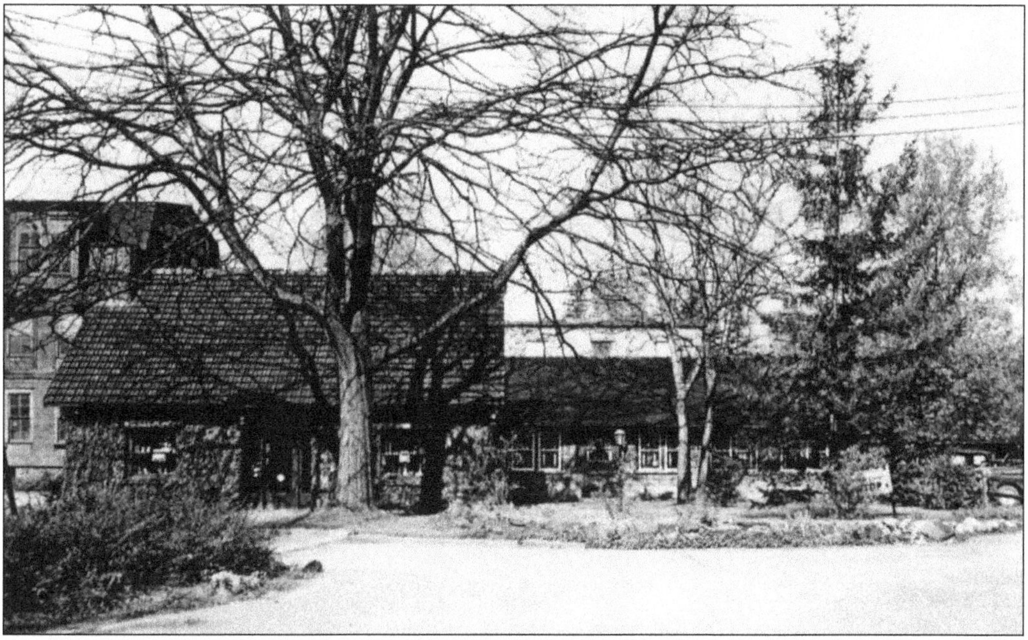

The Copper Shop on the campus has continually operated as a gift shop since first being leased to the Zink family of East Aurora in 1936, when copper production stopped. This card is from the 1960s, when it was recognized as one of the finer shops in Western New York to shop for wedding gifts of china and silver.

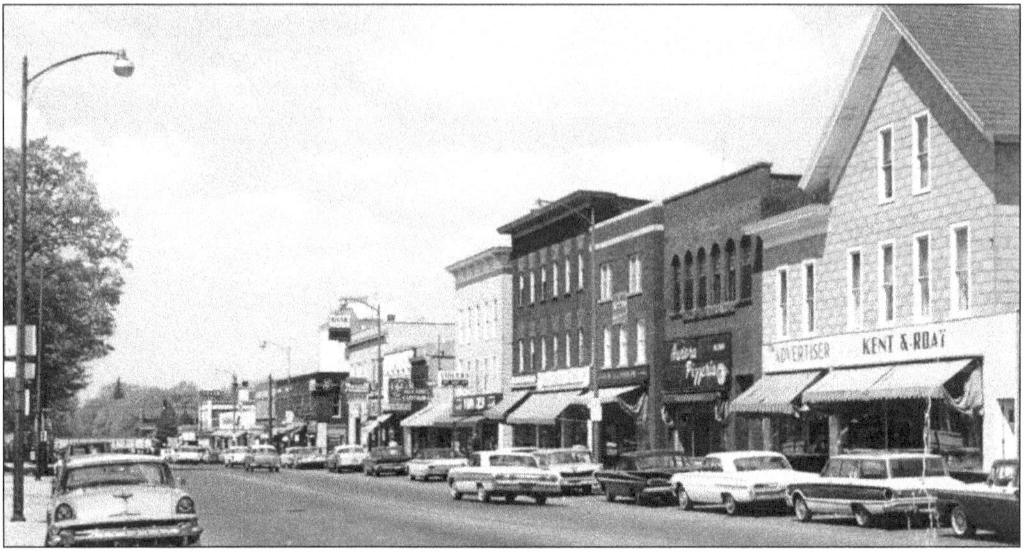

This view along Main Street in East Aurora from the early 1960s shows a prosperous small town with many locally owned businesses. The most famous of these businesses is Vidler's 5 and 10. Opened during the Depression, it is a step back in time and is still run by the third generation of the Vidler family, one of the few such operations in the United States today. East Aurora has been able to maintain its Main Street while many other nearby towns and villages have not. It has fought and won against the intrusion of Walmart and other superstores, which would destroy this fragile economy that makes the village so special today.

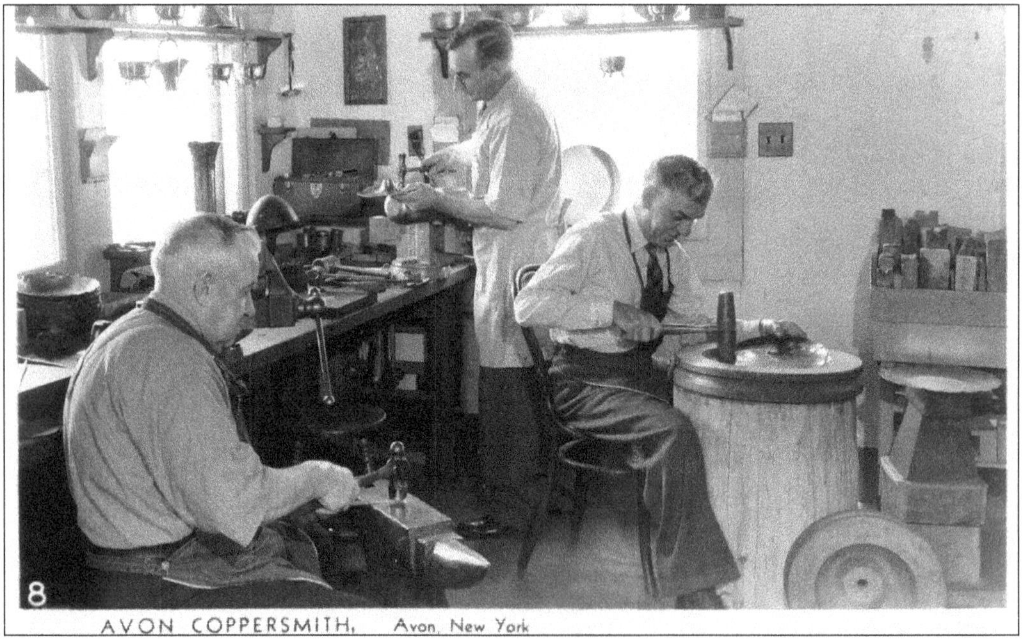


Other collectible postcards for the enthusiast are real-photo cards of the Roycroft craftsman after the shops closed in 1938. This image is from nearby Avon, New York, south of Rochester along Route 20 inside of Art Cole's Avon Coppersmith Shop. Many workers continued their crafts long after they left East Aurora. In addition to Art Cole in Avon, New York, Walter U. Jennings, Leon Varley, and others sold their fine bowls and jewelry into the 1960s.

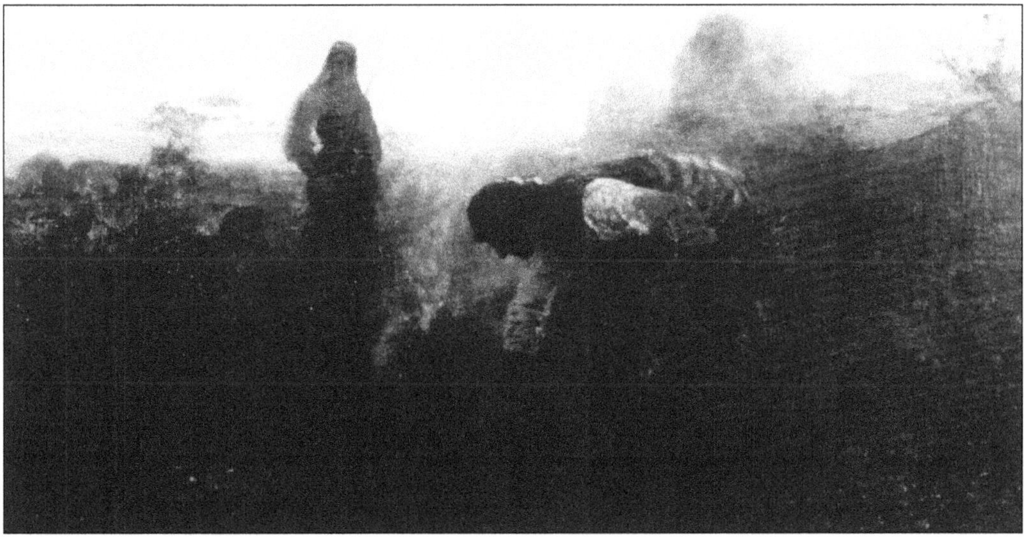

This large full-color card was sent out announcing the major retrospective of the work of Alexis Jean Fournier in December 1985. Held in the gallery of the James J. Hill House, it had over 70 paintings from collections throughout the United States and Canada. Fournier had been rediscovered as a major American Impressionist and Barbizon. Works from East Aurora, Indiana, Connecticut, Italy, and France were included. The largest painting exhibited was the Roycroft's own *Entrance to the Grand Canal, Venice 1901,* removed from the dining room of the inn.

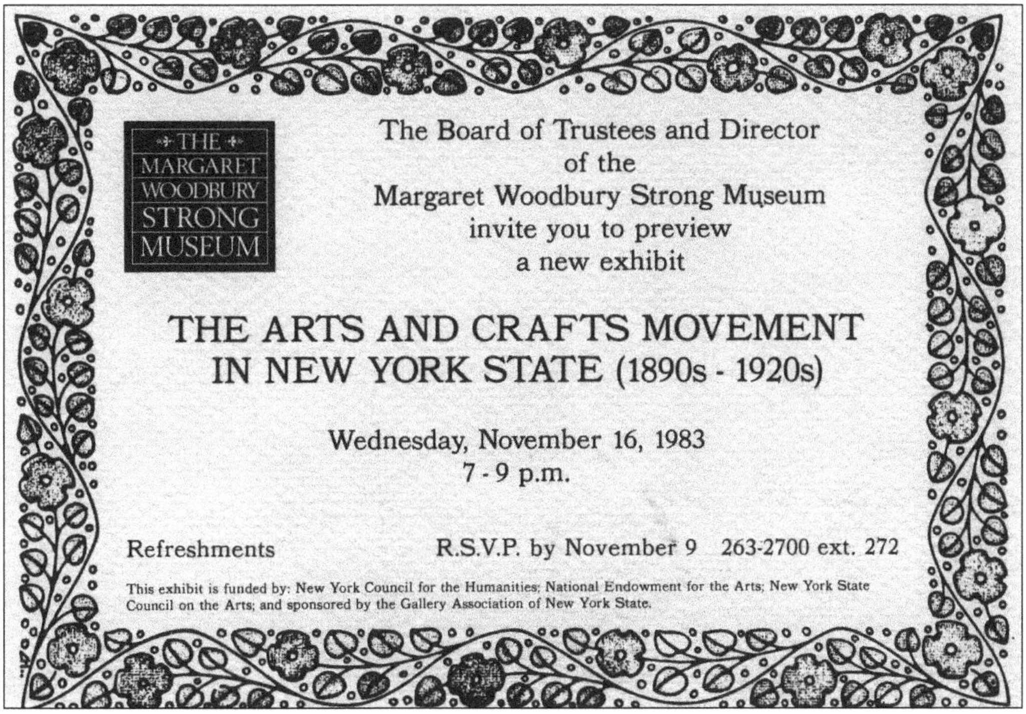

THE MARGARET WOODBURY STRONG MUSEUM

The Board of Trustees and Director
of the
Margaret Woodbury Strong Museum
invite you to preview
a new exhibit

THE ARTS AND CRAFTS MOVEMENT
IN NEW YORK STATE (1890s - 1920s)

Wednesday, November 16, 1983
7 - 9 p.m.

Refreshments R.S.V.P. by November 9 263-2700 ext. 272

This exhibit is funded by: New York Council for the Humanities; National Endowment for the Arts; New York State Council on the Arts; and sponsored by the Gallery Association of New York State.

In 1983, the first traveling exhibition to spotlight the Arts and Crafts Movement in New York State was assembled by Dr. Coy Ludwig of Oswego. Roycroft had a major representation in this exhibit that travelled to Albany, Rochester, Buffalo, Long Island, Syracuse, and Dartmouth College in New Hampshire through 1985.

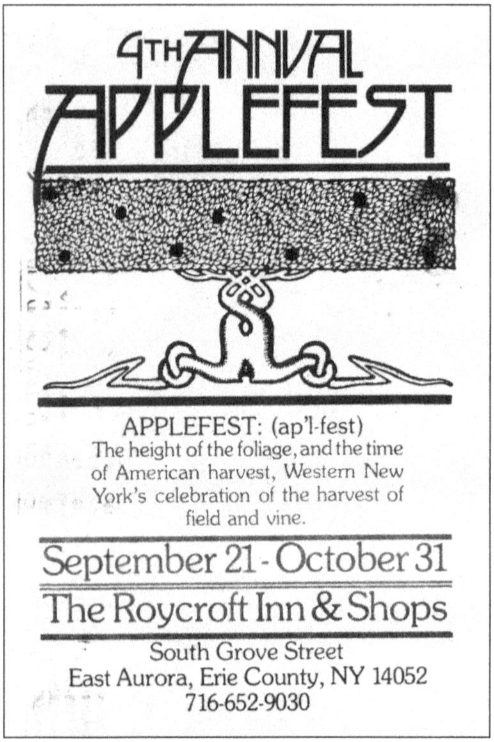


With the campus's revival starting in the late 1970s, many new activities and events were created to draw visitors. Applefest was a food and wine event hosted by the inn that started in the fall of 1982. Roycroft wine, a private label, was created in 1983 by the Woodbury Winery in Sheridan, New York, which became very popular with the local community.

In 1993, a major exhibition to help celebrate the 100th anniversary of the Roycroft's founding was put together at the Burchfield Penney Art Center in Buffalo. Borrowing from local collectors and a huge gift from Charles Rand Penney of Roycroftiana, this traveling decorative arts exhibit was entitled Roycroft Desktop in tribute to Hubbard, his advertising genius, and the fine craftsmanship of his many workers. It was presented in Columbia, South Carolina; Traverse City Michigan; Buffalo, New York; Columbus, Ohio; and Erie, Pennsylvania, over the space of two years.

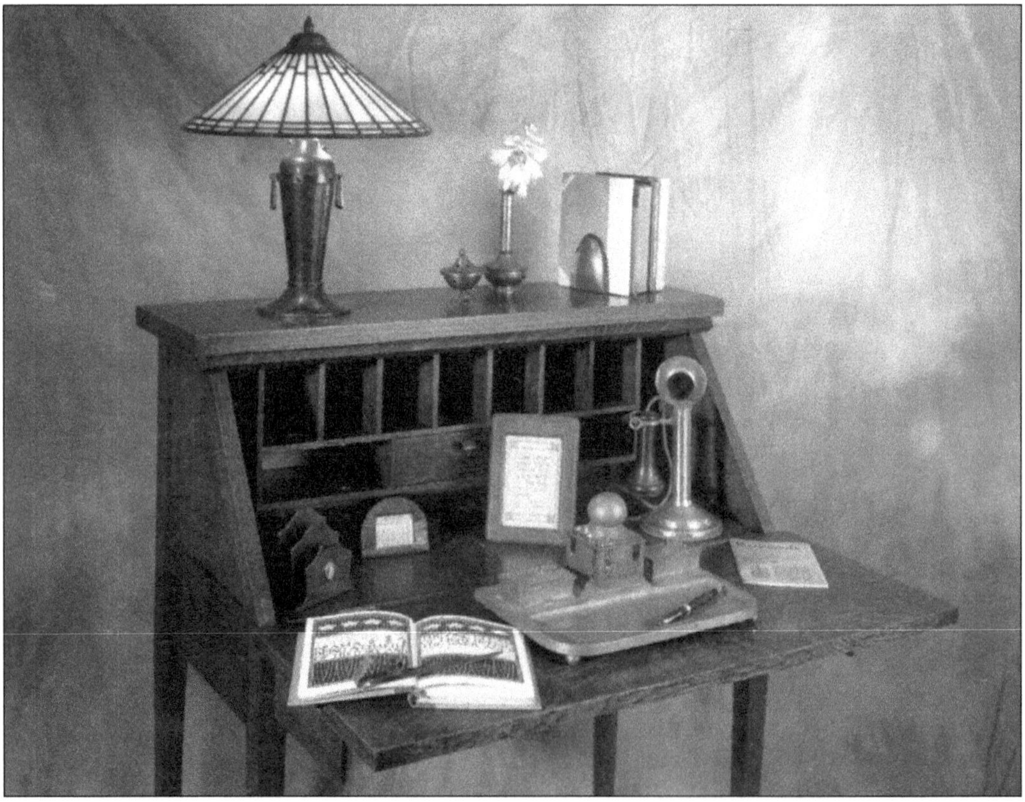

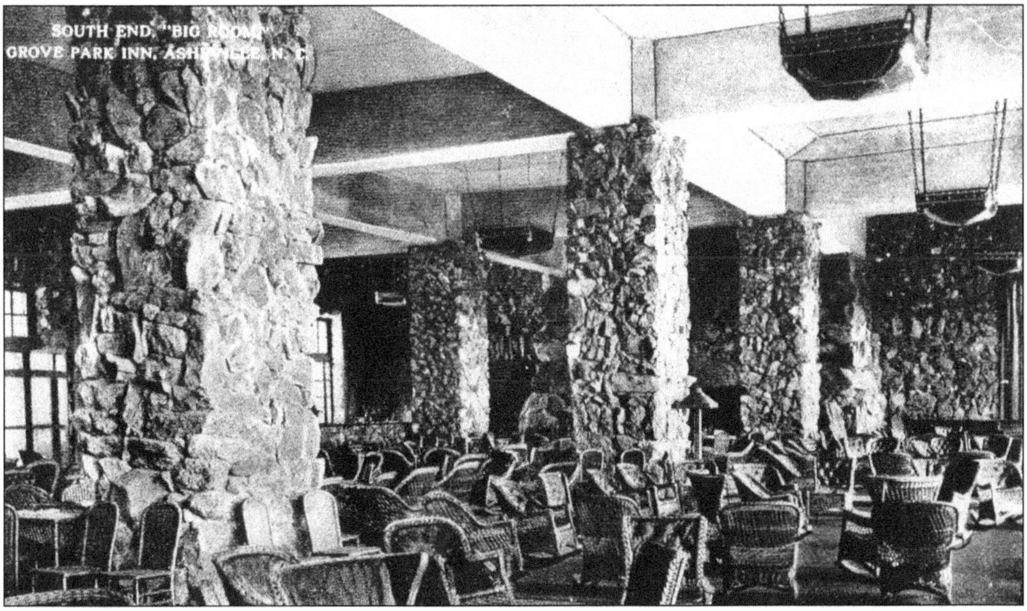


One of the major catalysts to the Arts and Crafts Movement revival has been the annual Arts and Crafts Conference founded in 1988 at the Grove Park Inn in Asheville, North Carolina. Founded by Bruce Johnson and still ongoing after 26 years, it brings together scholars and craftspeople from throughout the world to share their enthusiasm for this period in history. The inn is filled with Roycroft-made items that were created for the inn in 1913.

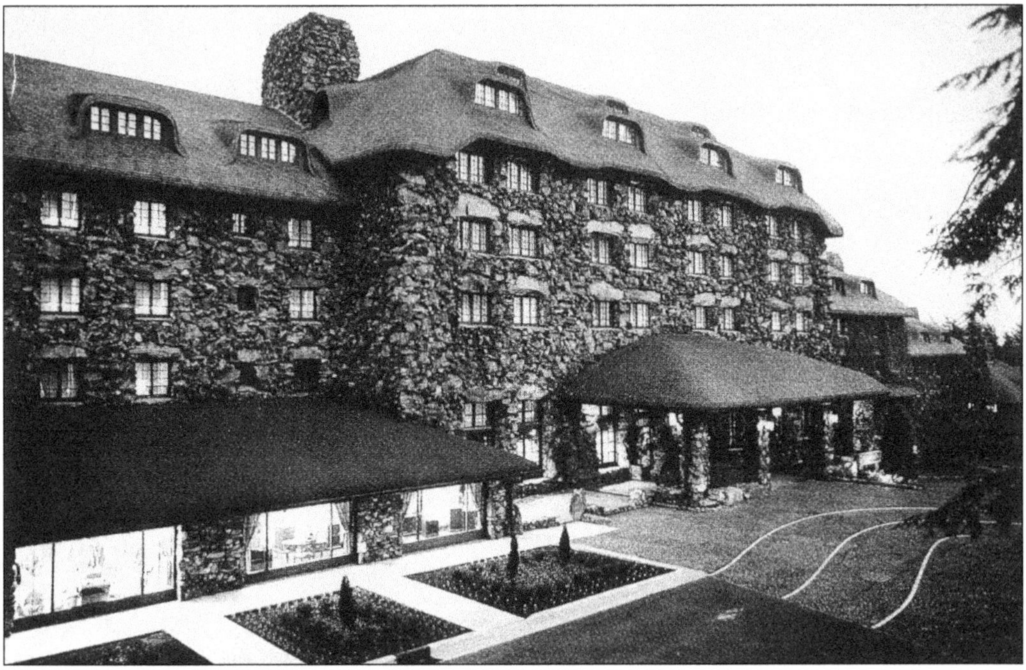

Inside the Grove Park Inn, visitors can find hundreds of Mission-style furniture items and dozens of Roycroft copper lighting fixtures. Over 2,500 people attend the annual conference, and Roycroft items can always be found for sale, both original and reproductions, and even newly inspired handcrafted items by Roycroft Renaissance–licensed men and women.

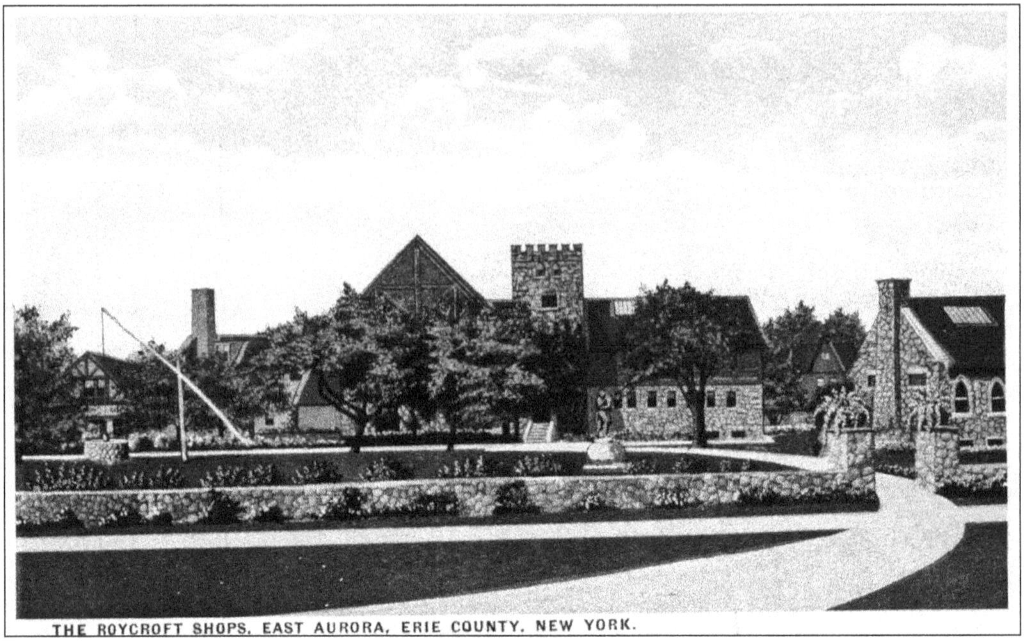


This view, a reprint of an Alexis Fournier oil painting, is the idyllic view of the Roycroft Campus most imagined in 1910. It may yet look like this, if the community-run nonprofits can meet their goals and assemble all of the buildings as a single-owner campus once again filled with craftspeople and museum exhibitions much like Williamsburg does for the Colonial era.

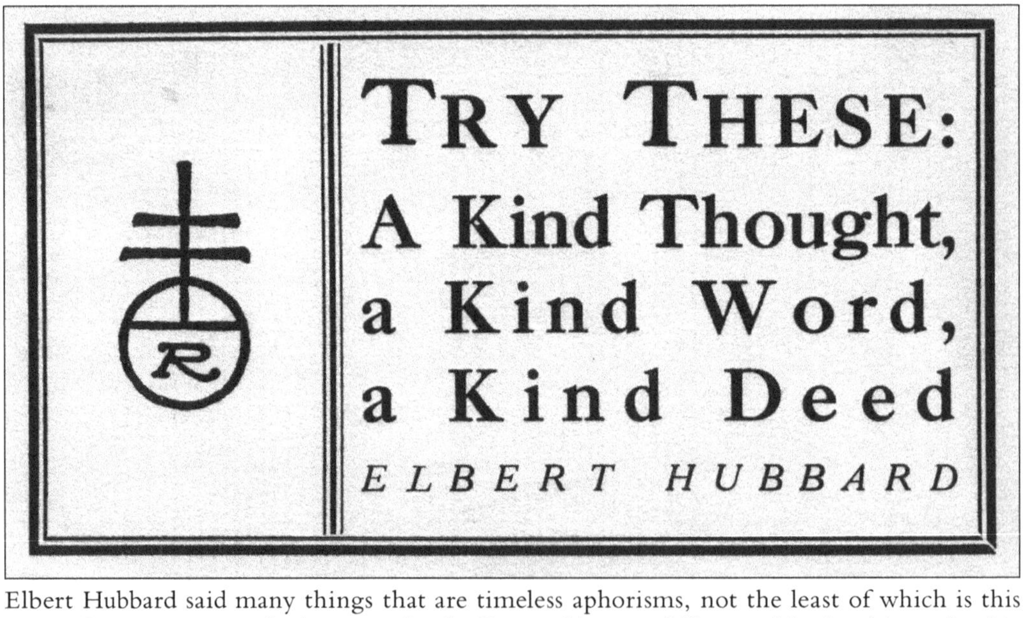


Elbert Hubbard said many things that are timeless aphorisms, not the least of which is this motto. It was sent out and taken away by the Roycroft's many followers. Not just his work ethic epigrams, but many of his words, some borrowed from others, are as appropriate in the 21st century as they were in the 19th century.

# Bibliography

Champney, Freeman. *Art and Glory: The Story of Elbert Hubbard.* Kent, Ohio: Kent State University Press, 1983.

Hamilton, Charles Franklin. *As Bees in Honey Drown Elbert Hubbard and the Roycrofters.* South Brunswick, NJ: A.S. Barnes, 1973.

Lane, Albert. *Elbert Hubbard and his Work: A Biography, a Sketch, and a Bibliography.* Boston, MA: The Blanchard Press, 1901.

Rust, Robert C., and Kitty Turgeon. *The Roycroft Campus.* Charleston, SC: Arcadia Publishing, 1999.

Via, Marie, and Marjorie Searl. *Head, Heart and Hand: Elbert Hubbard and the Roycrofters.* Rochester, NY: University of Rochester Press, 1994.

Walsdorf, John J. *Elbert Hubbard: William Morris's Greatest Imitator.* Council Bluffs, IA: Yellow Barn Press, 1999.

White, Bruce A. *The Philistine, A Periodical of Protest (1895–1915).* Lanham, MD: University Press of America, 1989.

www.ingramcontent.com/pod-product-compliance
Lightning Source LLC
LaVergne TN
LVHW071613240926
848761LV00043B/435
* 9 7 8 0 7 3 8 5 9 9 0 6 9 *